Selective Publication in the U.S. Courts of Appeals

Selective Publication in the U.S. Courts of Appeals

The Invisible Norm that Perpetuates Inequality

RACHAEL K. HINKLE
Professor
Department of Political Science
University at Buffalo, SUNY

OXFORD
UNIVERSITY PRESS

OXFORD
UNIVERSITY PRESS

Oxford University Press is a department of the University of Oxford. It furthers the University's objective of excellence in research, scholarship, and education by publishing worldwide. Oxford is a registered trade mark of Oxford University Press in the UK and certain other countries.

Published in the United States of America by Oxford University Press
198 Madison Avenue, New York, NY 10016, United States of America.

Library of Congress Cataloging-in-Publication Data
Names: Hinkle, Rachael K., author.
Title: Selective publication in the U.S. Courts of Appeals : the invisible norm that perpetuates inequality / Rachael K. Hinkle.
Other titles: Selective publication in the United States Courts of Appeals
Description: New York : Oxford University Press, 2024. |
Includes bibliographical references and index. |
Identifiers: LCCN 2024015073 | ISBN 9780197770085 (hardback) | ISBN 9780197770108 (updf) |
ISBN 9780197770092 (epub) | ISBN 9780197770115 (online)
Subjects: LCSH: Appellate courts—United States. | Appellate procedure—United States. | Court records—Access control—United States. | Court rules—Publishing—United States. | Citation of legal authorities—United States. | Equality before the law—United States.
Classification: LCC KF9052 .H56 2024 | DDC 347.73/243—dc23/eng/20240409
LC record available at https://lccn.loc.gov/2024015073

DOI: 10.1093/oso/9780197770085.001.0001

Printed by Marquis Book Printing, Canada

For Judge David W. McKeague, who gave me the opportunity that sparked my enduring curiosity about the federal circuit courts.

Summary Contents

Detailed Contents

Figures

Tables

Acknowledgments

I have long known the U.S. Courts of Appeals would be a central focus of my academic career. Even before I finished graduate school, I planned to explore the vast array of opinions generated in such courts. While it was necessary to carve out a manageable slice for my dissertation, the mountain of text beckoned. I'm famously bad at resisting the temptation to tackle mountains. So even as I was writing my dissertation, I set about the task of collecting a comprehensive set of opinions. By the time I earned my PhD, I had more than a decade worth of raw data.

It was not until a few years later that I turned my attention to that data. While I continued to write on a variety of topics related to circuit courts, I also ground away at sorting the wheat from the chaff, extracting important metadata, and hand-coding where no computational techniques were sufficient to suit my purposes. Throughout this process, my excitement about the many interesting questions I could answer with such extensive and comprehensive data kept me going. After such a long haul, the process of writing this book has truly been a labor of love as well as a journey of discovery. Tackling the questions in each chapter was reminiscent of the childhood joy of jumping in a large pile of leaves after a long afternoon of rigorous raking.

This book has been enriched by the contributions of so many people. After laboring over the data on my own for years, a grant from the Baldy Center for Law and Social Policy enabled me to hire two fantastic research assistants—Anthony Taboni and Avery Weissman—to finalize the extensive coding. Another RA, Sarah Krzemien, provided invaluable assistance by proofreading the entire manuscript. I have also benefited from feedback from many colleagues and friends (with apologies in advance for those I have forgotten to list here): Christy Boyd, Paul Collins, Christoph Engel, Morgan Hazelton, Lisa Holmes, Chuck Lamb, Michael Livermore, Lynn Mather, Michael Nelson, Jim Spriggs, Logan Strother, and Chris Zorn. I am also indebted to panel participants and discussants at the 2021 Southern Political Science Association meeting, the 2019 and 2022 Midwest Political Science Association meetings, and the 2022 Journal of Institutional and Theoretical Economics Symposium, as well as seminar participants at Penn State's Department of Political Science and the Max Planck Institute for Research on Collective Goods.

A variety of people in both my personal and professional worlds have made this book possible. On this occasion, I would like to particularly thank the many professors who have provided me with both the skills and example to be the scholar and teacher that I am today. My undergraduate education, as a history major, was primarily guided by Dr. Michelson and Dr. Brautigam. I had the incredibly good fortune to take multiple courses with each and to enjoy spirited weekly history department lunches. I recall learning editing annotation for book manuscripts in my Research Methods course and thinking that was a skill I would never need. How wrong I was. In law school, I was equally fortunate. In nearly every class I took, the professor was incredibly talented and engaging. Professors Hill, Fenton, and Young stand out the most. They all balanced providing an intellectual challenge in an environment that was still supportive and productive. They also provided wisdom with application well beyond the classroom or academy. Finally, my PhD experience would not have been the same without Jim Spriggs and Andrew Martin. It was quite the stroke of luck to have not one, but two, fantastic mentors on the last leg of my journey to academia. During my recruitment visit, Jim Spriggs told me, "We take our work seriously, but we don't take ourselves seriously." I hope the same can be said for me as well.

Table of Cases

TABLE OF STATUTES

TABLE OF COURT RULES

1
The Rise of Invisible Cases

Introduction

In the 1980s, Steven Johnson, an inmate in Maryland, applied for work in the education department of his prison. After being denied the job, he filed a federal lawsuit asserting that he did not get the job because a prison guard told the head of the department, Dr. Knable, that Johnson was a homosexual (Slavitt 1995). The trial court initially dismissed Johnson's complaint, but the U.S. Court of Appeals overruled that dismissal and stated the following: "If Johnson was denied a prison work assignment simply because of his sexual orientation, his equal protection rights may have been violated."[1] An appellate federal court hinting that sexuality could be a protected class seems like the kind of case that would have made quite a splash in the legal community. Except for one critical fact. The opinion was designated by the judges who issued it as an "unpublished" ruling. This designation meant that it was not binding precedent. As a result, it generated little discussion. *Johnson v. Knable* illustrates that virtually any case can be rendered largely invisible simply by not being published.

Why are some rulings declared to be "unpublished"? How did this norm arise? In the federal circuit courts this practice became a mainstream feature of judicial administration by the end of the 1970s. The 1960s and 1970s saw a tremendous increase in the workload appellate courts faced, which led to the development of several practices designed to allow judges to dispose of cases more quickly. One of those was the norm of selective publication, the process of including only some opinions[2] in printed law reports. Judges save time drafting decisions that are designated as unpublished because they do not have to carefully craft their reasoning with an eye toward future application of their words. Consequently, writing unpublished opinions takes far less time, effort, and agonizing (Wald 1995). As Baker (1994, 129) explains: "Some pride of authorship and all concerns for future application are eliminated with a nonpublished, noncitable opinion."

Since its inception, the practice of selective publication "has proven to be a watershed event in the history of federal court case law" (Hannon 2001, 201).

[1] *Johnson v. Knable*, 862 F.2d 314 (4th Cir. 1988).

[2] Some jurisdictions make a technical distinction between "opinions" and "orders." In this book, I use "opinion" in a more general sense that includes any written disposition of a case.

Selective Publication in the U.S. Courts of Appeals. Rachael K. Hinkle, Oxford University Press.
 DOI: 10.1093/oso/9780197770085.003.0001

Richman and Reynolds (1995, 275) argue that it is equivalent to agenda control stating that "the circuit courts have become certiorari courts." In short, a considerable portion of the circuit courts' work takes place in the shadows. Like the Supreme Court's shadow docket (see, e.g., Vladeck 2023), publication norms have fallen under criticism from a variety of quarters. Early debates surrounded the practice of prohibiting citation to unpublished opinions. In 2007, a change to court rules put this debate to rest by requiring that all circuits permit citation to any opinion going forward. Yet this did not bring the criticism to an end. Various scholars and commentators continued to decry the lack of transparency and accountability that accompanies unpublished decisions. In this chapter, I provide an overview of this history including the circumstances surrounding the emergence of unpublished opinions, the debate over no-citation rules, criticisms leveled at selective publication, and insights from existing empirical research. Next, I describe the comprehensive original dataset I have compiled. Finally, I conclude with a road map of the book that foreshadows how I utilize empirical data to address key debates that continue to swirl around selective publication today.

The Origins of Selective Publication

Historical Background

Discussion of how U.S. Courts of Appeals came to distinguish between rulings that were suitable for publication and those that were not often begins in the 1960s and focuses on the courts of appeals. However, a brief look further back in time and to other common law systems provides valuable perspective. Failure to publish the entire complement of written rulings issued by a court has ample precedent. Hoffman (1981, 405) points out that "[h]istoric English and American practice was to decide most cases by handing down judgments orally from the bench; the selective transcription of these oral judgments was left to unofficial reporters." However, as printing was established and became increasingly cost-effective, legal practice adjusted to keep up with the changing technology (Surrency 1981). Written opinions and official reporters emerged as the logistics and costs for those options became practical (Hoffman 1981). For example, legal rulings in the United States were not published at all until the end of the eighteenth century (Surrency 1981).

The emergence of law reporters necessarily generated the question of what they should include. In 1863, Sir Nathanial Lindley, QC, remarked that an opinion should not be published if it is "valueless as precedent" or "substantially repetitious of what is reported already" (Magrath 2019, 227). However, this general sentiment did not address the issue of who should make that determination. In England, there is a long history of private parties selecting opinions for publication and choosing only a small percentage of cases for inclusion in the law reports (Baker 1994; Magrath 2019). Similar approaches are used in Australia, New Zealand, and Canada as well (Pether 2004, 1439).

In the United States, the West Publishing Company, founded in 1876, quickly dominated the field of legal reporting. West took a different approach than private law reporters in England and many of her colonies. Brenner (1990, 495) describes how West "seems to have decided very early that success lay in publishing a comprehensive system of reports." Rather than selecting which cases to report, West simply published everything they obtained from the courts (Reynolds and Richman 1981, 576). This approach led to ever-expanding volumes of caselaw. During the late 1800s, the American Bar Association (ABA) frequently referred to the problems this caused in their annual reports (Brenner 1990). In 1898, they noted that it might be advisable to tell reporters to only include interesting cases, but they also expressed concern about who should determine which opinions to include (American Bar Association 1898). Some jurisdictions did try selective publication around this time, but it did not catch on (Surrency 1981). Up until the 1950s, most appellate judicial opinions in the United States were published in law reports (Kuersten and Songer 2001).

The Caseload Explosion

Starting in the 1960s there was drastic growth in the number and complexity of federal appeals (Reynolds and Richman 1981). From 1924 to 1960 the caseload doubled, and it took only four more years to double again (Carrington 1968). By 1970, the caseload had tripled (McAlister 2019). In 1962, there were 1,800 appeals filed in the U.S. Courts of Appeals and that number increased to 14,500 in 1972 (Gignoux 1978). There were not enough circuit judgeships created during this time to keep up with the increasing caseload (McAlister 2019). In fact, in 1978, a report submitted to the Judicial Conference noted that there had been no new judgeships since 1968 (Gignoux 1978).

The massive increase in caseload over a short period of time likely came from growth in four areas: (1) population, (2) economic activity, (3) new causes of action provided by federal law, and (4) Warren Court jurisprudence that extended rights for the criminally accused (Carrington 1968; Richman and Reynolds 2013). It is also possible that the increase in the number of federal trial court judges during this time might have sped up trial litigation, thereby reducing the incentive to settle and ultimately leading to more appeals (Carrington 1968). The large crop of new trial judges may also have been more mistake-prone in their early years, leading to more appeals (Carrington 1968). However, most commentators point primarily to the rise in civil rights litigation generated by both federal legislation and Supreme Court doctrine (Barrow and Walker 1988; Richman and Reynolds 2013). There were more causes of action and more complex cases as a result (Barrow and Walker 1988). The changing nature of the circuit courts' docket can be seen by looking at the type of litigants who appeared before them. Kuersten and Songer (2001) note that before 1950 an individual was on at least one side in about half of cases, and since 1950 an individual appeared in 76% of cases (Kuersten and Songer 2001, 181). This shift is consistent with the idea that the 1960s signaled a move toward considerably more rights-based appeals being brought in federal courts. These types of cases are not always greeted by judges with great enthusiasm. For example, Judge Edith Jones of the Fifth Circuit has remarked that "the docket is 'dumbed-down' by an overwhelming number of routine or trivial appeals" (Jones 1995, 1493). She likened the job of a judge having to resolve numerous civil rights cases to "that of a competitive tennis player forced to spend the bulk of his time rallying with novices" (Jones 1995, 1493).

The massive increase in caseload without a significant increase in the number of appellate judges created two serious issues (Beske 2018; Murrah 1973). The first was that the burgeoning caseload made it very difficult for circuit courts to complete their mission in a timely manner. Litigants in federal trial courts have a right to at least one appeal (Bowie et al. 2014). This means that circuit courts must render a decision in every case brought before them (see Federal Rules of Appellate Procedure, Rule 4). If the trial courts make an error, it is up to the Courts of Appeals to correct it (Baker 1994). Yet, error correction is not their only task. Since the Supreme Court's capacity to resolve cases is fairly fixed, any increase in the number of overall federal appeals necessarily also means an increase in the number of cases in which circuit judges must shape legal policy (Richman and Reynolds 2013, 5). Having a huge caseload makes it difficult to do both error correction and lawmaking well (Carrington 1968). Carrington (1968, 542) summarized the situation as follows: "The federal courts of appeals were designed to relieve the acute congestion in the Supreme Court, but the doctor has caught the disease."

The caseload explosion also pushed a second serious issue to the foreground that had been simmering below the surface for some time; the challenges posed by an ever-increasing body of precedent. Concerns about how lawyers and judges dealt with a rapidly increasing number of precedents were nothing new (Richman and Reynolds 2013, 10). West's approach to publishing all opinions generated complaints as far back as the 1800s (Surrency 1981). As Brenner (1990, 500) describes, "after comprehensive reporting prevailed, reports proliferated, producing fears that decisional law was becoming unmanageable." In 1895, the

Annual Report of the ABA (354) stated the following: "It is not at all clear but that it would be highly beneficial to the profession, the bench and the client if the fate of the Alexandria library should befall very much the larger portion of the reports of adjudicated cases in all English-speaking countries." The ABA's Annual Report in 1898 (442) followed up by warning that cases were increasing so fast that "the burden will soon become intolerable." Whitehair (1947) took on the topic of too many "unnecessary opinions" being published and noted that over one hundred others had previously written on the same topic, indicating widespread agreement that there was a serious problem. Prince (1962) further elaborated on the same issue, illustrating the problem by pointing out that in 1960 the L.A. County Law Library had eleven miles of bookshelves and the law library in the Library of Congress had thirty-nine miles of shelves. With 2.25 million American opinions, Prince (1962, 134) asserted that "[l]awyers know that there are too many law books."

Against this backdrop, the tremendous increase of federal appeals that occurred in the 1960s and 1970s also created a concomitant explosion of precedent that was very concerning (Chanin 1974). The Committee on Use of Appellate Court Energies reported that "[c]ommon law in the United States could be crushed by its own weight if the rate of publication is not abated" (Murrah 1973, 6). Martineau (1994, 144) stated that "[t]hose who argue that opinion proliferation is not a problem are ignoring or are unaware of the facts." In 1971, the Federal Judicial Center (FJC) noted in its annual report that many people thought there were too many opinions going in reporters (Murrah 1971). The expansion of caselaw created a problem because many felt legal professionals were already nearly at (or over) capacity in terms of what they could process (Murrah 1973). Observers outlined several problems created by a huge body of precedent. Prince (1962, 135) remarked that "[t]here is no way to estimate the vast amount of lawyers' time wasted in searching out cases from so stupendous a mass." Others pointed out that so much precedent can be overwhelming to judges, lawyers, litigants, and the public and that "an overabundance of precedent may muddy the waters with confusing or contradictory precedent" (Brown et al. 2021, 94). Judge Edith Jones remarked that "[i]n my view, a cacophony of precedent is just as troublesome as conflicting precedents" (Jones 1995, 1498).

The vast number of opinions being published in law reporters also posed financial and logistical barriers since "[l]ibrary expenses increase with volume" (Baker 1994, 129). In 1964, the Judicial Conference noted that the increased cost of libraries was becoming a problem (Olney III 1964, see also Murrah 1973). No lawyer could afford their own library (Prince 1962). Law reports were simply too voluminous for a small law practice to afford (Whitehair 1947). The Committee on Use of Appellate Court Energies also noted that the greater number of cases required more "law-finding devices" such as digests that also kept getting bigger and more expensive (Murrah 1973).

The massive increase in workload experienced by the federal courts of appeals, together with West's practice of publishing all judicial opinions, created substantial pressure. Something had to give. Without staffing or institutional changes, the time to adjudicate an appeal would become unacceptably long. A key change to address this crisis was the shift to selective publication.

A (Not So) Modest Proposal

The modern practice of selective publication in the U.S. Courts of Appeals can be traced back to a proposal and recommendation from the Judicial Conference in 1964 (Arnold 1999; Beske 2018; Chanin 1974). A subcommittee was tasked with collecting data and studying how best to deal with the increasing caseload and cost of library materials (Olney III 1964). After receiving this subcommittee's report, the March 1964 Report of the Judicial Conference included the following passage:

> In view of the rapidly growing number of published opinions of the courts of appeals and of the district courts of the United States, and the ever increasing practical difficulty and economic cost of establishing and maintaining accessible private and public law library facilities, the Committee presented the following resolution which was approved by the Conference:
> RESOLVED: That the judges of the courts of appeals and the district courts authorize the publication of only those opinions which are of general precedential value and that opinions authorized to be published be succinct (Olney III 1964, 11).

This relatively brief passage amid a fifty-three-page report ultimately worked a significant change in the operation of circuit courts. Notably, the reasons mentioned in this initial proposal focused on the complications created by a burgeoning amount of precedent as justification for selective publication. However, other arguments soon emerged as well. Before long, the unwieldy expansion of precedent took a back seat to the argument that overwhelmed judges could save much-needed time by quickly writing short, unpublished opinions. Other themes also entered the discussion alongside the efficiency and precedent-based arguments such as that there is simply no need to publish all rulings.

Current discussions of publication rules often focus on reducing judicial workload as the primary motivation and justification. Yet as the initial proposal of selective publication in 1964 indicates, concerns about the amount of precedent played a fundamental role in the origins of this institution (Keele et al. 2009; Martineau 1994; Pether 2004). Such concerns were multifaceted. Commentators argued that a plethora of precedent could have several ill effects. First, too many precedents could result in conflicts and overall lack of cohesion in legal doctrine (Gignoux 1978, 8). A key function of circuit courts is framing a coherent body of law (Carrington 1968). The Committee on Use of Appellate Court Energies asserted that publishing all opinions is "a burden and a threat to a cohesive body of law" (Murrah 1973, 6). Cohen (2002) reported that judges say unpublished opinions avoid areas of law getting "cluttered." Second, the excessive growth of precedent requires both lawyers and judges to spend more time doing legal research (Gignoux 1978). Hoffman (1981) stated that a critical argument for selective publication was keeping the amount of law reasonable for legal research. Songer et al. (1988, 964) similarly noted that "[t]he debate on curtailing publication stemmed from a legitimate concern over maintaining a manageable body of law." Third, the expanding books in which opinions were published made it increasingly expensive to acquire and house a law library (Gignoux 1978, 8). Not publishing all cases is cheaper and more practical from a logistical standpoint (Cleveland 2009).

Perhaps the most pressing issue created by the caseload explosion was simply how judges were going to find the time to resolve cases. Selective publication provided a sorely needed remedy by allowing the disposal of many cases with considerably less time and effort (Hoffman 1981). In 1978, a key subcommittee report stated that "[t]he primary concern which has led to the rules recently developed with respect to the non-publication of opinions is the need to conserve the time of judges during a period of expanding appellate litigation" (Gignoux 1978, 7). This efficiency rationale is frequently the main argument of judges who support selective publication; they say it is required by heavy caseloads (Brown et al. 2021). Published opinions take more resources (Beske 2018; Robel 1989). Writing to develop law takes more time and effort (Bowie et al. 2014; Murrah 1973). Opinion writing makes up about half of the time judges spend on cases, so streamlining that task has substantial benefits (Hruska 1975). The time saved in cases where the ruling is not published can be invested in more important cases (Cohen 2002). Murrah (1973) noted that judges are short on time to work on interesting cases. Pether (2004, 1444) argued that a less public dimension of this argument was judges' "dismay and irritation at the volume of appeals emerging from civil rights litigants and prisoners making *pro se* postconviction appeals."

Lastly, arguments in favor of selective publication also routinely referenced the simple lack of necessity of publishing all opinions. In its 1971 Annual Report, the FJC noted that the need to provide reasons for the litigants or the record does not mean all opinions should be published (Murrah 1971). The Hruska Report noted in 1975 that "while some cases require elaborate explanation, in others brevity better serves the cause of justice" (Hruska 1975, 113). Others similarly noted that many easy cases could be resolved with short opinions (Carrington 1968). Supporters of selective publication pointed to other countries that used the same practice, even going so far as to note that the American practice of publishing all rulings seemed ridiculous in other countries (Prince 1962). Chanin (1974) noted that the Court of Appeal, Criminal Division in England published only 15% of its cases. Much of this discussion relied on the distinction between writing opinions and publishing them. Opinions are written to explain reasons to the parties, help the judge think through the issues, and to develop law, but only the last reason requires publication (Murrah 1973). Robel (1989) makes a similar point by asserting that the two functions of the courts of appeals—error correction and policymaking—naturally lend themselves to two distinct kinds of opinions, unpublished and published. Finally, the opinion of the legal community regarding the lack of necessity of publishing all decisions was proffered in support of selective publication. Carrington (1968, 560) reported that "[d]istinguished judges have suggested that as few as one-tenth of the appeals involve significant substantive issues" (see also Murrah 1973). The Hruska Commission reported that attorneys surveyed agreed many opinions do not need to be published (Hruska 1975, 140). For all these reasons, the move toward selective publication met little resistance.

Circuits Develop Publication Rules

Although many agreed that the 1964 proposal to limit publication was sensible, the general recommendation left a host of details to be fleshed out. In facing this problem, the FJC reported that "[t]here is not, however, any consensus about how to limit publication to those opinions that serve the general needs of the law and the public" and acknowledged that "[t]he problem of translating knowledge and promising ideas into action has always confounded judicial reformers" (Murrah 1971, 8). The Board of the FJC recommended in 1971 that the Judicial Conference tell circuits to overhaul their publication practices and recommend citation to unpublished decisions be prohibited (Richman and Reynolds 2013, 12–13). In 1972, the Judicial Conference did as asked and approved sending a recommendation on publication to all circuits and asking each to formulate a publication plan by January 1, 1973 (Kirks 1972). Circuits were asked to submit not only plans but also statistics for evaluation (Gignoux 1978). The idea was that individual circuits could serve as laboratories and provide data on how well different kinds of publication plans worked (Gignoux 1978).

In 1973, a committee analyzed all of the existing rules, including those from states that had addressed the issue of selectively publishing opinions in their intermediate courts of appeals (Murrah 1973). States were facing some of the same pressures as the federal courts, and a handful had already turned to limiting publication. New Jersey established a committee of judges to determine which decisions should be published (Murrah 1973). New York and Georgia court rules specified that the judges who resolved a case also determined whether the decision would be printed in the official law reports, but neither provided any criteria for that decision (Murrah 1973). Washington identified cases "having precedential value" as those which should be published (Murrah 1973, 28). California had the most specific criteria—providing that a ruling should only be published if it criticized, modified, or made new law or if the issue was of "continuing public interest" (Murrah 1973, 24). After canvassing the possibilities, the committee proposed a Model Rule, pointing out that every circuit having their own publication criteria going forward would not be ideal (Murrah 1973). In 1975, the Hruska Report concluded that the topic of publication was best left to the Judicial Conference, and that experimentation and evaluation should continue (Hruska 1975). After a five-year trial, the "experimentation" did not produce a clear best approach that people agreed on, so circuits continued to use their own rules and no consistent approach was adopted (Hoffman 1981; Gignoux 1978, 407).

The publication plans developed across the circuits varied in the particulars, but they did address common issues. Three key elements arose in these plans: the criteria for determining which opinions would be published, the precedential status of unpublished opinions, and whether citation to unpublished opinions was permitted. The Model Rule set forth four criteria for publication, did not address the issue of precedent, and stated that unpublished rulings could not be cited by or to any court (Murrah 1973). The criteria for publication in the Model Rule were establishing or modifying a legal rule, addressing an issue of continuing public interest, criticizing existing law, or resolving a conflict (Murrah 1973). The circuits adopted different combinations of these elements, and some left the question of precedential status somewhat or entirely unaddressed in the early years.[3]

In the early publication plans, the Fourth, Seventh, Eighth, Ninth, and Tenth Circuits were the only ones that contained specific lists of the criteria for publication (Chanin 1974). The four criteria included in the Model Rule were largely incorporated, albeit in slightly different forms, by all of these circuits. Other criteria, such as a nonduplicative exposition of legal or legislative history, appeared in the list for more than one circuit. Still others were used only by a single circuit. For example, the Ninth Circuit provided for an opinion to be published if there was a

[3] The Sixth Circuit adopted an interim publication plan but refused to make it available to the public (Chanin 1974, n. 30).

separate opinion authored by a judge who preferred publication (Chanin 1974). The Eighth Circuit mandated that an opinion be published if the ruling below was published and the appellate panel did not accept the trial court's reasoning (Chanin 1974).

In some common law systems, including Australia, Canada, and New Zealand, opinions excluded from the law reporters have the same precedential status as those that are included (Pether 2004, 1439). However, in the United States, making a distinction in such status quickly entered the discussion. The earliest publication rules did not explicitly state that unpublished rulings were not legally binding, but "within a few years, most federal court rules made these unpublished cases nonprecedential" (Cleveland 2009, 698). In fact, Kagan et al. (2017, 687) note that "the terminology of publication and precedent are often used synonymously." Unpublished cases still resolve disputes, but they do not make law (Slavitt 1995). Today, all circuit rules say that unpublished rulings are not precedent (McAlister 2019, n. 79). This is often a point of criticism (Brown et al. 2021).

Finally, early publication rules addressed whether attorneys and litigants would be allowed to cite unpublished rulings. Local rules split on this issue. While some circuits did not mention any restrictions, citations to unpublished decisions were prohibited by the First, Sixth, Eighth, Ninth, and Tenth Circuits. The Fourth Circuit rules stated that unpublished decisions would not be cited by them and that they "prefer" attorneys and parties not use such sources in their arguments to the court. The Seventh Circuit declared that unpublished orders could not be cited as precedent. Over time, these provisions restricting citation became the target of vociferous criticism.

The Citation Kerfuffle

The publication plans adopted in the 1970s have largely developed as they began, haphazardly with continued variation among circuits. While circuits occasionally revisit their individual rules with respect to publication, only one major change has taken place that has moved selective publication practice in a more unified direction. This change was the result of intense and protracted debate (Brown et al. 2021; Schiltz 2005a, b). In 2007, the Federal Rules of Appellate Procedure, which govern all circuits, were amended to abolish restrictions on citation to unpublished rulings.[4] The decades of debate that ultimately led to this development are an important chapter in the history of selective publication.

[4] Circuits were allowed to continue prohibiting citation to unpublished decisions issued prior to 2007 (Cleveland 2010; McAlister 2019).

The official designation of opinions as unpublished created the key question of how they could be used (Steinstra 1985). As early as 1978 there was disagreement on this point (Gignoux 1978). A key subcommittee that studied the issue had notable internal dissension about the advisability of no-citation rules; while there was criticism of those in place in seven circuits, others felt the policies were justified (Gignoux 1978). Such disagreements continued for decades. As Steinstra (1985, 10) pointed out, "many noted the difficulties that arise either when citation is prohibited or when it is permitted." By the early 2000s there were still four circuits that did not allow citation to unpublished rulings (1st, 2nd, 9th, Fed.) (Morande 2003). In 2003, the Advisory Committee on the Federal Rules for Appellate Procedure proposed a rule that would allow unpublished rulings to be cited and received a flurry of over five hundred comments vehemently supporting and opposing the proposal. Schiltz (2005a, 30), who served as the Reporter to the Advisory Committee during this time, remarked that "[w]hen over 500 of the best judges, lawyers, and law professors in America get into a fight over a proposed rule, no stone will be left unturned."

The proponents of requiring all circuits to permit citation to unpublished decisions made several key arguments. Many were focused on the utility of such rulings for making legal arguments. Robel (1989, 944) pointed out that "[l]awyers are trained to use opinions." A survey of federal agencies showed that many used unpublished rulings to make the decision to appeal (Robel 1989). Others focused on noting problems raised by noncitation rules (Schiltz 2005b). For example, Vladeck and Gulati (2005, 1671–72) argued that such rules "stifle the development of the law, fuel suspicions that courts are not scrupulously obeying the rule of law, and give both judges and lawyers incentives to engage in strategic game-playing." Finally, support for the new rule was buttressed by the results of a survey conducted by the FJC in which the circuit judge respondents generally reported that they did not anticipate the new rule would make unpublished rulings longer or more time-intensive to draft (Schiltz 2005a).

Opponents of the proposed rule raised several counterarguments. Contrary to the results of the FJC survey, many argued that allowing citation would negate most of the timesaving features of nonpublication (Hoffman 1981). They asserted that the cost savings of unpublication only apply if lawyers don't use such opinions (Robel 1989). According to Schiltz (2005a, 36), commenters claimed that the rule would "force judges to spend as much time drafting unpublished opinions as they now spend drafting published opinions." A second major argument was that permitting citation to unpublished rulings favored more privileged participants who were able to access such resources (Martineau 1994; Steinstra 1985). For example, commenters asserted that the proposed rule would "particularly disadvantage pro se litigants and prisoners, who often do not have access to the Internet or to the *Federal Appendix*" (Schiltz 2005a, 39).

After extensive and vigorous debate, Rule 32.1, "one of the most controversial proposals in the history of federal rulemaking," went into effect on January 1, 2007 (Schiltz 2005a, 24). Any ruling issued by a federal circuit court from that point forward may be cited in any federal court. The aftermath of this change was rather anticlimactic. Nonpublication rates went down a small amount in the immediate wake of the rule change, but then continued the overall increasing trend (Brown et al. 2021). An Administrative Office study examined two years before and after the rule went into effect and found no evidence of a change in time to disposition (Schiltz 2005a). Nor did unpublished decisions get longer after the rule change, as some opponents had anticipated (Brown et al. 2021).

Continuing Criticisms of Selective Publication

The rule change in 2007 addressed only some criticisms of selective publication. Other controversies continue to swirl. For example, McAlister (2019) argues that the idea that unpublished opinions save time is a myth. Hoffman (1981) points out that survey results show attorneys like selective publication less than judges. However, there have been judges that adamantly oppose it as well. Judge Richard S. Arnold of the Eighth Circuit wrote the following about selective publication: "This practice disturbs me so much that it is hard to know where to begin in discussing it" (Arnold 1999, 222). Others have raised concerns about the fact that the procedure was adopted "without serious internal reflection on the consequences" (Richman and Reynolds 2013, 7). While there are a wide range of criticisms, the bulk of them can be organized into three groups: concerns about diminished judicial accountability, the quality of unpublished rulings, and inequalities created by the system of selective publication (Martineau 1994).

Diminished Accountability

Selective publication creates three ways in which appellate judges are arguably less accountable than they were when all opinions were published. First, there is virtually no oversight of the publication decision. The judges themselves decide whether to leave a ruling unpublished, and there is no procedural mechanism to appeal that determination. Even in the circuits that have specific criteria for publication, applying them in each case still leaves considerable room for discretion. One study looked at publication decisions in the D.C. Circuit and concluded that the determination of suitability for publication was questionable in 40% of cases (Wald 1995, 1374). Others point to the presence of unpublished reversals as evidence of problematic publication decisions, arguing that reversing the lower court makes a case sufficiently important to justify publication (Hannon 2001). Law (2004, 826) notes that "[f]ailure to publish reversals, in particular, has been identified repeatedly as a form of underpublication." Unpublished rulings that are not unanimous have also been criticized (Slavitt 1995). Overall, observers have expressed concern that the publication decision is made with little transparency and, therefore, may undermine circuit courts' legitimacy (Brown et al. 2021, 103).

Second, after the publication decision the opinions that are not published receive little to no scrutiny from observers outside the case. In some circuits, such rulings are not even circulated to other circuit judges who did not participate in the case (Robel 1989; Steinstra 1985). As a result, some argue that there is little accountability and transparency for the substance of unpublished rulings (Martineau 1994; Vladeck and Gulati 2005). Slavitt (1995, 122) asserts that "[n]onpublication makes the opinion and the rule it develops disappear." Hannon (2001, 240) expresses a similar concern: "The most visible action of these courts is deciding cases appealed to them. Since the mid-1970s, however, this most visible action has been increasingly hidden because many of these decisions are issued in unpublished opinions."

Third, critics point out that by designating a ruling as unpublished, circuit judges can quite effectively insulate it from further review (Martineau 1994). All dispositions issued by a three-judge panel can potentially be reviewed by the full circuit in an en banc proceeding[5] or by the Supreme Court (Hellman 2007). However, both types of review are discretionary, and permission is almost never given when the panel decision is not published (Beske 2018; Hazelton et al. 2016). There is little motivation to invest scarce resources to review decisions that are not precedential and, therefore, do not shape legal policy (Hazelton et al. 2016). Moreover, potential reviewing courts can save time by using publication status as a signal for whether a case involves salient or unusual legal issues (Black and Owens 2009). The consequence is that nonpublication results in another type of loss of accountability—when judges choose not to publish, they virtually never have to answer to a higher court. This concern has been raised by scholars and at the highest level of the judiciary (Hazelton et al. 2016; Law 2004; McAlister 2019). For example, in a 1991 dissent, Justice Harry A. Blackmun wrote, "Nonpublication must not be a convenient means to prevent review" (Liptak 2015).

[5] Due to its size, the Ninth Circuit hears en banc cases with a subset of eleven judges (Berdejó 2013).

Decreased Quality

McAlister (2019, 533) reports speaking with a judge who said unpublished opinions are "not safe for human consumption." This quote poignantly summarizes concerns raised by a variety of sources about the quality of unpublished rulings (Reynolds and Richman 1981). Since a key justification for nonpublication is efficiency, some critics point out that spending less time on a subset of cases in the interests of efficiency may well also mean that the quality of judicial work will suffer (Davies 1981). The result may be problematically subpar unpublished decisions (Reynolds and Richman 1981). Of particular concern are rulings that lack reasons or give insufficient reasons for the disposition of the case. Reynolds and Richman (1981, 603) argue that providing thorough justification is important because "[j]ustice must not only be done, it must appear to be done." Brown et al. (2021, 91) similarly state that "[r]eason-giving is intimately linked to the system's legitimacy and perceptions of procedural justice." Furthermore, there is experimental evidence that indicates the process of writing down reasons can reduce bias in decision-making (Liu 2018).

In addition to concerns about poorly reasoned rulings reducing legitimacy or containing bias, critics also claim that limiting the time invested in writing unpublished decisions can have a negative impact on the clarity and coherence of law (Dragich 1994). Nonpublication makes it harder to keep circuit law uniform and resolve intra-circuit conflicts (Hoffman 1981). As a result, the law becomes less predictable (Pether 2004, 1504). The accumulation of inconsistent circuit rulings over time can create challenges for both litigants and trial courts (Ricks 2006). As the law in a circuit becomes increasingly murky, that uncertainty may lead to fewer settlements and more appellate litigation (Ricks 2006, 222). In short, the very mechanism designed to efficiently address increasing caseloads may actually be contributing to continued growth, thereby undercutting the efficiency justification (Ricks 2006, 222).

Inequality

McAlister (2019, 533) asserts that "[t]he creation of the inferior unpublished decision also has created an inferior track of appellate justice for a class of appellants—indigent litigants." Considerable criticism of selective publication elaborates on this general point; when some groups are more likely than others to have opinions in their case published, this raises equal protection concerns (Hoffman 1981; Reynolds and Richman 1981). Hoffman (1981) points out that treating different cases differently is not a problem, but treating different types of litigants with the same type of case differently is problematic. Several scholars argue that "have nots" such as prisoners and those with fewer resources do not get the same appeal as others; instead, they get little more than a rubber-stamp of the trial court ruling (McAlister 2019). Brown et al. (2021, 98) argue that the selective publication "procedure itself can create or reinforce inequities in the judicial system." Along similar lines, Cleveland (2010, 60) states that the way selective publication operates creates a "sense of injustice."

The criticism of inequality is directed at how selective publication decisions are made rather than at the fact of the institution. Songer et al. (1988, 982) point out that how important a case is can be "a very subjective criterion which may be subtly affected by unarticulated attitudes regarding the status of the parties." Davies (1981) posits that appellate judges find work on civil appeals more rewarding than work on criminal appeals. As a result, there is a greater tendency to publish opinions in civil appeals and spend more time on those cases compared to criminal appeals (Davies 1981, 380). Songer and Davis (1990, 308) report that in interviews, some judges "specifically denied that the characteristics of the appellant would have any effect on the decision to publish." However, the data tell a different story. Songer et al. (1988, 981) find that 58% of cases with a government or corporate appellant are published compared to only 40% for other appeals. Slavitt (1995) finds that rulings in prisoner rights and Social Security cases and prisoner petitions are published less frequently than others. Pro se appeals are also less likely to be published (Pether 2004; Robel 1989). In sum, "less important cases and weaker litigants" get less "judicial attention" and "receive less (and different) justice" (Richman and Reynolds 1995, 275).

Inequalities in the distribution of judicial resources can lead to three distinct harms: legal development that disproportionately favors the privileged, decreased legitimacy for the courts, and a loss of dignity for some types of litigants. First, the decision to publish in different issue areas can affect legal development (Brown et al. 2021). Moreover, Slavitt (1995, 119) argues that repeat players with long time horizons and more resources are in a position to use selective publication to shape law to suit their purposes. Second, publication decisions that systematically treat different types of litigants differently risk harming the legitimacy of the court (Dragich 1994). Vladeck and Gulati (2005, 1676) assert that "[i]f like cases are not decided in a like manner in an open and public process, it is a danger signal that perhaps justice is not being done." Furthermore, "[n]onpublication can create the appearance of arbitrariness" (Slavitt 1995, 132). As a result, litigants may perceive the system as less fair (Reynolds and Richman 1981). Finally, the unequal use of selective publication can affect how litigants experience the legal system (McAlister 2019). Brown et al. (2021, 7) claim that "[t]his differential treatment may also exacerbate dignity harms caused by nonpublication." Others similarly argue that having a ruling be unpublished could leave a litigant feeling short-changed and like their case is perceived as not having much value (Brown et al. 2021; Slavitt 1995).

Evaluating Selective Publication

Many of the foregoing criticisms (and responses to them) are based on foundational assumptions and claims that are susceptible to empirical testing. How often are unpublished opinions reviewed? Are they written poorly? How do a litigant's resources and privilege impact whether their case is published? However, collecting the data to conduct such analyses can be quite challenging (Brown et al. 2021; Carlson et al. 2020). To date, there is surprisingly little in the way of widespread empirical analysis of the effects of selective publication. Much of the debate has generated more heat than light (Brown et al. 2021; Hoffman 1981). However, a handful of scholars have forged the trail by examining various facets of publication. Though logistical difficulties have limited the extent of investigation, these scholars have provided glimpses behind the curtain drawn by selective publication. This section summarizes some highlights from this work to provide a backdrop for the rest of the book. In particular, I examine work that looks at the link between selective publication and efficiency, whether publication criteria are followed, what other factors affect the publication decision, and how published and unpublished rulings differ.

In 1981, the FJC commissioned a study of publication and productivity that looked at the 1978–79 reporting year (Richman and Reynolds 2013). Reynolds and Richman (1981) examined about twelve thousand cases, locating published opinions in the *Federal Reporter* and counting the number of unpublished decisions listed in Administrative Office data. They found a small positive correlation of about 0.10 between the productivity of a circuit and the percentage of decisions it designated as unpublished (Reynolds and Richman 1981). However, they added a caveat that this simple correlation did not control for other factors that might be important (Reynolds and Richman 1981). Other scholars sought to establish a link between unpublication and efficiency by looking at the time taken to resolve the two types of cases. Hoffman (1981) conducted a ten-month study in the Seventh Circuit and showed that the time frame from oral argument to opinion was ninety-eight days for published opinions on average, and fifty-seven days for unpublished rulings (Hoffman 1981). Szmer et al. (2012) built a multivariate model of the time taken to dispose of cases and estimated that even accounting for other relevant factors, publication adds seven weeks to the time to dispose of a case. However, McAlister (2019) analyzed twenty years of data from the Administrative Office and reported that the use of unpublished decisions increased even when caseload did not. This suggests that efficiency is not necessarily the primary motivation for not publishing (McAlister 2019).

Other work has focused on whether publication criteria laid out in court rules are followed. In 1977, the newsletter of the federal judiciary reported on research on selective publication in California courts, which use similar criteria to federal courts (Third Branch 1977). The work showed that, for the most part, the publication criteria were being followed (Third Branch 1977). Songer et al. (1988) conducted a detailed study using all Eleventh Circuit cases from 1986. They theorized that if the publication criteria were followed, then unpublished opinions should primarily be unanimous affirmances, ideology should not predict votes in unpublished cases, and publication rates should be similar across judges (Songer et al. 1988). After empirically evaluating these three hypotheses, Songer et al. (1988) found no evidence for any of them and concluded there was no indication that judges were following publication rules. Merritt and Brudney (2001) examined the publication process using a dataset of about twelve hundred labor law cases from 1986 to 1993 and observed that circuits with similar publication criteria have substantially different publication rates, which casted doubt on the efficacy of the criteria (Merritt and Brudney 2001).

Scholars have also looked beyond formal publication criteria to explore more generally what types of factors affect which cases get published. Davies (1981) reported that in California intermediate appellate courts a larger percentage of civil cases were published compared to criminal cases. Brown et al. (2021) looked at FJC data and a sample of about fourteen hundred unpublished rulings from six circuits from 2008 to 2018. They found that pro se cases were rarely published, while those with the United States as a party were more likely to be published than others (Brown et al. 2021). A study of the Ninth Circuit in 1998 also found that pro se cases were more likely to be unpublished and reported that publication was unlikely in cases without oral argument (Wasby 2001). Other research examines whether ideology plays a role in the publication decision. Berdejó (2013) analyzed all Ninth Circuit cases available in Lexis (an electronic legal database) with named judges from 1991 to 2006 (nearly sixty-three thousand) and reported that liberal opinions were more likely to be published. However, Law (2004) conducted a study of asylum law in the Ninth Circuit from 1992 to 2002 (nearly two thousand cases) and specifically examined whether judges were more likely to publish rulings that are consistent with their own policy preferences. He found no such evidence of ideology impacting the publication decision (Law 2004).

Finally, some empirical work has begun to take on the important question of how published and unpublished decisions vary and how the dynamics of judicial decision-making work in these two types of cases. Most of what we know about the circuit courts is based on research that examines exclusively published opinions (Berdejó 2013). It is worth considering how much of this important knowledge is similarly applicable when circuit courts are resolving cases without publishing (Siegelman and Donohue III 1990, 1136). Law's (2004) asylum study provides evidence that ideology is a significant predictor of judicial votes on the merits in unpublished cases just like we know it is in published ones. Berdejó's (2013) study of the Ninth Circuit more broadly indicates that ideology has a bigger impact in published cases. Keele et al. (2009) explored 227 circuit cases involving the U.S. Forest Service from 1989 to 2002 and reported that judicial ideology was significant for published, but not unpublished, cases. In another exploration of Ninth Circuit caselaw, Rempell (2016) examined asylum cases from 2009 to 2014. According to legal doctrine in that circuit, a showing of physical harm to the applicant means asylum should be granted (Rempell 2016). However, when looking only at cases with an allegation of persecution, asylum was granted in 78% of published cases, but only 27% of unpublished cases (Rempell 2016).

The Comprehensive Circuit Court Panel Opinion (C^3PO) Database

The existing empirical work highlights how careful data collection and analysis can shed light on a host of important questions. However, our current understanding is limited by the scope of the available data. Existing studies are based on particular circuits, issues, or both, and often cover a very limited time span. This book steps into this important gap and introduces an expansive novel dataset of circuit court panel opinions from 2002 to 2012. Rulings were collected by downloading every available U.S. Court of Appeals opinion from Lexis during the time frame.[6] Nondispositive rulings on motions and other interim matters were excluded as well as the small number of en banc opinions. Many key variables of interest for circuit court cases were obtained from the FJC's Integrated Database.[7] The resulting dataset contains more than two hundred thousand cases drawn from all twelve geographic-based circuits. Hereinafter, I refer to this as the Comprehensive Circuit Court Panel Opinion (C^3PO) database.

[6] As others have noted, collecting unpublished rulings can be challenging (Carlson et al. 2020; Merritt and Brudney 2001). Not all unpublished opinions are in electronic databases (Kagan et al. 2017; Keele et al. 2009). However, since the E-Government Act of 2002 (Pub. L. 107-347, 116 Stat. 2899, 44 USC §§3501 et seq.), the circuits have been required by federal law to make all opinions publicly available online, which is how providers such as Westlaw and Lexis obtain them (McAlister 2020; Morande 2003; Ricks 2006).

[7] These data are available at https://www.fjc.gov/research/idb. I merged the dataset of decisions to the Integrated Database using the first listed docket number in each case.

The C³PO database is not only extensive in terms of the number of cases but is also well developed with respect to the information gathered on each individual case. Exploring the implications of selective publication requires a wide range of variables. These were derived from the text of the rulings downloaded from Lexis in addition to the data available in the FJC Integrated Database. The variables include myriad details about the case, litigants, judges, and features of the decision itself. Case-level variables include information such as the circuit, year, issue area, and—most critically—whether the disposition was published.[8] Issue area is coded into one of eight categories: administrative; civil, civil rights; civil, tort; civil, other; criminal; prisoner petition; bankruptcy; and original jurisdiction. Important litigant features include whether the appellant and appellee are a national government, subnational government, organization, person, or indigent or pro se person.

The identity of participating judges was extracted from the text of the ruling and merged with the FJC's Biographical Database. As a result, a wide range of judicial characteristics are incorporated into the C³PO database, including demographics, experience, and seniority. I also identified the specific role of each judge in each case in terms of authoring majority or dissenting opinions. Finally, obtaining the text of the rulings themselves made it possible to calculate several quantities of interest using computational text analytic techniques. In addition to the simple word court of each decision, I calculated frequently used measures such as the readability of the text. I also relied on computational techniques to extract all citations from each ruling and identify whether each citation was to binding or nonbinding precedent. Using this information, I calculated what proportion of all citations in a decision is to nonbinding precedent. A higher value of this variable reflects greater legal novelty. While these variables are illustrative, this list is not exhaustive. The C³PO database makes possible a series of investigations into not only how publication rules and norms operate but also into some of their unintended consequences.

Road Map of the Book

In Chapter 2, I begin with a broad overview of how selective publication operates. Thorough evaluation of the criticisms leveled at the practice is difficult without a clear picture of how it affects judicial output. In this chapter, I use the C³PO database to paint such a picture. To begin, I explore variation across space and time.

[8] By circuit rule, unpublished opinions must bear a specific notation such as "NOT FOR PUBLICATION." I compiled a list of all such notations and used a series of regular expressions to identify that text in opinions and, thus, code publication status.

Publication rates vary by circuit from only 6% in the Fourth Circuit all the way up to 81% in the First Circuit. The frequency of publication also varies over time, although less dramatically, ranging between 20% and 25% overall, from 2002 to 2012. These differences are not necessarily surprising considering that each circuit has its own set of rules that govern the publication decision, and they are sometimes changed. I discuss how rules have been amended over time, summarize key differences and similarities between circuit rules, and examine whether circuit-level publication practices map onto differences or changes in formal rules. Next, I explore features of rulings themselves to describe how published and unpublished decisions vary in terms of a range of features including length, clarity, complexity, and use of binding and persuasive precedent.

Chapter 3 addresses a foundational empirical question: What factors shape the publication decision? Explicit legal rules almost assuredly play a substantial role. As a result, cases with novel and particularly important legal issues should be published. But judges are human, and we know that they are affected by a variety of extralegal factors, including implicit biases and their own ideological preferences. As a result, publication decisions may be influenced by several factors beyond those stated explicitly in circuit rules. A group of judges with divergent viewpoints may use nonpublication as a tool of compromise. Cases with litigants or legal issues that judges do not view as a high priority might be less likely to result in a published opinion. Judges may be more willing to publish decisions that reflect their own ideological preferences. Finally, judges may leave rulings unpublished when they anticipate the possibility of hostile review. In short, there are reasons to theorize that the publication decision is shaped by rules, diversity of views, litigant status, issue area, judicial ideology, and strategy. The empirical evidence reveals support for several of these explanations. Specifically, there is evidence that publication rules, judicial ideology, and both internal and external strategic considerations shape publication decisions. Some of these findings raise concerns about disparities that can be generated as a result of selective publication.

Chapters 4, 5, and 6 focus on how inequalities in power and privilege are affected by selective publication. Chapter 4 begins by focusing on litigants. In 1974, Galanter famously theorized that society's "haves" are more likely to be successful in litigation than "have-nots" due to both their greater resources and more extensive familiarity with the legal system. Scholars have found evidence of precisely this empirical pattern in a wide variety of courts, including federal circuit courts. Litigants such as government actors, who have more resources and experience, are more likely to be successful than litigants with fewer resources and less experience like individuals. I theorize that depending upon the mechanism driving the resource advantage, this discrepancy might be either larger or smaller among cases with unpublished decisions. The data reveal that while have-nots are at a disadvantage in unpublished cases, the size of that deficit is smaller than in published cases. This undermines the most benign explanation for the resource advantage, that it is simply a product of uninformed litigants making bad decisions to bring weak appeals. The remaining explanations for why wealth and experience help win cases are more troubling.

In Chapter 5, I explore how the selective publication norm distributes benefits among judges. Simply bringing more women and minorities to the bench does not guarantee that they experience the same level of power as their historically privileged white, male counterparts. This chapter investigates two elements of how power is distributed. Published cases make law, which means both participating in such cases and authoring such opinions are important metrics of judicial power. The data reveal that female and minority judges wield disproportionately low amounts of power on both dimensions. Diverse groups often find a need to accommodate varying viewpoints, and women and judges of color are more likely to find themselves in such diverse groups. Consequently, nonpublication as a tool of compromise results in white men participating in a disproportionately high number of cases with policymaking implications. Even when participating in a case where the ruling is published, judges from historically underrepresented groups find themselves less likely to be assigned to write the opinion. Yet they dissent more frequently. The picture that emerges is clear. Judges from demographic groups that have been historically excluded from the federal judiciary (as well as many other aspects of society) are clamoring for a voice. They write dissenting opinions despite the effort and time that requires. Yet those same voices are muted when circuit courts pronounce law.

The disparities generated by selective publication do not end when the decision is issued. Chapter 6 examines how they continue to manifest at the next stage of litigation as well. A ruling by a three-judge circuit panel is not always the end of the road. The litigants may request review en banc by the full circuit, or they may ask the Supreme Court to grant a writ of certiorari. Such review is a rare prize. Unsurprisingly, publication status is a key element in which cases get reviewed. In this chapter, I summarize and evaluate both how often litigants request review of the two types of decisions and how frequently those requests are granted. Both are rarer in unpublished cases. Further examination shows that the resources of litigants also affect which cases are reviewed. In this way, disparities generated by selective publication can also create further downstream distributional consequences with respect to review. For example, the haves are not only more likely to win, they are also more likely to get a second bite at the apple in the cases where they lose. Finally, I go on to examine the results in cases that are granted discretionary review and explore whether the publication status in the case below has any correlation to success during discretionary review.

Conditional on review being requested and granted, those seeking review of unpublished rulings are actually *more* likely to be successful on the merits.

The final chapter brings the book to a close by outlining the normative implications of the empirical findings. Selective publication both generates and reveals disparities in power and privilege. Now what? The most optimistic takeaway is that sometimes becoming consciously aware of discriminatory patterns is sufficient to work toward dismantling those differences (Patton and Smith 2017). It is more likely that this knowledge is only a first step. After all, knowing is only half the battle. In this case, what is the other half? The answer to that question is far from easy. The most straightforward approach might be to do away with the concept of publication entirely. Since hard-copy law reporters are no longer part and parcel of everyday legal practice, there is less reason to make hard decisions about what rulings are worthy of sacrificing trees. The circuit courts could, instead, simply make all rulings available online without distinction. All decisions would be legally binding throughout the circuit. However, without also addressing staffing levels, this "fix" would likely cause other problems. The most comprehensive solution would also need to include increasing staffing levels, including the number of circuit judges, quite substantially to provide a high-quality level of legal analysis to all litigants who come before the circuit courts. Other, less extensive, reforms have been suggested as well. This chapter summarizes such proposals and highlights how the empirical findings from throughout the book shed light on such debates about institutional structure. In summary, the problems caused by selective publication are not simple to solve, but they do exist. As a result, we must grapple with the costs and benefits of potential solutions.

2
Publication Policies and Practices

Introduction

Fuzzy, Junior, and Tatoo [*sic*] Billy were members of a motorcycle gang known as "the Breed." In 2007, they were all convicted on counts of conspiracy to distribute crystal meth. Their appeals to the Third Circuit were consolidated into one case, which the court disposed of with an opinion that was over forty-three thousand words long and contained 262 citations to caselaw.[1] In spite of the extensive nature of this opinion, the circuit designated it as unpublished. At the other end of the spectrum, in 2009 the Eighth Circuit disposed of a case with a published opinion that was less than two hundred words long and contained no citations to caselaw. After a one-line description of the procedural posture, the court concluded, "[f]or the reasons set forth in the order issued by the district court, we affirm."[2] Yet the court deemed it suitable for publication.

These cases are not representative of typical unpublished and published rulings. However, such extreme examples are often used by critics of selective publication to highlight the inconsistencies in how the norm is applied (see, e.g., Arnold 1999). Yet individual anecdotes only tell a small part of the story. Effective evaluation requires a look at the bigger picture. In short, empirical research on courts is important (Sassman 2019). While there is a substantial amount of empirical work on the courts of appeals, the bulk of it uses the Songer Court of Appeals database, which only includes published opinions (Kuersten and Songer 2001, 45). This invaluable resource has contributed immeasurably to our understanding of circuit courts, but there are gaps in what we know as a result of what is excluded from that dataset (Sassman 2019; Szmer et al. 2012). As Carlson et al. (2020) show, published opinions are not a random sample of all cases, nor do they make up the majority of circuit cases. For example, in 2010, 84% of dispositions were not published (Epstein et al. 2013). The sheer volume of unpublished opinions makes it important to extend empirical research beyond published decisions exclusively (Songer et al. 1988). However, the same volume that raises the importance of such work also makes it more difficult (Brown et al. 2021, 41). I have taken on this challenge. The Comprehensive Circuit Court

1 *United States v. Heilman, et al.*, 377 Fed. Appx. 157 (3rd Cir. 2010).
2 *McKinzy v. Union Pacific Railroad*, 569 F.3d 345 (8th Cir. 2009).

Selective Publication in the U.S. Courts of Appeals. Rachael K. Hinkle, Oxford University Press.
 DOI: 10.1093/oso/9780197770085.003.0002

Panel Opinion (C^{3}PO) database provides the necessary data to empirically examine broad trends instead of being limited to eye-catching anecdotes.

Incorporating unpublished rulings into empirical research is not just important because of the large volume of such opinions. They are also central to understanding an important procedure within an influential institution. The U.S. Courts of Appeals formulate federal legal policy on a variety of topics left unaddressed by the Supreme Court (Wald 1995). Circuit courts have emerged as "the de facto courts of last resort" in the federal system (Bowie et al. 2014, 26). As a result, studying them has become increasingly important. While many scholars have taken up this task, little attention has been paid to how federal circuit judges exercise what Bachrach and Baratz (1962) famously call the "second face of power," that is, the ability to prevent policy from being made. Scholars have long recognized the importance of understanding how the U.S. Supreme Court exercises its agenda-setting power (see, e.g., Perry 1991; Boucher and Segal 1995; Ulmer 1984). In the judiciary, as in other policymaking arenas, understanding the determinants of how topics get on the agenda is a fundamental element of understanding how policy is ultimately made. Selective publication is analogous to direct agenda control because it involves determining which cases make policy (Wasby 2001). As Morande (2003, 780) points out, "[t]he publication decision carries with it important consequences." Understanding these consequences requires looking beyond anecdotes to explore the overall view.

Thorough evaluation of selective publication is difficult without a clear picture of how it operates. In this chapter, I provide a broad overview of the rules, procedures, and empirical patterns related to selective publication in the geographically based federal circuit courts from 2002 to 2012. I begin by describing the relevant rules within each circuit over this time span, highlighting both differences and similarities. Next, I describe the general process of how judges decide whether to publish the opinion in each individual case. After establishing these foundational elements, I turn to examine empirical patterns within the data. Publication rates vary across both circuits and time. There are also key differences between published and unpublished cases, along several dimensions of interest. I document how issue area and litigant type differ, as well as how the two kinds of opinions vary in their content in terms of length, clarity, and the use of precedent. Finally, I conclude by summarizing key findings and discussing how these patterns and metrics lay the groundwork for empirical analyses in Chapters 3 through 6.

Variation in Publication Rules

Title 28, Section 2071(a) of the United States Code establishes that all courts created by Congress "may from time to time prescribe rules for the conduct of their business." The Federal Rules of Appellate Procedure, which govern all circuits, are silent on the criteria for publication (Bowie et al. 2014). As a result, each circuit may use its rule-making power to fill in this gap however they see fit. The result is substantial variation across circuits (and time) in the rules related to determining which opinions should be published (Brown et al. 2021). Various scholars have discussed the nature and extent of such rules at different points in time (Cleveland 2010; Merritt and Brudney 2001; Morande 2003; Pether 2004; Richman and Reynolds 2013; Serfass and Cranford 2001). Here, I provide a summary with two specific objectives. The first is to describe the rules in effect during the time frame of my empirical analysis: 2002 to 2012. Therefore, I will discuss how rules changed over this time span within circuits as well as how they vary between circuits. Second, I provide an overview of the rules with an eye to classification that will be useful in empirical testing.

A minority of circuits explicitly declare a preference for either publication or nonpublication.[3] The First Circuit states: "In general, the court thinks it desirable that opinions be published."[4] The Seventh and Eleventh Circuits state the opposite preference. The Seventh Circuit explicitly declares a policy of avoiding unnecessary publication.[5] The Eleventh Circuit's emphasis on this issue is the most expansive:

> The policy of the court is: The unlimited proliferation of published opinions is undesirable because it tends to impair the development of the cohesive body of law. To meet this serious problem, it is declared to be the basic policy of this court to exercise imaginative and innovative resourcefulness in fashioning new methods to increase judicial efficiency and reduce the volume of published opinions.[6]

These provisions can be summarized in two binary variables: *Circuit Prefers Published*, which equals one only for First Circuit cases, and *Circuit Prefers Unpublished*, which equals one for Seventh and Eleventh Circuit cases. For all other circuits, these two variables equal zero.

Perhaps the most fundamental question raised by selective publication is which rulings should be published. Yet some circuits provide surprisingly little guidance for their judges when making this decision. After 2006, the Seventh Circuit's rules contain no discussion of which types of cases should be published. The Eighth Circuit's rules are similarly devoid of guidance after 2007. The

[3] Unless otherwise specified, the rules discussed were in effect from 2002 to 2012.
[4] First Circuit Rule 36.0(b)(1).
[5] Seventh Circuit Rule 32.1. Prior to 2007, this provision was located at Seventh Circuit Rule 53(a).
[6] Eleventh Circuit Rule 36-3, I.O.P. 5.

Tenth Circuit does not list any criteria but does mention that rulings are usually published when the decision being appealed was published.[7] Three other circuits provide only a brief description of what merits publication. The Second Circuit's rules state that nonpublication is appropriate for unanimous rulings that serve "no jurisprudential purpose."[8] The Third Circuit provides the less-than-helpful proviso that a decision should be designated precedential (i.e., published), when it has precedential value.[9] The Eleventh Circuit similarly provides that decisions with "no precedential value" should not be published.[10] Only six of the twelve geographic circuits provide a detailed list of criteria in their rules for when publication (or nonpublication) is appropriate throughout the time frame from 2002 to 2012.[11] The Seventh Circuit provided such a list from 2002 to 2006,[12] and the Eighth Circuit did so from 2002 to 2007.[13] Table 2.1 lists the various criteria that appear and shows which circuit rules include which criteria. It also notes the overall number of criteria provided by each circuit.

While there is substantial overlap among the publication criteria listed in court rules, there is still notable variation both in the number and content. The Fifth Circuit provides the highest number with nine. The most commonly adopted provision is that cases which make new law, or alter or clarify existing law, should be published. Even circuits with more vague standards discuss the importance of precedential value for deciding publication. This amounts to much the same thing since an opinion that makes new law would have undeniable value as precedent in future cases. The next most frequently adopted proviso is that opinions relating to issues of significant public interest ought to be published. Observers often note that publication criteria leave substantial room for discretion (Bowie et al. 2014; Hoffman 1981), and this criteria is particularly susceptible to interpretation.

Two other groups of criteria are adopted in various combinations across circuits. The first is a series of features of the law involved in the case and how it is discussed. Some deem a ruling worthy of publication if it applies existing law to new facts, criticizes the current law, includes a useful discussion of the historical background of a law, calls attention to an overlooked law, or creates or addresses a conflict in the law within or across jurisdictions. Another type of criteria is directed at the procedural posture of a ruling. Selected circuits deem

[7] Tenth Circuit Rule 36.2.

[8] Second Circuit Rule 32.1(a). Before 2009, this provision was located at Second Circuit Rule 0.23.

[9] Third Circuit I.O.P. 5.2.

[10] Eleventh Circuit Rule 36-3, I.O.P. 6. Before 2007, this provision was located at Eleventh Circuit Rule 36-3, I.O.P. 5.

[11] First Circuit Rule 36.0(b)(1), Fourth Circuit Rule 36(a), Fifth Circuit Rule 47.5.1, Sixth Circuit Rule 206(a), Ninth Circuit Rule 36-2, D.C. Circuit Rule 36(a)(2)

[12] Seventh Circuit Rule 53(c)(1).

[13] Eighth Circuit Appendix 1(4).

Table 2.1 Publication Criteria by Circuit from 2002 to 2012. ✓ indicates that a criterion is mentioned in the relevant circuit's rules, and an "x" indicates that the rules explicitly state that a factor is *not* determinative of publication. After 2006 and 2007, respectively, the Seventh and Eighth Circuit local rules and internal operating procedures did not list any criteria for publication. (Source: Rachael K. Hinkle 2024)

	1st	2nd	3rd	4th	5th	6th	7th (02-06)	8th (02-07)	9th	10th	11th	D.C.
New, changed, or clarified law	✓			✓	✓	✓	✓	✓	✓			✓
Precedential/jurisprudential value		✓	✓								✓	
Issue of public interest				✓	✓	✓	✓	✓	✓			✓
Law applied to new facts	✓				✓	✓		✓				
Current law criticized				✓	✓		✓		✓			✓
Historical discussion of law				✓	✓		✓	✓				
Calls attention to overlooked law									✓			✓
Creates or resolves a conflict				✓	✓	✓	✓	✓				✓
Separate opinion		✓	x		✓	✓			✓			
Reverse or affirm on different grounds			x		✓	✓						
Appealed ruling was published						✓			✓	✓		
Published ruling reversed							✓	✓				✓
Remanded from Supreme Court					✓	✓	✓		✓			
Significant guide to future litigants	✓											
Number of criteria	3	2	1	5	9	8	7	6	7	1	1	6

public disagreement among the panel or with the court below sufficient to justify publication. The Third Circuit takes the opposite tack and explicitly notes that such features do not necessarily preclude leaving a ruling unpublished.[14] Some rules indicate that when the lower court disposition under review was published, the circuit opinion should be as well. Yet other circuits combine these criteria and recommend publication when a published ruling is reversed or affirmed on different grounds. Finally, in some instances, the criteria specify that opinions issued after a case has been remanded from the Supreme Court must be published.

The Process of Deciding on Publication

The day-to-day practice of determining which rulings will be published varies from the formal rules in two respects. First, unlike court rules, which are publicly available and straightforward to access, the informal norms of how courts make these decisions are less visible. Second, the evidence from scholars who have interviewed judges and otherwise investigated how the process works behind closed doors indicates that there is substantially more similarity across circuits in practice than there is in the court rules. In the circuit courts, appeals are resolved by rotating panels of three judges. While their home offices are scattered across multiple states, panels periodically meet in the same location, generally for about a week at a time (Kuersten and Songer 2001). In addition to hearing oral arguments, the three judges have private conferences to discuss a variety of matters regarding both the cases that were argued and other cases assigned to the panel. It is at these conferences when the publication decision is usually made (Bowie et al. 2014; Hazelton et al. 2016). Bowie et al. (2014) conducted extensive interviews of circuit judges about the details of each stage of the appellate process, and they report that, overall, their interviews indicate "a widespread informal norm" of publication if even one panel judge wants the opinion to be published.

Although the decision to publish is usually made in conference, it can be changed at any time up until the opinion is released (Murrah 1973).[15] However, the efficiency rationale of selective publication dictates that most of the time the decision is made as early in the process as possible (Robel 1989; Wasby 2001). This is especially true for unpublished decisions (Murrah 1973). After all, one can only save time and effort in the drafting process if one knows prior to writing the opinion that it does not need to stand up to the rigors of scrutiny that accompany binding precedent. As Robel (1989, 954) states, "the determination not

[14] Third Circuit I.O.P. 5.3.

[15] In rare instances, panels have even changed publication status after an opinion has been issued.

to publish occurs very early in the appellate process, and necessarily so." Once an opinion is issued, if the litigants are unhappy about the publication status of the ruling, they have limited recourse. The decision to not publish cannot be appealed. The parties may file a motion requesting publication, but winning such motions is rare (Brown et al. 2021). Ultimately, the decision of the panel regarding publication is final.

Variation in Publication Rates

Having examined the rules within circuits and the process by which publication decisions are made, I now proceed to explore broad trends in how these foundational elements manifest in the aggregate. This section begins by exploring variation in publication rates. During early debates over publication, Bell (1970, 242) wrote that "[i]t is not contemplated that the order [i.e., unpublished] form of decision will receive undue use." However, that is an empirical question. The percentage of cases that are published may well vary by circuit and rule type as well as over time. In the following analyses, I provide a chronological summary of publication rates in each circuit as well as by different types of rules.

Publication Rates Across Circuits

In the decade after publication rules were introduced, Reynolds and Richman (1981) argued that while the circuits could be viewed as laboratories, insufficient attention had been given to such data. In the spirit of this observation, I begin my descriptive analysis of publication rates in the C^{3}PO database by examining each circuit on its own. Figure 2.1 illustrates overall publication rates by circuit in map form, and Figure 2.2 shows the average publication rate in each circuit in each year. While some circuits, such as the Fourth Circuit, have remained consistent across the time span, others reveal the importance of examining developments over time. The exceptionally high publication rates for the Fifth and Eleventh Circuits in the early years of the data may reflect that these circuits were slow to comply with the E-Government Act of 2002[16] that mandated all opinions be posted on circuit websites (thereby making them accessible for collection by providers such as Lexis) (McAlister 2020). Other interesting patterns emerge as well. The First Circuit has consistently maintained a high publication rate around 80%, while the Third, Fourth, Fifth, and Ninth Circuits have low publication rates below 15%.

[16] Pub. L. 107-347, 116 Stat. 2899, 44 USC § 3501 et seq.

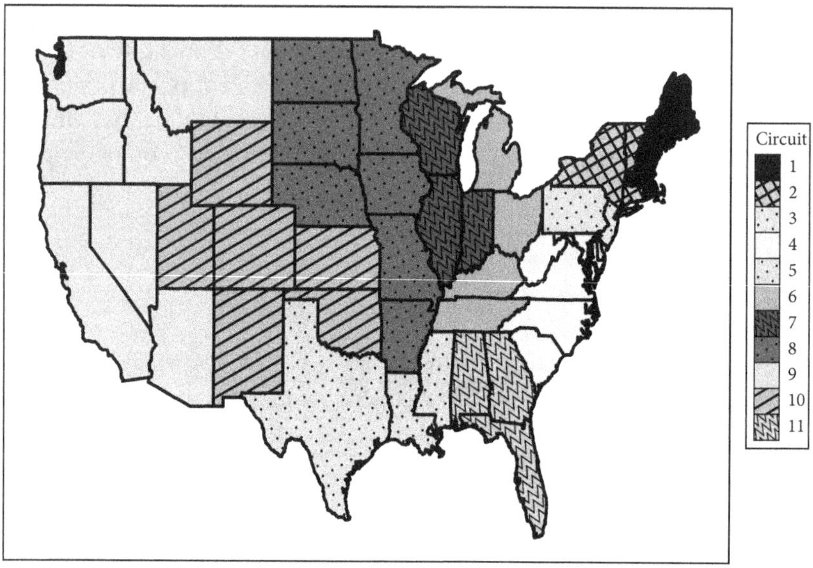

Figure 2.1 Map of Publication Rate by Circuit: Different patterns are used to identify the circuits, and darker background shading indicates a higher rate of publication (Source: Rachael K. Hinkle 2024)

Publication Rates by Rule Type

In 1981, Reynolds and Richman conducted a study of publication and found that a presumption against publication in the rules did not have a discernible empirical effect and vague standards led to more published opinions. The description of the various circuit rules summarized in Table 2.1 makes it possible to conduct a similar analysis for the time frame from 2002 to 2012. First, I examine the impact of an explicitly stated preference to publish or not publish. Figure 2.3 shows that, as expected, the highest publication rates occur where the rules state an a priori preference for publishing. Since only one circuit has this rule, the right panel shows the publication rate in the First Circuit. The lowest incidence of publication occurs in the circuits that have no indication of favoritism one way or the other. The publication rate in circuits with a stated default of nonpublication is a bit higher. Reynolds and Richman (1981) found that a presumption of not publishing appeared to depress the publication rate from 45% to about 33%. It is possible that the opposite finding here is due to parsing out the First Circuit into a separate category, or perhaps the dynamics have changed over time.

The other feature of circuit rules that may affect the publication rate is the specificity of the criteria for publication. Table 2.1 outlines the number of such

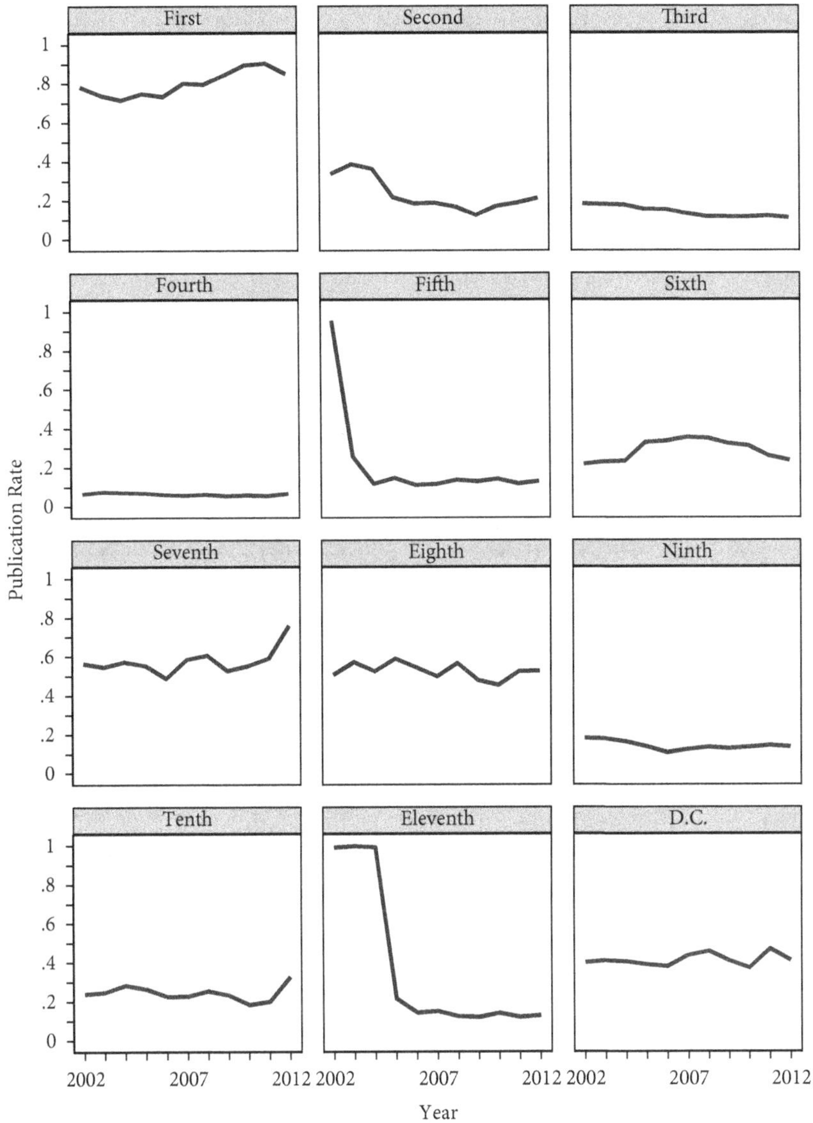

Figure 2.2 Publication Rate by Circuit and Year: 2002 to 2012 (Source: Rachael K. Hinkle 2024)

criteria for each circuit, including how the number changed in the Seventh and Eighth Circuits. The circuits vary from zero to nine listed criteria. Figure 2.4 shows the publication rates for the circuits with vague (0–2 criteria), moderate (3–5 criteria), and specific (6 or more criteria) publication guidelines. While

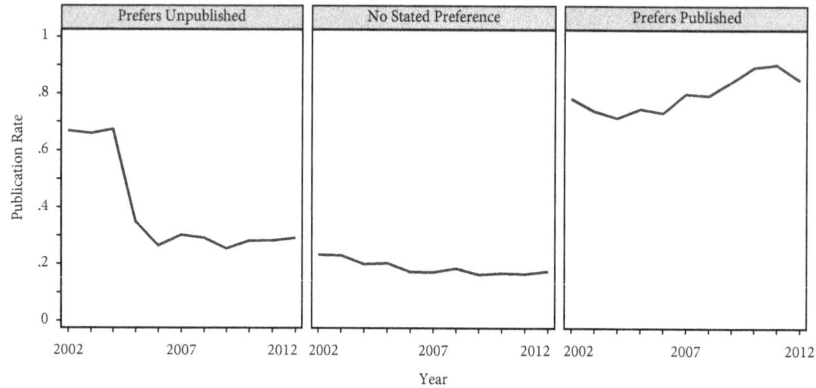

Figure 2.3 Publication Rate by Circuit's Stated Preference for Publication: 2002 to 2012 (Source: Rachael K. Hinkle 2024)

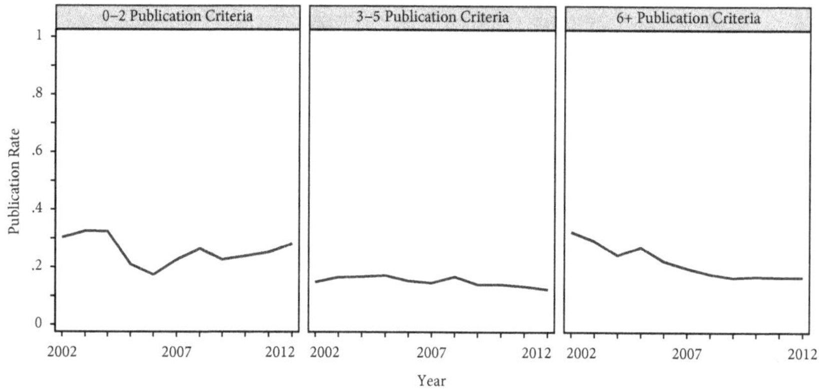

Figure 2.4 Publication Rate by Circuit's Number of Criteria for Publication: 2002 to 2012 (Source: Rachael K. Hinkle 2024)

Reynolds and Richman (1981) found that vaguer rules with fewer criteria led to higher publication rates, I do not find such a consistent pattern. Rather, publication rates are lowest when the rules give a moderate amount of guidance and a bit higher both when rules are vague and highly specific. This suggests that perhaps this element of circuit rules has minimal constraining effect.

Differences Between Published and Unpublished Cases

Next, I turn to examine differences between published and unpublished rulings. Many scholars have pointed out that these should be distinct (Robel 1989;

Siegelman and Donohue III 1990), although some types of differences may have more concerning normative implications than others. McAlister (2019, 564) points out that "[r]easoned explanations matter not only as an indicator of trustworthiness and neutrality, but also as a sign of dignity and respect." Consequently, it is important to understand both when published opinions, with their more extensive justification, are provided and to what extent unpublished decisions can still provide such explanations. I begin by comparing how publication is distributed among issue area and litigant type, and then I proceed to compare elements of the content of rulings by publication status.

Issue Area

Various scholars have noted that publication is often dependent upon the type of legal issue a case involves. According to Brown et al. (2021, 39), "[i]nherent in the decision to publish is a normative decision that the subject of the opinion is important." Carlson et al. (2020, 225) claim that "some types of cases may be more likely to lead to a published opinion than others." Davies (1981, 380) argues that publication is more likely in civil than criminal cases, citing a judge he interviewed who stated, "[C]ivil appeals offer appellate judges more interesting, more satisfying, and more prestigious work than criminal appeals." Davies (1981) goes on to point out that it is not likely that all criminal appeals are either routine or frivolous. The data suggest both that this is accurate and that judges do not necessarily overwhelmingly relegate criminal appeals to unpublished status. Figure 2.5 shows the distribution of cases by issue area within each type of opinion.[17] Because there are many more unpublished rulings than published, looking at the percentage of each issue area within each type of opinion provides a useful point of comparison. While 34% of unpublished opinions are criminal appeals, that is also the most common category among published opinions, where criminal appeals make up 30% of cases. Prisoner petitions constitute 14% of unpublished rulings, which is understandably greater than the 8% of published opinions they make up. Administrative appeals show an even larger difference, accounting for only 10% of published opinions compared to 18% of unpublished ones. This is arguably another category of cases that are relatively mundane and less interesting to judges. Bankruptcy, tort, and other civil appeals occupy a larger portion of published cases compared to unpublished. In fact, the percentages are at least doubled in published cases. Civil appeals that involve civil rights issues and original jurisdiction cases are similarly represented for both types of opinions.

[17] Appendix 2.A provides details regarding how issue area was coded.

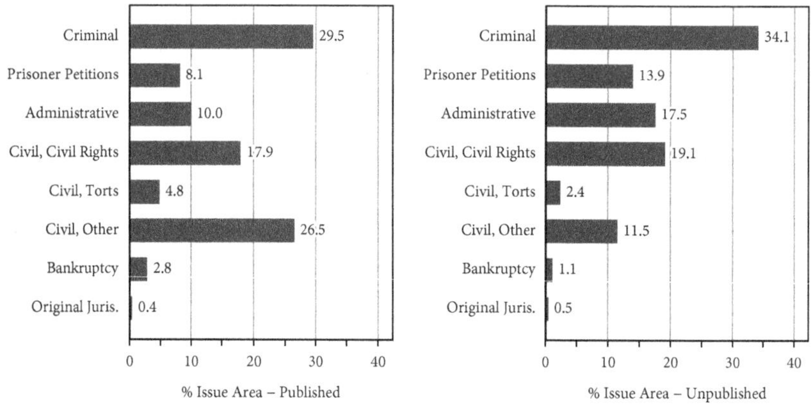

Figure 2.5 Breakdown of Issue Area in Published and Unpublished Cases (Source: Rachael K. Hinkle 2024)

Litigant Type

One of the reasons for the move toward selective publication was judges' assertion that some cases are not important (Murrah 1973). While the assessment of which cases are important may be driven by legal considerations or the issue area, it is also possible that the type of litigants involved in a case may shape the perception of importance. This may also be related to the preferences and priorities of the litigants themselves. Some parties might want a fast resolution more than reasons (Brown et al. 2021). Richman and Reynolds (2013, 162–63) assert that "[f]or most small, one-time litigants, error correction is all that matters; by contrast, rich and powerful governmental and business entities, whose activities may spread across the country or around the world, care a great deal about consistent law declaration." However, Songer and Davis (1990, 308) note that "[i]n interviews with the author, three of the judges on the Eleventh Circuit specifically denied that the characteristics of the appellant would have any effect on the decision to publish." Figure 2.6 suggests this is not necessarily the case. The distribution of types of appellant is rather different when rulings are published compared to when they are not. Most notably, appeals brought by indigent prisoners or people representing themselves pro se make up 36% of unpublished rulings, but only 10% of published ones. Conversely, the percentage of published opinions involving appellants that are organizations is quadruple what it is for unpublished opinions. For state and local governments, the portion of published opinions is nearly five times greater, and for the United States as an appellant it is over six times greater. Interestingly,

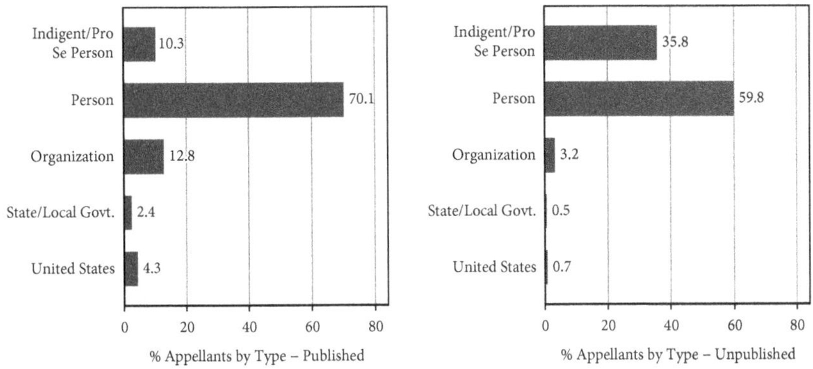

Figure 2.6 Breakdown of Appellant Type in Published and Unpublished Cases (Source: Rachael K. Hinkle 2024)

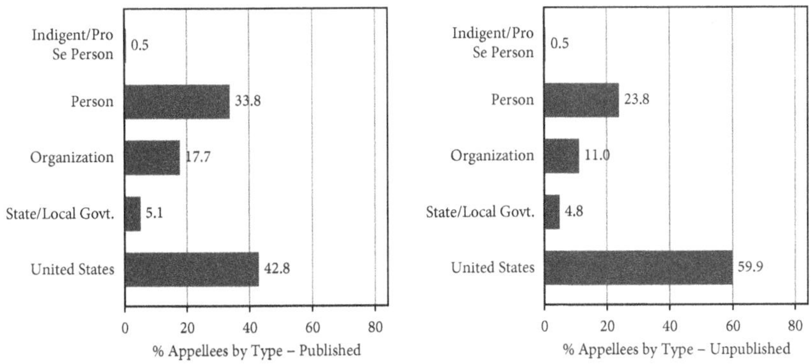

Figure 2.7 Breakdown of Appellee Type in Published and Unpublished Cases (Source: Rachael K. Hinkle 2024)

regular people who bring appeals and are represented by counsel make up a larger share of published cases (70%) than unpublished ones (60%).

While appellant type is arguably most relevant because appellants make the decision about whether to bring the appeal, it is also possible that the characteristics of the appellee might matter as well. Figure 2.7 shows both how different appellees are from appellants and how appellees vary by publication type. The United States is frequently on the receiving end of appeals, but they make up a larger portion of unpublished rulings than published, 60% compared to 43%. Persons, organizations, and state/local governments still have a larger share of published cases, although the gaps are relatively smaller.

Opinion Content

There is substantial reason to believe that the content of opinions will depend greatly on whether they are published. Early on, Murrah (1973, 5) advised that "[n]on-published opinions can be short. They do not need to cite all of the law." Bowie et al. (2014, 118) interviewed a judge who told them, "When you decide to publish, a lot more work goes into the opinion." Others have similarly noted that writing published opinions takes far more time and effort (Martineau 1994; Schiltz 2005a; Wald 1995). It seems likely that such a difference in effort will produce noticeable differences in the nature of the content. To quantify such variation, I compare the distribution of opinion length, writing clarity, and the use of precedent across opinion types.

It is well accepted that unpublished opinions are generally shorter than their published counterparts (Bowie et al. 2014; Richman and Reynolds 2013). Reynolds and Richman (1981) examined a sample of 891 cases and reported that 55% of unpublished opinions were less than three hundred words. Brown et al. (2021) reported that unpublished opinions are about one-fifth of the length of published ones. Figure 2.8 displays the magnitude of the difference between the length of published and unpublished decisions from 2002 to 2012. The average length of a published opinion is 5,922 words, compared to 1,309 for unpublished. This is roughly comparable to Brown et al. (2021)'s finding. However, unlike Reynolds and Richman (1981), in this dataset only 11% of unpublished opinions are less than three hundred words.

Posner (2017, 225) writes that "[c]larity and brevity, not eloquence, are the only attainable, though rarely attained or even attempted, literary goals of modern judicial writing." To probe this claim a bit, I next summarize the clarity of circuit court opinions. Specifically, I calculate the reading grade level of each opinion and compare the distributions to see the extent to which published and unpublished decisions vary on this dimension.[18] Figure 2.9 shows that both kinds of opinions are pitched at similar levels. Both tend to be complex, with reading grade levels that correspond to the junior or senior year of college. While unpublished decisions are somewhat more readable, the difference from published opinions is only one grade.

A third feature of the content of opinions is how much and what type of caselaw they cite. The greater amount of time and effort judges devote to crafting published opinions is likely to result in a more extensive use of previous rulings in addition to resulting in longer opinions. Figure 2.10 shows that this is, indeed, the case.

[18] Specifically, I use the SMOG index (McLaughlin 1969), which generates a number equivalent to the appropriate reading grade level for a text. "SMOG" is an acronym for "Simple Measure of Gobbledygook."

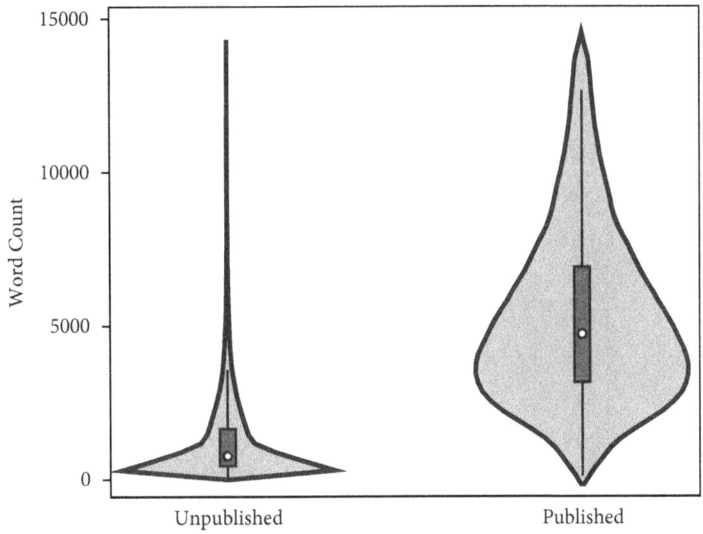

Figure 2.8 Distribution of Opinion Length by Publication Status (Source: Rachael K. Hinkle 2024)

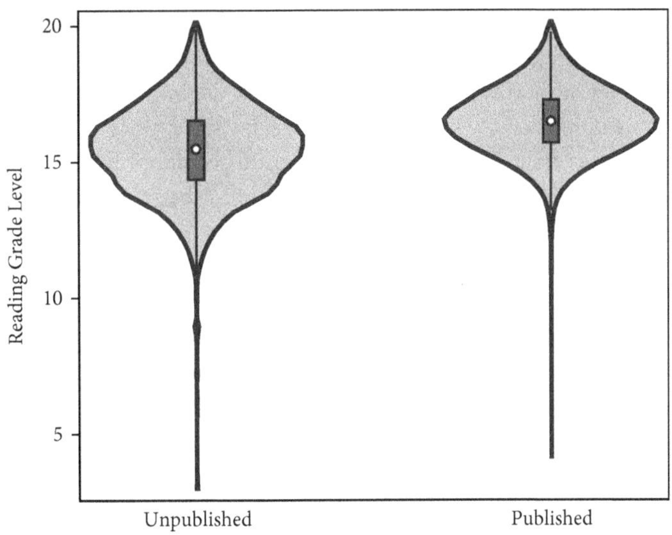

Figure 2.9 Distribution of Reading Grade Level by Publication Status (Source: Rachael K. Hinkle 2024)

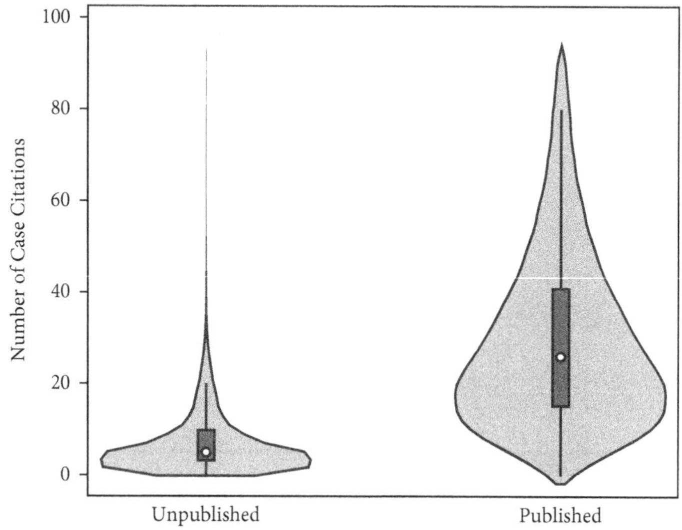

Figure 2.10 Distribution of Case Citations by Publication Status (Source: Rachael K. Hinkle 2024)

The average number of case citations in a published opinion is thirty-five compared to eight in unpublished rulings. Moreover, the distribution for unpublished cases is heavily concentrated at the low end of the scale. Ninety-three percent of such rulings have fewer than twenty citations, and 74% are in the single digits. There are also some opinions with no citations to caselaw. Seven percent of unpublished opinions, and less than 1% of published rulings, do not cite any cases.

The type of caselaw cited in published and unpublished decisions is also likely to vary. Not all precedents carry the same weight; some are binding, while others are only persuasive. According to legal doctrine, published circuit opinions are binding for all subsequent panels in the same circuit (Songer, Sheehan, and Haire 2000). Of course, Supreme Court opinions are also binding precedent. All other caselaw only has persuasive value in federal circuit courts. Since unpublished rulings are intended to be used in cases with well-settled legal principles, most of the caselaw cited in such opinions should be binding. When there is clear binding precedent, judges have little reason to go further and also cite persuasive precedent. However, when a point of law has not previously been addressed in a circuit, there may be little binding authority available. This often means a court will discuss any persuasive caselaw that addresses a similar issue. Since cases of first impression are the classic type of case where publication is expected, published opinions should tend to cite a higher concentration of persuasive caselaw compared to unpublished opinions. In order to evaluate this element of the content of opinions, I generate a metric, *Legal Novelty*, which is the proportion of precedents cited in an opinion that are to persuasive authority. Therefore,

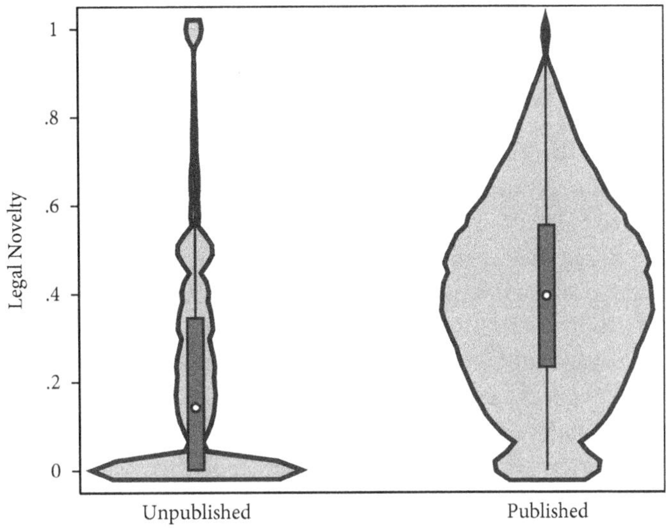

Figure 2.11 Distribution of Legal Novelty by Publication Status (Source: Rachael K. Hinkle 2024)

an opinion that cites only binding precedent equals zero, and an opinion that cites only persuasive precedent equals one.[19]

Figure 2.11 shows how the type of precedent used varies by publication status. As expected, published opinions use a noticeably higher proportion of persuasive precedents compared to unpublished decisions. The average published opinion uses 40% persuasive caselaw compared to about half that amount, 21%, for the average unpublished opinion. However, the distribution shows that the difference is even more dramatic because of the large concentration of unpublished cases with very low measures of *Legal Novelty*. In fact, 42% of all unpublished opinions contain no citations to persuasive precedent at all. Conversely, 31% of all published opinions contain more references to persuasive authority than to binding precedent. These patterns are precisely what one would expect given the emphasis in court rules and scholarly discussion on the link between legal novelty and publication.

Conclusions

Anecdotes raise interesting questions, but they are only a starting point. By looking at rules, procedures, and empirical practice, this chapter takes the

[19] Opinions that dispose of a case without citing any caselaw at all are typically easy cases in which the law is quite clear, so such opinions are coded as zero on the *Legal Novelty* scale.

next step and provides the broad overview necessary to understand how selective publication operates. One pattern that stands out is that while circuit rules and publication rates vary quite substantially, there is little link between the two. The First Circuit does have a stated preference for publication and a high publication rate. But there is not a clear pattern between a stated preference for nonpublication and publishing fewer rulings. Nor does increasing specificity in the criteria for publication uniformly increase or decrease the relative frequency with which circuits decide to publish.

This chapter also summarizes differences in issues, litigant types, and opinion content based on publication status. The distribution of issues within the two kinds of cases varies as expected, but not quite as dramatically as some scholarly commentary might suggest. For example, criminal cases make up a larger percentage of unpublished cases, but only 4% more than their share of published cases. The distribution of litigants, especially appellants, also follows expectations. Pro se or indigent appellants constitute 36% of unpublished cases compared to 10% of published ones, while appeals brought by the United States are 4% of published cases and less than 1% of unpublished ones. Opinion content also carries few surprises. Published opinions are longer, contain more citations to caselaw, and cite a larger percentage of persuasive precedents (which indicates more novel legal issues). However, it is interesting to note that both types of opinions are drafted with similar levels of complexity.

Much like the anecdotes surrounding publication that are often discussed, the broad patterns described in this chapter are also only a starting point for an even more detailed discussion. The descriptive summaries here suggest the importance of continued exploration and rigorous empirical testing of how selective publication affects a variety of ways in which both litigants and judges exercise power within an important institution. The rest of the book takes up this challenge, beginning with the foundational question of how judges decide which opinions are published.

Appendix 2.A: Coding Issue Area

Issue area is coded using a combination of the appeal type (APPTYPE) variable and the "nature of suit" (NOS) code from the FJC's Integrated Database. APPTYPE identifies whether an appeal is administrative, civil, criminal, bankruptcy-related, or a matter of original jurisdiction. NOS codes can take on nearly one hundred different values, but I only used a subset here to designate three additional issue areas: prisoner petitions, civil cases involving civil rights issues, and civil cases involving tort claims. Table 2.A.1 provides a list of all NOS codes used to create each of these three issue areas, as well as the title assigned to each NOS code. For a complete list of NOS codes and more detailed descriptions, see https://www.uscourts.gov/sites/default/files/js_044_code_descriptions.pdf (accessed December 10, 2020).

Table 2.A.1 NOS Codes Used to Create Issue Area Variable (Source: Rachael K. Hinkle 2024)

NOS Code	NOS Title	Issue Coding
510	Motions to Vacate Sentence	Prisoner Petitions
530	Habeas Corpus—General	Prisoner Petitions
535	Death Penalty	Prisoner Petitions
540	Mandamus & Other	Prisoner Petitions
440	Other Civil Rights	Civil, Civil Rights
441	Voting	Civil, Civil Rights
442	Employment	Civil, Civil Rights
443	Housing/Accommodations	Civil, Civil Rights
444	Welfare	Civil, Civil Rights
550	Prisoner Civil Rights	Civil, Civil Rights
555	Prison Condition	Civil, Civil Rights
195	Contract Products Liability	Civil, Torts
240	Torts to Land	Civil, Torts
245	Tort Product Liability	Civil, Torts
310	Torts: Airplane	Civil, Torts
315	Airplane Product Liability	Civil, Torts
320	Torts: Assault, Libel, & Slander	Civil, Torts
330	Torts: Federal Employers' Liability	Civil, Torts
340	Torts: Marine	Civil, Torts
345	Marine Product Liability	Civil, Torts
350	Torts: Motor Vehicle	Civil, Torts
355	Motor Vehicle Product Liability	Civil, Torts
360	Other Personal Injury	Civil, Torts
362	PI: Medical Malpractice	Civil, Torts
365	PI: Product Liability	Civil, Torts
368	Asbestos PI Product Liability	Civil, Torts
370	Personal Property Fraud	Civil, Torts
385	Property Damage Product Liability	Civil, Torts

3

Visible Rules, Invisible Norms

The Determinants of Publication

Introduction

In 1997, Suzanne Conti was hired as an executive at American Axle, a corporation that specialized in manufacturing automobile parts. After nearly a decade of being promoted more slowly, paid less, and given less prestigious titles than her male peers, she filed a gender discrimination lawsuit. During discovery, the trial judge refused permission for her to depose the CEO, whom she alleged was the source of discriminatory culture and practices at American Axle. On appeal, the Sixth Circuit reversed the trial court and ruled that Conti was entitled to conduct the deposition.[1] The appellate opinion reversed the trial court, was not unanimous, and contained a lengthy and substantial discussion of the issues. It was over eleven thousand words long and contained more than one hundred citations. Yet the panel chose not to publish the ruling. While leaving such an opinion unpublished is unusual, it is not the only one of its kind. Various scholars point to similar situations in which rulings that appear to merit publication are not given such status (Arnold 1999; Brown et al. 2021; McAlister 2019).

One of the central concerns raised with respect to how judges make publication decisions is the sheer amount of discretion they are given. Law (2004, 866) argues that "[s]imply to assume that judges can and do apply inherently vague publication criteria to precisely their intended effect, in a consistent manner untainted by considerations of ideology or strategy, is wishful thinking." Supreme Court justices have openly complained that circuit judges use nonpublication to avoid review (Liptak 2015). While Judge Patricia Wald of the D.C. Circuit has asserted that there is not enough time to resolve every case in great detail, she also believes that selective publication "allows for deviousness and abuse" (Wald 1995, 1374). At a minimum, judges could make mistakes regarding publication simply because they are human and "error-free application of publication guidelines cannot be achieved" (Morande 2003, 753).

[1] *Conti v. American Axle and Manufacturing, Inc.*, 326 Fed. Appx. 900 (6th Cir. 2009).

Selective Publication in the U.S. Courts of Appeals. Rachael K. Hinkle, Oxford University Press.
 DOI: 10.1093/oso/9780197770085.003.0003

Assessing the extent to which publication decisions are "correct" is quite challenging. It is especially difficult to provide evidence of how many important cases are left unpublished (Hoffman 1981). Scholars have generally noted such a phenomenon without estimating its frequency (Arnold 1999; Brown et al. 2021; McAlister 2019; Songer et al. 1988). Reynolds and Richman (1981) concluded that refusing to publish opinions that could be important did not seem to be a major problem and estimated that it happened in less than 1% of cases. However, a bar study in the D.C. Circuit reviewed publication decisions and the participants questioned nonpublication in 40% of the cases studied (Wald 1995). This surprisingly high number suggests that publication decisions may be substantially more complex than simply applying circuit rules.

What is at stake when a panel decides whether to publish? Why is it worth the effort to investigate? For litigants like Suzanne Conti, whether the opinion in their case is published can affect them in various ways. The status of the opinion reflects the amount of court attention and resources that were devoted to resolving a case (Davies 1981, 373). Refusing to publish an opinion "may send an especially strong signal to the litigant about the perceived low value of her case" (Brown et al. 2021, 102). Furthermore, the decision has far-reaching implications for how much a ruling will impact future cases. Although unpublished opinions are sometimes cited (Hannon 2001, 225), Brown et al. (2021) report that there are thirty published opinions cited (by circuit courts) for every one unpublished decision. The reasons for this practical reality are directly linked to legal doctrine. When a ruling is not published, it is not binding precedent (Arnold 1999; Law 2004; Vladeck and Gulati 2005). However, published opinions are binding on all subsequent circuit panels (Beske 2018).

The power to withhold precedential status is important in its own right. Speaking of the law, Slavitt (1995, 109) observed that "[l]ike a sculpture, it is shaped as much by what is removed as by what is added." In the federal circuit courts, selective publication provides such power. Litigants at the trial level have a right to at least one appeal (Bowie et al. 2014). This means that circuit courts must render a decision in every case brought before them (see Federal Rules of Appellate Procedure, Rule 4). Consequently, they do not have agenda control in the same sense as an apex court with discretionary jurisdiction (Hinkle 2023). However, circuit judges have control over their policy agenda through the combination of selective publication and circuit rules that state unpublished rulings are not precedent (Epstein and Jacobi 2010). Judges may exercise what Bachrach and Baratz (1962) famously call the "second face of power" by deciding when to simply resolve a dispute without shaping the law. As a result, exploring how publication decisions are made is key to understanding the exercise of this important negative power as well as how litigants experience the circuit courts.

This chapter is focused on answering a foundational empirical question: What factors shape the publication decision? Like judicial decisions more generally, there are multiple broad categories of influences that might shape such determinations. I build on existing judicial decision-making theory and formulate hypotheses with respect to how law, ideology, strategy, and case characteristics influence the publication decision. Explicit legal rules almost assuredly play a substantial role. As a result, circuit rules, legal novelty, oral argument, and disagreement among judges should all affect the likelihood of publication in various ways. But judges are human, and we know that they are affected by a variety of extralegal factors, including their own preferences, strategic calculations, and implicit biases. As a result, publication decisions may be influenced by several factors beyond those stated explicitly in circuit rules. Judges may be more willing to publish decisions that reflect their own ideological preferences. A group of judges with divergent viewpoints may use nonpublication as a tool of compromise. Judges may leave rulings unpublished when they anticipate the possibility of hostile review. Finally, cases with topics or litigants that judges don't view as a high priority might be less likely to result in a published opinion. After developing these hypotheses, I describe the research design and then discuss the results. Finally, the chapter concludes with a discussion of overall patterns and their implications for how we understand the work of the circuit courts.

How Law Affects Publication

One of the fundamental tenets of a court system is that judges make decisions by applying the law. While empirical evidence of legal constraint is challenging to isolate, there is evidence of its operation in the circuit courts (see, e.g., Hinkle 2015). Like other decisions judges make, publication is likely shaped by the controlling legal doctrine (although not necessarily to the exclusion of other influences). While the effect of law is often difficult to nail down, in the case of publication decisions, the formal circuit rules governing the process provide a basis for establishing which empirical patterns are consistent with legal constraint. Moreover, the variation in the rules (discussed in detail in Chapter 2) provides leverage to determine if different rules lead to different publication behavior. In this section, I first analyze how the various types of rules might be expected to make publication more or less likely in general. Then I proceed to link specific publication criteria to the impact they would be expected to have if judges take them seriously.

There is often skepticism that circuit rules regarding publication have a substantial impact. Judge Wald has stated that "in my experience the criteria are vague and infinitely maneuverable" (Wald 1995, 1374). Bowie et al. (2014, 121) report that after conducting interviews, the overall impression from judges is that the criteria for publication "take different concrete meanings in the minds of different judges." There is not clear empirical evidence of judges following publication rules (Songer et al. 1988). Merritt and Brudney (2001) note that circuits with similar rules have very different publication rates, which perhaps suggests that rules do not matter. However, research to date has not undertaken a large-scale investigation of the myriad ways rules might matter. It is possible that some aspects of the rules do affect judges even if others do not.

There are several ways that circuit rules might affect how judges make publication decisions. First, the clearest potential implication is that circuits with an explicit default preference for either publication or nonpublication should have a higher rate of the preferred type of opinion than circuits that do not state a preference. When Reynolds and Richman (1981) examined whether a presumption against publication in the rules mattered, they found no discernible difference (Richman and Reynolds 2013). Nevertheless, it is possible that more recent data contain the expected pattern.

Second, the specificity of the publication criteria might have an impact. Here the direction of the impact is not immediately obvious. It is possible that listing more reasons for publishing an opinion would lead to more frequent publication overall. However, a long line of literature on the difference between rules and standards establishes that providing more detailed criteria constrains a decision maker more effectively (Cross et al. 2012; Montgomery et al. 2021). From this perspective, a small number of publication criteria might leave circuit judges more discretion to publish cases whenever they prefer, while more specific criteria limit judges' ability to publish to only the subset of cases that fit the listed criteria. Consistent with this explanation, Reynolds and Richman (1981) found that vague standards led to more published opinions (Richman and Reynolds 2013). Based on their finding, I hypothesize that more extensive publication criteria will constrain the impulse to publish, and, therefore, more criteria will be associated with a lower probability of publication.

Third, prior to 2007 some circuits prohibited citation of unpublished opinions.[2] Such policies arguably allowed judges to produce opinions with less effort since any mistakes could not be aired in future litigation. This added benefit to nonpublication may have led to judges using it more frequently when the rules would insulate their work from later examination. Put differently, I expect that prohibiting citation to unpublished opinions decreased the publication rate.

[2] Prior to the adoption of Federal Rule of Appellate Procedure 32.1, such citation was prohibited (with narrow exceptions) in the First, Second, Third, Fourth, Seventh, Eighth, Ninth, and Tenth Circuits. The Sixth Circuit adopted a rule prohibiting citation in 2006.

In addition to the overall type of rules each circuit employs, several of the specific criteria in use provide opportunities to measure the extent to which publication decisions fall in line with legal doctrine. The most frequently mentioned criterion is whether there is some new issue of law that needs to be decided. Many circuits list new, changed, or clarified law as a criterion for publication, while others refer to the precedential or jurisprudential value of a case. Scholars also often point out this key link between publication and whether law is unsettled or clearly established (Carlson et al. 2020; Fischman 2021; Ricks 2006; Wald 1995). The original justification for selective publication was largely driven by the idea that many cases involved clear and well-settled law, thereby rendering a published opinion a redundant and unnecessary expenditure of resources. As Ricks (2006) points out, the efficiency gains produced by selective publication are contingent on the foundational assumption that there is really nothing new at all in unpublished cases. In short, the strongest expectation from legal doctrine is that cases with more novel legal issues should be more likely to be published. This element is so pivotal that I expect it to operate across all circuits and years, including those where the publication criteria are so vague that it is not explicitly mentioned.

There are seven circuits that mention issues of substantial public interest justify publication.[3] While this is a complicated concept to measure, both cases with oral argument and those in which third parties participate as amici are more likely to involve issues of widespread importance to the public. Several scholars have noted that cases in which there is oral argument are more likely to result in published opinions (Songer, Sheehan, and Haire 2000; Wald 1995; Wasby 2001). Previous scholars have not investigated whether amicus participation operates in the same way, perhaps because it is relatively rare in the circuit courts. However, that rarity makes it an excellent indicator of public importance. I hypothesize that in circuits where public importance is a criterion for publication, both oral argument and amicus participation will increase the probability of publication compared to circuits where it is not a listed criterion. I expect that both factors will still increase publication rates in circuits without this criterion (albeit to a lesser degree). There are two reasons for this. First, the concepts formalized in one circuit might have an informal impact in others through a process of policy diffusion. Second, there can be overlap between cases that are important to the public and those that involve novel legal issues. To the extent that oral argument and amici signal unsettled legal issues, they may increase publication for that reason as well.

[3] However, two of these circuits only included such a criterion for a subset of the years in the dataset. For details of all criteria by circuit, see Table 2.1 in Chapter 2.

The next three publication criteria I will use to test for the effect of legal doctrine on publication decisions have the advantage of being straightforward to measure. They are the presence of separate opinions, reversal of the lower court, and the lower court opinion being published. Four circuits list separate opinions (or, more generally, lack of unanimity) as a reason for publication. A variety of scholars have also noted that dissents and concurrences in unpublished opinions seem questionable and should at least be quite rare (Hannon 2001; Reynolds and Richman 1981; Songer, Sheehan, and Haire 2000). Empirical research generally reports such patterns (Brown et al. 2021). For example, Reynolds and Richman (1981) found separate opinions in only 0.5% of unpublished cases compared to 12.4% for published ones. As a result, I expect that cases with a dissent or concurrence will be more likely to be published. While previous research has not specifically looked at the impact of particular rules, I also anticipate that the proportion of cases with a separate opinion that are published will be higher in circuits that explicitly list separate opinions as a criterion for publication.

Five circuits mention reversal or affirming on other grounds as a basis for publishing.[4] Like separate opinions, this factor is frequently discussed in the literature. A popular argument is that reversal implies precedential value because it indicates disagreement among judges on the underlying legal issues (Hannon 2001; Law 2004; Reynolds and Richman 1981). Brown et al. (2021) point out that reversals are published more than affirmances. Kuersten and Songer (2001) report only 8% of reversals in unpublished cases compared to 38% in published ones. As with separate opinions, I expect that reversals are more likely to be published and that this distinction is more notable in circuits that explicitly mention it as a publication criterion.

Finally, though this factor is raised less often by scholars, six circuits mention the publication status of the opinion being appealed as a relevant criterion. Three indicate that any appeal from a published district court ruling should be published, while the other three state that reversals of a published lower court ruling ought to be published. Steinstra (1985, 33) reports that "according to the clerks in the Eleventh and D.C. Circuits, the judges in practice publish an opinion when the decision below was published." This is particularly interesting since the Eleventh Circuit rules do not contain any reference to lower court publication as a criterion for the publication decision. This suggests that, once again, there is reason for lower court publication to increase the probability of publication across all circuits. However, I again anticipate that mention of the criterion in the rules will result in trial court publication having a larger effect compared to circuits where it is not mentioned.

[4] Three of these five circuits specifically reference reversing a *published* lower court ruling. However, for the sake of parsimony, I set this nuance aside and treat all five circuits the same.

Ideological Motivations to Publish

There are a range of ways that the rules regarding publication may affect judges' decisions. However, as Merritt and Brudney (2001, 79) note, "[b]ehind these formal rules stands a thicket of circuit practice that may affect publication rates." That practice may be motivated by many extralegal factors, including ideology (Carlson et al. 2020). Law (2004, 820) details such a possibility as follows:

> [T]he fact that they [judges] choose which of their opinions will be binding in future cases offers them a further opportunity to advance their preferences by engaging in what amounts to selective lawmaking: they may attempt to steer the evolution of the law in a particular ideological direction by publishing opinions they like, while burying in unpublished form those they do not.

Others have similarly posited that judges may use nonpublication to hide analysis (Arnold 1999; Richman and Reynolds 2013).

Empirical research shows extensive evidence of circuit judges behaving ideologically, including in their voting behavior and opinion drafting (Bowie et al. 2014; Hinkle 2015). While many of these studies are limited to the examination of published opinions, some scholars have found that ideology also shapes case outcomes in unpublished cases (Berdejó 2013; Law 2004; Merritt and Brudney 2001; but see Keele et al. 2009). Given the importance of ideology in appellate judicial decision-making and the high level of discretion in the publication decision, it is likely that judges' policy preferences influence publication. Neither publication nor nonpublication are inherently liberal or conservative. Nevertheless, judges seeking to further their policy goals may do so by making rulings that comport with their preferences binding precedent and leaving others to languish in obscurity. Consequently, I hypothesize that judges are more likely to publish opinions in which the case outcome is more closely aligned with their own ideological preferences. However, it is important to note that previous work seeking to find such evidence has come up empty (Law 2005; Merritt and Brudney 2001; Swenson 2004).

Strategic (Non)Publication

Virtually any judicial decision can potentially lend itself to strategic behavior, and publication is no different. There is considerable speculation that panel judges may be strategic when they decide which cases are published and which are not. McAlister (2019, 573) notes that there are some cases where "the court ultimately hides its work—and perhaps intentionally so." The previous section discusses why judges might ideologically hide cases. But there are strategic reasons to do so as well (Law 2004; Hinkle 2016). These can emerge from internal group dynamics or external relationships with potential reviewing courts.

Internal Strategy: Facilitating Compromise

One element of strategic behavior that can shape whether an opinion is published is the homogeneity or diversity of the group of judges hearing the case. Understanding how the publication decision is made requires accounting for the fact that it is made in a group context rather than by an individual decision maker. In federal circuit courts, there is substantial variation in the composition of panels because assignments rotate on a regular basis (Levy 2017). Some panels are composed of three judges with similar ideology and the same gender and race, while other panels are composed of three judges with varying levels of diversity on both ideological and demographic dimensions. Research has demonstrated that both the ideological and demographic composition of panels has important implications for case outcomes within cases with published opinions (see, e.g., Beim et al. 2016; Boyd et al. 2010; Cross and Tiller 1998). Diversity can also impact how opinions are crafted (Haire et al. 2013; Hinkle 2017) and the time it takes to resolve a case (Bowie et al. 2014, 110). Like these other elements of judicial behavior, there is evidence that diversity impacts publication decisions as well (Hinkle 2021).

One of the often observed correlates of diversity within a group setting is that differences in background, perspective, and experiences often generate a wider range of ideas than a homogeneous group. A panel composed of judges who share the same party affiliation, gender, and race or ethnicity may often be able to dispose of cases more easily than a group of three judges with diversity along one or more of those dimensions. Judges appointed by Republican presidents often differ from judges appointed by Democratic presidents in their perspective regarding what the law requires. Men and women experience society differently and, therefore, may bring different information and priorities to case deliberations (Boyd et al. 2010; Tillman and Hinkle 2018). Finally, a person's race also shapes their view of society and potentially the role of law within that society (Cox and Miles 2008; Tillman and Hinkle 2018). In this way, diverse panels are more likely to need to reach a compromise than homogeneous panels. One tool of compromise available is to leave the opinion unpublished so that the judge unhappy with the result can be assured it will at least not shape the law of the circuit (Brown et al. 2021; Carlson et al. 2020; Hazelton et al. 2016; Law 2004). Circuit judges themselves have noted that after internal negotiations difficult issues can get swept under the rug by leaving an opinion unpublished

(Arnold 1999; Wald 1995). Therefore, cases where there is more likely to be disagreement among judges are more likely to result in unpublished opinions. This, in turn, suggests that judicial diversity may be associated with lower levels of opinion publication. I expect this to be true with respect to ideological, gender, and racial diversity.

External Strategy: Avoiding Review

Publication decisions are not only made in a group context, they are also made within a hierarchical structure. Panel rulings (but not the publication decision) can be reviewed by their own circuit sitting as a whole in an en banc proceeding[5] or by the Supreme Court (Hellman 2007). However, such review is very rarely conducted when an opinion is unpublished (e.g., Black and Owens 2009; Beske 2018). Since such opinions do not establish binding precedent, there is less reason to incur the cost necessary to review (Law 2004). This creates the possibility that panels could choose to leave important decisions unpublished in an effort to escape scrutiny.

There have been high-profile accusations of panels engaging in such strategic behavior. In a 1991 dissent, Justice Harry A. Blackmun wrote, "[n]onpublication must not be a convenient means to prevent review" (Liptak 2015). Hazelton et al. (2016, 5) note that "[a]t least three judges who served on federal courts of appeals have published concerns that such strategic behavior is possible, likely, or occurring" (internal citations omitted). Scholars point to examples that suggest this kind of strategic behavior as well. For example, McAlister (2019) points out that in *Henry v. City of Mt. Dora*[6] the Eleventh Circuit issued a brief unpublished opinion affirming the lower court without further comment in a case that presented a complex legal issue that had already generated an extensive circuit split with six circuits on one side and four on the other.

If judges are willing to use nonpublication to dodge review as these anecdotes suggest, what patterns would emerge? Panels should be more concerned about review when they anticipate the probability of reversal is higher. Not all scholars agree that judges care very much about whether they are reversed (Bowie et al. 2014), but surely they do not object to being affirmed. There are a variety of reasons for judges to avoid reversal, including preserving their reputation, bolstering the legitimacy of the courts, or affirmation that they got the law "right" (Cameron et al. 2000; Klein and Hume 2003). Reversal is more likely

[5] Due to its size, the Ninth Circuit hears en banc cases with a subset of eleven judges (Berdejó 2013).

[6] 688 F. Appx. 842 (11th Cir. 2017).

when the reviewing court is more distant ideologically from the panel (George and Solimine 2001; Tiller 2015). Therefore, nonpublication due to strategically avoiding review would manifest as lower publication rates when a circuit panel is further from a potential reviewing court, whether that be the full circuit en banc or the Supreme Court. Hazelton et al. (2016) find empirical support for this proposition using a dataset of search and seizure cases from 2005 to 2008. They find that publication is less likely when the median of the panel majority is further from the full circuit (but no such evidence emerges for the Supreme Court) (Hazelton et al. 2016).

Case and Litigant Characteristics

Critics of selective publication often argue that inequalities can emerge in how judges distribute their time and attention. If judges view certain types of cases as less important and those cases also tend to involve less advantaged members of society, the result is to funnel judicial resources disproportionately toward those with more privilege. Songer et al. (1988, 982) point out that how important a case is can be "a very subjective criterion which may be subtly affected by unarticulated attitudes regarding the status of the parties." Davies (1981) argues that courts are like any organization and tend to give more time and attention to sources of support. In the case of judges, they get "support" in terms of reputation and prestige from various legal actors, including lawyers. More high-profile lawyers can provide more of such "support" and, therefore, their clients are more likely to secure the court's detailed attention in the form of published opinions (Davies 1981). Richman and Reynolds (1995, 275) argue that "less important cases and weaker litigants" get less "judicial attention." In short, it is possible that characteristics of the case or litigants might affect the publication decision.

Issue Area

A key feature of a case that can affect publication is the issue area it involves. Various scholars have noted that the probability an opinion is published varies for cases addressing different legal issues (Reynolds and Richman 1981; Songer et al. 1988; Wasby 2001). Because unpublished rulings do not constitute binding precedent in future cases, differences in publication rate also imply differences in the rate of legal development (Brown et al. 2021). As Wald (1995, 1376) states, "[t]he law is coming to be defined by the issues and situations that judges decide to write about."

So, what types of law do judges prefer to write about? Davies (1981) asserts that lawyers in civil appeals tend to have more prestige than those who represent criminal defendants, so judges will tend to focus their attention on civil cases. Criminal appeals may also be viewed less positively by judges, and therefore published less often, because they are seen as boring and usually unmerited. Davies (1981, 374) points out that "[b]oth judges and commentators see the Warren Court's due process decisions as giving indigent criminal appellants a 'free ride' on appeals—as creating incentives to appeal which are not balanced off by any costs or disincentives." Along similar lines, Jones (1995) notes that criminal, habeas, and prisoner civil rights cases are both numerous and usually easy to resolve because of the incentive structure for those types of cases. Such cases should be less likely to be published, and there is evidence that such is the case. Brown et al. (2021) report that 2.1% of pro se cases and 5% of prisoner civil appeals are published, compared to 17.4% of all civil appeals and 37.9% of cases where the United States brings the appeal.

I hypothesize that criminal cases and those involving prisoner petitions will be less likely to be published compared to other cases and that civil cases will be more likely to be published. However, it is important to note that such a pattern could emerge for two different reasons. First, judges may publish fewer criminal and prisoner-related cases because the incentive structure leads to more meritless claims than other issue areas. Second, judges may have preconceived notions (perhaps based in real empirical patterns) that such cases are not worth their time and effort and are subsequently less likely to publish compared to other kinds of cases. And, of course, some combination of the two is possible.

Litigant Type

Finally, there is a possibility that the nature of the litigants has an impact on publication. Swenson (2004) has shown that district judges are more likely to publish when a case involves more powerful litigants or counsel. Although the publication decision is rather different at the trial level,[7] this finding is still instructive. Other research has indicated that in the circuit courts, appeals brought pro se (without representation by counsel) are more likely to be unpublished (McAlister 2019; Richman and Reynolds 2013; Robel 1989; Wasby 2001). Criticisms of such patterns abound. McAlister (2019, 537) reports that "[a]fter his abrupt resignation, [Judge] Posner told the New York Times that 'most judges regard these people'—pro se and indigent litigants—'as kind of trash not worth the time of a federal judge."' Richman and Reynolds (1995, 277) assert that "those

[7] District court opinions are not binding outside the case at hand even if published, so in that institutional context the publication decision does not have implications for precedent and legal development.

without power receive less (and different) justice," and Richman and Reynolds (2013, 54) continue to argue that "the system works in favor of those who have resources and knowledge." McAlister (2019, 536) claims that for litigants with less power and fewer resources, "the promise of an appeal as of right has become little more than a rubber stamp: 'You lose.'" Songer et al. (1988, 308) conducted interviews on this topic and "three of the judges on the Eleventh Circuit specifically denied that the characteristics of the appellant would have any effect on the decision to publish." However, the data told a different story. Songer et al. (1988, 308) found that appeals brought by governments or corporations were more likely to be published (58%) than all other cases (40%). They concluded that "[t]his finding suggests the presence of subtle biases in the judicial decisionmaking processes in that certain litigants and their concerns are considered more important than other litigants" (Songer et al. 1988, 981). Taken together with findings about pro se appeals being published less frequently, I hypothesize that frequency of publication will be ordered from lowest to highest for the following categories of appellants: indigent or pro se individuals, other individuals, organizations, state and local government, and the federal government. While there is little discussion of the type or status of the appellee, it is possible that judicial biases could operate with respect to them as well. To the extent they do, I would anticipate the same ordering of importance and, therefore, publication.

Research Design

The foregoing discussion develops a variety of hypotheses, which are outlined for convenience in Table 3.1. I test these hypotheses using the C^{3}PO database that contains opinions from 2002 to 2012. I analyze all three-judge panel opinions, and the unit of analysis is the case. The outcome variable is whether the ruling disposing of the case was published. By circuit rule, unpublished opinions must bear a specific notation such as "NOT FOR PUBLICATION." Any opinion that does not bear the applicable label is coded as published. Since this outcome variable is binary, I estimate a probit regression model.

Testing the hypotheses listed in Table 3.1 requires a wide array of explanatory variables. I begin with those used to test whether and how law shapes publication decisions. The first four explanatory variables describe elements of each circuit's local rules regarding publication. *Circuit Prefers Published* equals one if the circuit rules explicitly state a preference for publication and zero otherwise. Conversely, *Circuit Prefers Unpublished* equals one if the circuit rules explicitly state a preference for nonpublication and zero otherwise. The number of criteria listed in the rules is captured in the variable *Number of Publication Criteria*. When the circuit rules indicate that citation to unpublished opinions

Table 3.1 Summary of Hypotheses (Source: Rachael K. Hinkle 2024)

Factor	Hypothesis
Law	Rules Prefer Published, ↑ Publication
Law	Rules Prefer Unpublished, ↓ Publication
Law	More Criteria, ↓ Publication
Law	Citation of Unpublished Prohibited, ↓ Publication
Law	Legal Novelty, ↑ Publication
Law	Pr(Pub.|Oral Arg. + Rule) > Pr(Pub.|Oral Arg.) > Pr(Pub.|No Oral Arg.)
Law	Pr(Pub.|Amicus + Rule) > Pr(Pub.|Amicus) > Pr(Pub.|No Amicus)
Law	Pr(Pub.|Sep. Opin. + Rule) > Pr(Pub.|Sep. Opin.) > Pr(Pub.|No Sep. Opin.)
Law	Pr(Pub.|Reversal + Rule) > Pr(Pub.|Reversal) > Pr(Pub.|No Reversal)
Law	Pr(Pub.|LC Published + Rule) > Pr(Pub.|LC Published) > Pr(Pub.|LC Unpublished)
Ideology	Panel Ideological Alignment with Case Outcome, ↑ Publication
Strategy	Ideologically Split Panel, ↓ Publication
Strategy	Gender-diverse Panel, ↓ Publication
Strategy	Race-diverse Panel, ↓ Publication
Strategy	Panel Ideological Distance to Full Circuit, ↓ Publication
Strategy	Panel Ideological Distance to Supreme Court, ↓ Publication
Issue	Criminal and Prisoner Petition, ↓ Publication
Issue	Civil Cases, ↑ Publication
Appellant	Pr(Pub): Pro se/Indigent < Person < Organization < State/Local Govt. < Nat. Govt.
Appellee	Pr(Pub): Pro se/Indigent < Person < Organization < State/Local Govt. < Nat. Govt.

is prohibited or strongly disfavored, the variable *Citing Unpublished Prohibited* equals one and is zero otherwise.[8]

The next explanatory variables measure elements of a case that reflect specific criteria associated with publication. Perhaps the most important of these is whether a case requires the resolution of a new legal issue. While a nuanced concept to capture empirically, it can be approximated by assessing the precedent used in an opinion. When a case involves rote legal issues, frequently addressed

[8] Due to the adoption of FRAP 32.1, this variable equals zero from 2007 forward.

in the past, the court will be able to cite primarily binding precedent on the topic. However, when a new issue arises, there is, by definition, little to no binding caselaw available to provide direction. For circuit panels, binding precedents are previous published opinions from the same circuit and those issued by the Supreme Court. Following Hinkle (2021), I measure *Legal Novelty* on a scale from 0 to 1 that is calculated using the proportion of cases cited in the circuit opinion that are not legally binding.[9]

While new legal issues are universally considered to be a justification for publication, other criteria may not apply across the board. Some circuits instruct that opinions addressing issues of substantial public importance should be published, while others do not. I leverage two features of a case that can indicate its importance. First, oral argument is typically only granted in cases considered to be at least somewhat important. Second, outside groups are likely to invest the resources necessary to participate in litigation as amicus curiae ("friends of the court") only in important cases. Both *Oral Argument* and *Amicus Participation* equal one if the element is present in a case and zero otherwise. I expect them to have an impact in all circuits because both features may also be associated with novel legal issues. However, to the extent that publication criteria have an impact, I expect these to matter more in the circuits that include public importance as a criterion for publication. Consequently, I also interact each of these measures with *Criteria: Public Importance*, which equals one if the circuit rules in the applicable year and circuit include such a criterion and zero otherwise.

Three publication criteria are quite clear-cut to measure: separate opinions, reversal, and whether the lower court ruling was published. However, the first two require caution as it is not clear that these decisions occur before the publication decision. They are both related to the outcome on the merits, which is announced at the same time the publication decision is made public. A judge who disagrees with the panel in whole or part may well save their time and go along with an unpublished ruling but take the time to write separately if the majority is published (Hazelton et al. 2016). In this way, publication can influence dissent or concurrence, which means including separate opinion in the model would create a very real possibility of biasing the results. Reversal is less problematic since the proper resolution of a case is not likely to be influenced by the publication decision. For example, a panel would not be likely to first decide to publish and then write an opinion that reversed the lower court simply because that would justify publication. Rather, to the extent that publication is more frequent in cases involving reversals, it is much more plausible that a panel first decided to reverse and then decided the reversal justified publication. Therefore,

[9] Rulings that do not cite any caselaw are coded as zero on the *Legal Novelty* measure because such opinions indicate issues so well settled that no citation is needed.

including reversal in the model does not risk post-treatment bias. In summary, I include indicator variables for whether a panel reversed the lower court (in full or in part) and whether the lower court judge published the ruling. I also interact each variable with a variable that captures whether the relevant circuit rules include the relevant criterion. Once again, this allows me to distinguish between the overall impact of these factors and the impact attributable to the presence of a criterion in circuit rules. Although I cannot formally evaluate the separate opinion hypothesis, I include bivariate descriptive statistics that compare separate opinion rates by publication status and whether separate opinions are listed as a publication criterion.

The next broad factor that can impact publication is ideology. I employ a continuous measure of panel median ideology, specifically Judicial Common Space (JCS) scores (Boyd 2010; Giles et al. 2001; Epstein et al. 2007).[10] However, knowing how conservative or liberal a panel is does not directly inform whether they may be more or less inclined to publish. Theory predicts that how much a panel likes or dislikes a case outcome will shape that decision. In order to capture this, I first develop a measure, *Direction of Case Outcome*, that equals −1 if the case was resolved in a liberal manner, 1 if it reached a conservative outcome, and zero if there was a split outcome or the ideological direction could not be clearly classified.[11] Then I construct the variable *Panel Alignment with Outcome* by multiplying the panel median JCS score by *Direction of Case Outcome*. The greater the value of *Panel Alignment with Outcome*, the more the opinion tracks the personal policy goals of the panel.

Since the publication decision is made within a group and hierarchical context, strategy can also play a role. More diversity can lead to a need to compromise that can depress the probability of publication. I account for three types of diversity. *Ideologically Split Panel* is an indicator for whether a panel is ideologically split based on the party of the president who appointed each judge on the panel. This variable equals zero if all three judges share the same party affiliation and equals one otherwise. To account for demographic diversity, I use the variables *Gender Diverse Panel* and *Race Diverse Panel*, which are constructed along similar lines. They equal zero if all three judges share the same characteristic and one otherwise. Publication may be impacted by external as well as internal strategy. Greater distance to either the full circuit or the Supreme Court may depress the frequency with which a panel publishes. The variables *Ideological Distance: Panel to Circuit* and *Ideological Distance: Panel to Supreme Court* calculate the absolute value of the difference between the panel median

[10] JCS scores are based on the ideology of the political elites who appointed a judge and are located on a scale from −1 (liberal) to 1 (conservative).

[11] See Appendix 3.A for further details regarding how this variable was coded.

JCS score and the median JCS score of the potential reviewing court in the applicable year.[12]

The final explanatory variables capture the issue area and the type of litigants. Each case is classified into one of seven topics: criminal; prisoner petitions; administrative; civil, civil rights; civil, torts; civil, other; or bankruptcy.[13] For each case, the first named appellant and appellee were also manually classified into one of five categories: indigent or pro se persons, other persons, organizations, state or local government, and national government. The "organization" category includes both for-profit businesses and interest groups. This coding scheme was used because coding over two hundred thousand cases requires a streamlined approach. As a result, the categories correspond to more coarse-grained methods used in prior research (see, e.g., Sheehan and Randazzo 2012; Songer et al. 2000). Following the approach of other scholars, individuals listed in their official capacity are coded based on the entity they represent (Songer and Sheehan 1992; Songer et al. 1999).

Finally, I control for other factors that may affect the probability of publication and may also be correlated with the primary explanatory variables. Given the efficiency rationale for selective publication, an important factor that can shape publication is how busy judges are. Published opinions take considerably more time to craft (Bowie et al. 2014). Therefore, I control for the caseload per active judge in the applicable circuit and year. I also control for the year to account for any changes over time. Circumstances can vary by circuit as well. To estimate the determinants of publication across circuits as well as within them, I control for relevant circuit-level features rather than including circuit fixed effects. Specifically, in addition to caseload, I account for the overall publication rate in the applicable year and circuit.[14] Summary statistics for all variables are provided in Table 3.B.1 located in Appendix 3.B.

Results

The C^{3}PO database contains over two hundred thousand cases. Such a large amount of data creates the possibility that very small effects can be estimated with statistical significance. Therefore, it is especially important to focus on substantive significance as well. I do so by illustrating the changes in the predicted

[12] Circuit judges with senior status typically do not participate in en banc review, so this measure for the full circuit calculates the median of the active judges serving in a circuit.

[13] Details on how cases were coded are provided in Chapter 2 in Appendix 2.A. Note that the analysis here does not include original jurisdiction cases because those cases cannot be coded as reversing or affirming a lower court, nor is the publication of a lower court opinion applicable.

[14] Circuit-wide publication rates are calculated excluding the observation in question.

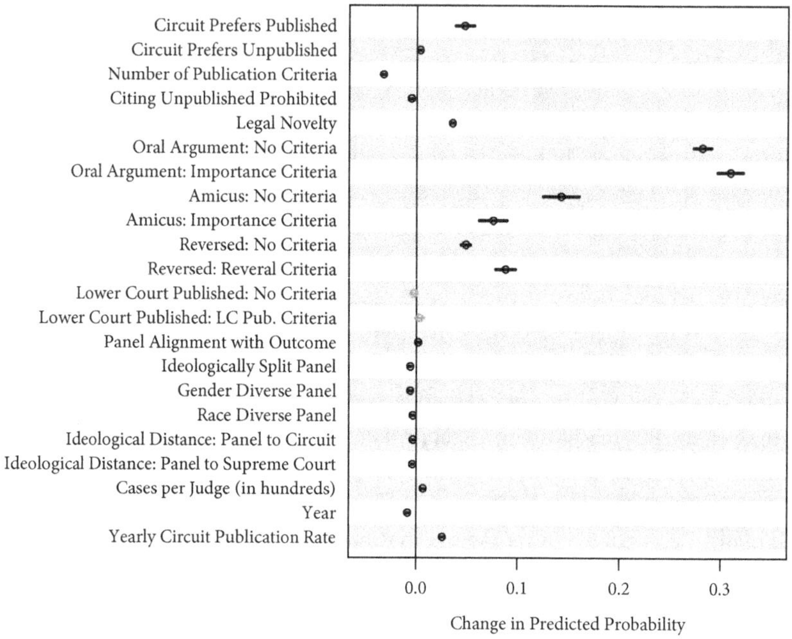

Figure 3.1 Changes in Predicted Probability of Publication: Estimates (and associated 95% confidence intervals) of the change in the predicted probability of publication generated by moving each variable from a low to high value while holding other variables at their median. Variables reflecting publication criteria are shown both when the relevant criterion is part of a circuit's rules and when it is not. Low and high values are 25th and 75th percentile for continuous variables, and zero and one for binary variables. Estimates and confidence intervals in gray (instead of black) indicate that the confidence interval includes zero. Full regression estimates are available in Appendix 3.C in Table 3.C.1. (Source: Rachael K. Hinkle 2024)

probability of publication that occur when each variable is moved from a low to high value and everything else is held at its median. Low values are zero for binary variables and the 25th percentile for continuous variables, while high values are one and the 75th percentile, respectively.[15] These changes and their 95% confidence intervals are plotted in Figure 3.1. The substantive importance of these effects must be interpreted in light of the overall likelihood of publication. When all the variables are set to their median or mode as applicable, the predicted probability of publication is quite low, only 0.03.[16] Therefore, even an effect size as small as 0.006 constitutes a 20% relative increase.

[15] Since this format does not lend itself to evaluating categorical values, I present the predicted probabilities for each value of issue area and litigant type in later figures.

[16] This should not be confused with the overall publication rate in the database, which is 22%.

Figure 3.1 shows that all but two estimates are statistically significant, and all but two significant estimates are in the hypothesized direction.[17] While there is widespread evidence for my hypotheses, there is interesting variation in the strength with which various factors shape publication decisions. The variables with the largest impact are all related to rules and legal doctrine. In circuits that state an explicit preference for publication in their rules, the predicted probability is higher by 0.05. Publication in such circuits is more than twice as likely as in those that do not overtly prefer publication. Interestingly, a stated preference for nonpublication is also associated with a higher publication rate, but by a much smaller amount of 0.003. Shifting the number of publication criteria from one to seven leads to a decrease of 0.03 in the publication rate. This confirms the expectation that providing judges with more specific directions tends to depress publication. Prohibiting citation to unpublished opinions also makes publication less likely as expected, although the decrease is only 0.005.

Next, I turn to examine the specific factors that should make publication more likely according to legal doctrine. As expected, cases with more novel legal issues are more likely to be published. The magnitude of this increase is 0.04; the likelihood of publication triples. I examine the remaining factors both when they are and are not mentioned in the circuit rules as criteria that merit publication. The results indicate that oral argument, amicus participation, and reversal all increase the probability of publication quite substantially. Oral argument has the largest effect by far, increasing publication by 0.31 when the rules identify public importance as a criterion and 0.28 when they do not. As expected, oral argument matters more in circuits that include important public issues in their rules compared to those that do not, and the difference is statistically significant ($p < 0.001$). The impact of reversal is also larger, as expected, when circuit rules list it as a publication criterion and this difference is also statistically significant ($p < 0.001$). The impact of both public importance and reversal criteria are somewhat similar in size, with a difference of 0.03 for oral argument and a difference of 0.04 for reversal.

The difference in change of publication rate generated by the presence of an amicus is 0.07 ($p < 0.001$), but not in the expected direction. Amicus participation has a larger impact on publication in circuits that do *not* list public importance as a reason for publication compared to circuits that do. Finally, whether the lower court ruling was published does not have a statistically significant impact either with or without the relevant criterion in the circuit rules. However, the estimate with the criterion is significantly higher than the estimate without ($p = 0.04$), but that difference is somewhat small at 0.006.

[17] All discussion of statistical significance throughout this book is at the 0.05 level.

As discussed previously, the presence of a dissenting or concurring opinion is another factor that is often listed in criteria for publication. While that factor cannot be included in the regression analysis because it may sometimes occur after the publication decision, Figure 3.2 shows how frequently cases with separate opinions are published in circuits with and without such a criterion. To the extent that formal rules constrain judges, we would generally expect that where separate opinions are mentioned as a reason for publication most cases with such opinions should be published. Interestingly, the data reveal no such pattern. When the rules mention lack of unanimity as a justification for publication, circuits leave over 40% of non-unanimous opinions unpublished. This is twice the percentage in circuits where separate opinions are not mentioned, which leave less than 20% of such rulings unpublished. While these descriptive data do not account for myriad other factors that pertain to publication, they suggest that the instruction to publish cases with disagreement largely falls on deaf ears.

Figure 3.1 reveals evidence for all hypotheses with respect to ideology and strategy, but the effect sizes are smaller compared to those discussed so far. Panels are more likely to publish outcomes that are more ideologically palatable, but the estimated difference is 0.002, which is only a 7% relative increase over the baseline predicted probability of publication. Internal strategy has a bit larger impact. Ideological and gender diversity decrease publication by 0.006 each and racial diversity does so by 0.003. External considerations affect the panel at a similar level. Greater distance to the full circuit and Supreme Court decrease the

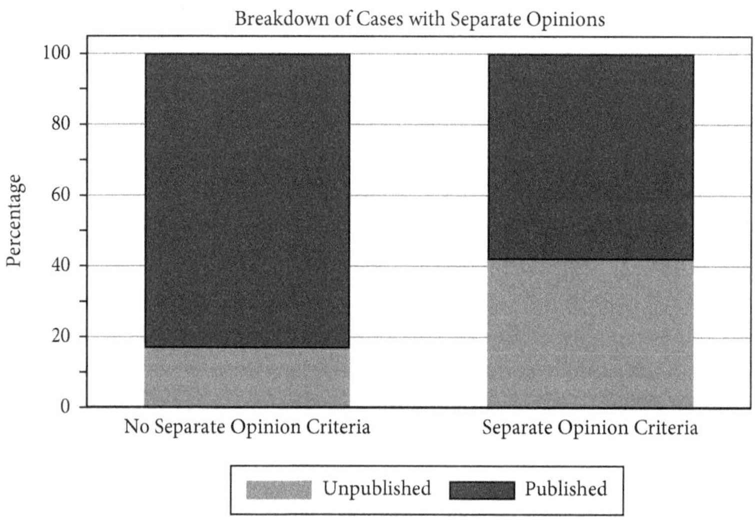

Figure 3.2 Summary of Publication in Cases with Separate Opinions (Source: Rachael K. Hinkle 2024)

predicted probability of publication by 0.003 and 0.004, respectively. It is important to note that even seemingly small effect sizes can have a remarkable impact given the large number of cases resolved in the circuit courts. For example, in this dataset an increase of 0.002 in the probability of publication translates into an estimated additional 462 published opinions that shape legal policy.

Finally, I turn to consider case and litigant characteristics. Since these variables are categorical, I present predicted probabilities of publication for each category (with the related 95% confidence intervals). Figure 3.3 presents these estimates for each issue area. I hypothesize that criminal cases and prisoner petitions are less likely to be published and civil cases are more likely to be published. Curiously, after controlling for the wide range of other variables in the model, no such links appear between publication and issue area. In fact, criminal and prisoner cases are somewhat *more* likely to be published than any of the three categories of civil cases. The one issue that stands out as being particularly likely to be published is bankruptcy cases. Such cases are not frequent, making up only 1.3% of the data. They also are procedurally distinct in that they begin in bankruptcy court and the first appeal is to a federal district court. Therefore, bankruptcy cases at the circuit level are typically at the second round of review rather than the first. This may be the reason they are more likely to result in publication.

Figures 3.4 and 3.5 show the likelihood of publication for each type of appellant and appellee, respectively. Theory suggests that litigants with the greatest amount of power and resources will be most likely to have their cases published.

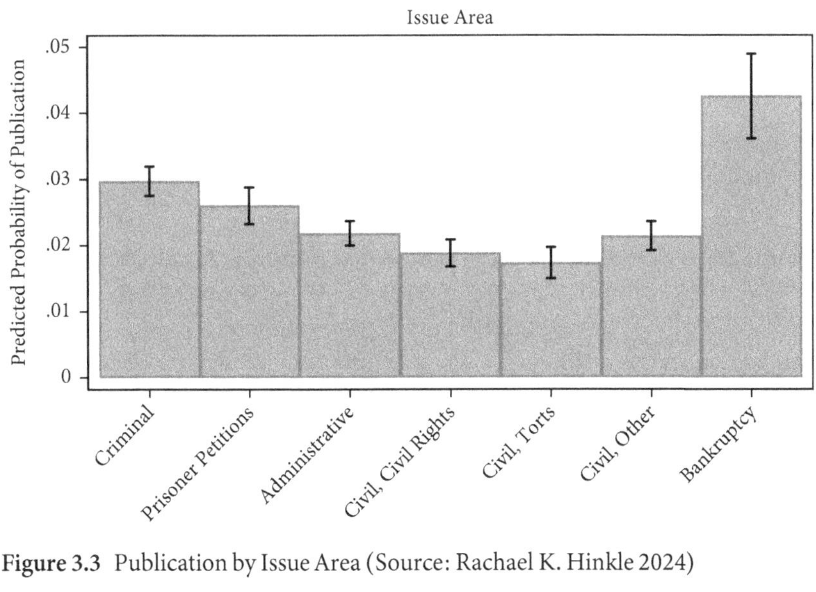

Figure 3.3 Publication by Issue Area (Source: Rachael K. Hinkle 2024)

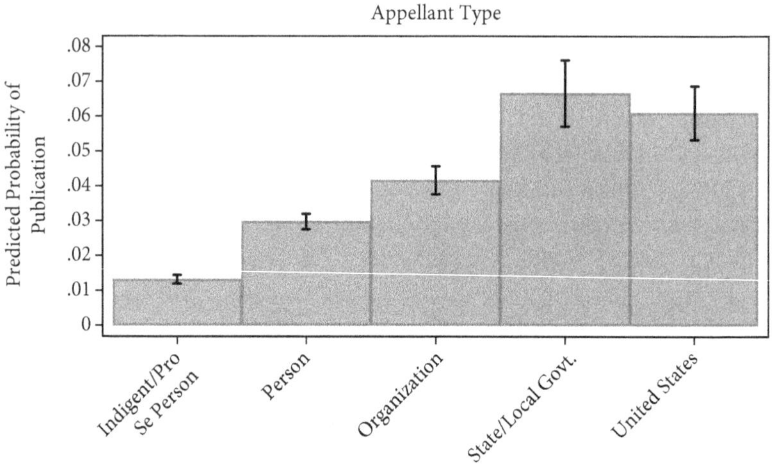

Figure 3.4 Publication by Appellant Type (Source: Rachael K. Hinkle 2024)

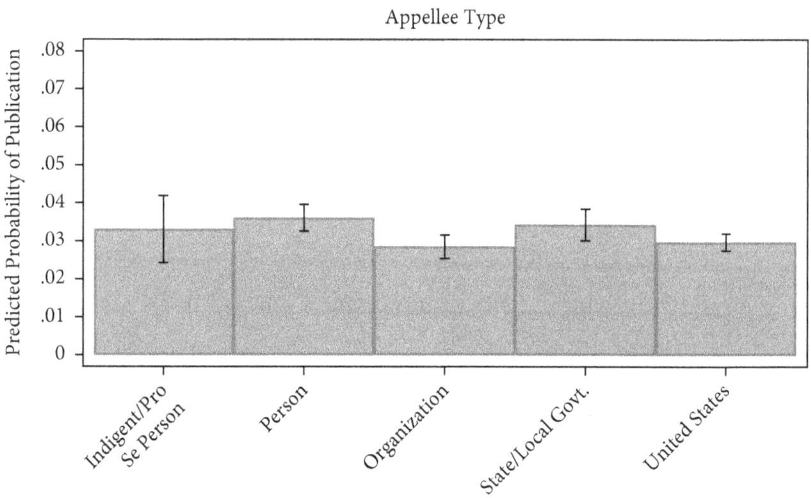

Figure 3.5 Publication by Appellee Type (Source: Rachael K. Hinkle 2024)

This pattern emerges with respect to appellants. Indigent and pro se individuals who bring an appeal have their cases published an estimated 1.3% of the time compared to 6% or more for local, state, and national governments. Other individuals and organizations fall in between those two extremes in the expected order. On the contrary, no pattern is observed for appellee type. All types of litigants on the receiving end of an appeal have the case published around 3% of

Table 3.2 Summary of Results: * indicates a finding in the opposite of the hypothesized direction. (Source: Rachael K. Hinkle 2024)

Factor	Variable	Impact on Publication
Law	Explicit Preference for Publication	+
Law	Explicit Preference for Nonpublication	+*
Law	Number of Publication Criteria	-
Law	Citation of Unpublished Prohibited	-
Law	Legal Novelty	+
Law	Oral Argument	+
Law	Amicus Participation	+
Law	Oral Arg. + Public Interest Criteria	> no criteria
Law	Amicus + Public Interest Criteria	< no criteria*
Law	Reversal	+
Law	Reversal + Reversal Criteria	> no criteria
Law	Lower Court Published	n.s.
Law	LC Published + LC Published Criteria	> no criteria
Ideology	Panel Ideological Alignment with Case Outcome	+
Strategy	Ideologically Split Panel	-
Strategy	Gender Diverse Panel	-
Strategy	Race Diverse Panel	-
Strategy	Ideological Distance: Panel to Pull Circuit	-
Strategy	Ideological Distance: Panel to Supreme Court	-
Case	Issue	Unexpected Order
Litigants	Appellant Type	Expected Order
Litigants	Appellee Type	n.s.

the time. For convenience, a summary of the evidence for all hypotheses is provided in Table 3.2.

Finally, the control variables shed some interesting additional light on the publication decision. Contrary to expectation, circuits with higher caseloads actually publish *more* frequently. This suggests that the caseload explosion in the 1970s that led to the adoption of selective publication out of sheer necessity to dispose of cases may no longer be the predominant dynamic in circuit courts today. The efficiency rationale for nonpublication rings somewhat hollow in a context where judges who have more cases to dispose of are not more likely to utilize that tool. During this time frame, judges have also become decreasingly likely to publish. In short, despite a weaker link to a key justification for nonpublication, its overall use is increasing.

Conclusions

Scholars have often recognized the importance of the moves policymakers do *not* make. So far, such analysis in the context of courts has primarily focused on the Supreme Court and its agenda-setting power. Such influential decisions are happening in the circuit courts as well. Our understanding of how legal policy develops in the federal court system is incomplete without a broad and comprehensive analysis of when circuit judges choose to publish their rulings. This chapter provides that long-needed analysis. The findings reveal that the publication decision is every bit as nuanced and complex as rulings on the merits.

Virtually all the major factors that political scientists and legal scholars would expect to influence judicial decision-making more broadly also shape the decision of whether to publish. Decades of theoretical development on the topic of what factors affect judges hold up remarkably well in this context. There is evidence that legal doctrine affects the publication decision, both in terms of rules having a notable effect and specific criteria operating as expected. But many other factors enter the process as well. Judges are more likely to publish cases that are aligned with their personal ideological preferences. They are also likely to lean on nonpublication as a strategic tool to manage disagreement either with each other or with potential reviewing judges. The impact of case characteristics is a bit mixed. Issue area matters to publication, but in ways that are somewhat surprising. There is no evidence that the type of the appellee matters to publication, but the appellant does so in entirely predictable ways. Government appellants are most likely to have the opinion in their case published, while poor or unrepresented individuals are least likely to.

The determinants of publication are many and varied. Some are entirely expected and create no qualms, but others raise normative concerns. While the purpose of this chapter was primarily to describe the publication decision, the next three chapters take up questions that address substantive concerns about how selective publication might perpetuate disparities or exacerbate privilege. Chapter 4 builds on the observation that the type of litigant bringing an appeal influences publication to further examine how selective publication and differences in litigant capabilities interact to affect how people experience the federal appellate courts. Chapter 5 focuses on questions raised by the findings regarding internal strategic deliberations in this chapter. If diversity creates the need to compromise and compromise often leads to nonpublication, that suggests that underrepresented members of the judiciary (who are more likely to be on diverse panels) may have disproportionately less influence over legal policy. The finding here that external strategic considerations can shape publication is the foundation of Chapter 6, which examines how selective publication leads to downstream disparities in who is able to obtain further review of their case and whether they win at the next level. A common thread runs through all these chapters: in federal appellate courts, who you are affects what you get.

Appendix 3.A: Coding Direction of Case Outcome

Measuring the ideological alignment between a panel and the case outcome requires coding the direction of each case outcome. Following the typical approach in judicial politics literature, I complete this task by using a combination of information about the issue area and the party that won. For example, a criminal case in which the defendant wins is coded as a liberal ruling. Table 3.A.1 provides a list of all coding rules. The issue area for civil cases which are neither tort cases nor civil rights cases is too homogeneous to use wholesale coding of ideological direction. Therefore, I used NOS codes to further classify these cases into subgroups. Table 3.A.2 lists all NOS codes and related titles used to create these issue subgroups.

In some cases, it was not possible to clearly classify whether the case outcome was conservative or liberal. In some cases, ambiguity was created by split rulings. In others, the issue of the case did not lend itself to ideological classification or the text of the opinion provided insufficient information about who won the appeal. Rather than drop these cases, the ideological alignment variable is created by multiplying the panel's ideology by *Case Outcome Direction*, which equals −1 for a liberal ruling, 1 for a conservative ruling, and zero otherwise. The Judicial Common Space scores used to capture judicial ideology are scaled so that larger numbers indicate greater conservatism. The multiplication by −1 when the decision is liberal flips the JCS scale to show how aligned judges are with a liberal outcome. The multiplication by zero when the direction of the outcome cannot be clearly coded allows for ideology to be excluded from consideration for such cases without dropping them from the analysis. However, this decision is not driving the conclusions. A model that does drop these cases produces remarkably similar results.

Table 3.A.1 Coding Direction of Case Outcome (Source: Rachael K. Hinkle 2024)

Case Outcome Direction	Issue/Issue Subgroup	Winner
Liberal	Prisoner Petition	Plaintiff
Conservative	Prisoner Petition	Defendant
Liberal	Civil Rights	Plaintiff
Conservative	Civil Rights	Defendant
Liberal	Civil, Tort	Plaintiff
Conservative	Civil, Tort	Defendant
Liberal	Bankruptcy Appeal	Other
Conservative	Bankruptcy Appeal	Government
Liberal	Original Jurisdiction	Plaintiff
Conservative	Original Jurisdiction	Defendant
Liberal	Criminal	Defendant
Conservative	Criminal	Government
Liberal	Administrative	Other
Conservative	Administrative	Government
Liberal	Consumer Protection	United States
Conservative	Consumer Protection	Other
Liberal	Anti-discrimination	United States
Conservative	Anti-discrimination	Other
Liberal	Labor Laws	United States
Conservative	Labor Laws	Other
Liberal	Economic Protections	United States
Conservative	Economic Protections	Other
Liberal	Environmental Regulation	United States
Conservative	Environmental Regulation	Other
Liberal	All remaining civil cases	Other
Conservative	All remaining civil cases	United States

Table 3.A.2 NOS Codes Used for Coding Direction of Case Outcome (Source: Rachael K. Hinkle 2024)

NOS Code	NOS Description	Issue Subgroup
371	Truth in Lending	Consumer Protection
410	Antitrust	Consumer Protection
430	Banks and Banking	Consumer Protection
450	Commerce	Consumer Protection
470	RICO	Consumer Protection
480	Consumer Credit	Consumer Protection
445	ADA—Employment	Anti-discrimination
446	ADA—Other	Anti-discrimination
710	Fair Labor Standards Act	Labor Law
720	Labor/Management Relations	Labor Law
730	Labor/Management Report & Disclosure	Labor Law
740	Railway Labor Act	Labor Law
790	Other Labor Litigation	Labor Law
791	ERISA	Labor Law
850	Securities/Commodities/Exchange	Economic Protection
891	Agricultural Acts	Economic Protection
892	Economic Stabilization Act	Economic Protection
893	Environmental Matters	Environmental Regulation
894	Energy Allocation Act	Environmental Regulation

Appendix 3.B: Summary Statistics

Table 3.B.1 Summary Statistics (Source: Rachael K. Hinkle 2024)

Continuous Variables	**Min.**	**25%**	**50%**	**75%**	**Max**
Number of Publication Criteria	0	1	5	7	9
Legal Novelty	0.00	0.00	0.20	0.42	1.00
Panel Alignment with Outcome	−0.60	−0.17	0.00	0.30	0.60
Ideological Distance: Panel to Circuit	0.00	0.05	0.13	0.39	0.91
Ideological Distance: Panel to Supreme Court	0.00	0.19	0.29	0.38	0.66
Cases per Judge (in hundreds)	1.16	3.40	4.40	5.04	7.40
Year	2002	2005	2007	2010	2012
Yearly Circuit Publication Rate	0.06	0.13	0.18	0.29	0.91
Dichotomous Variables	**0**	**1**			
Published	78%	22%			
Circuit Prefers Published	98%	2%			
Circuit Prefers Unpublished	87%	13%			
Citing Unpublished Prohibited	68%	32%			
Oral Argument	65%	35%			
Amicus Participation	98%	2%			
Criteria: Public Importance	57%	43%			
Reversed	91%	9%			
Criteria: Reversal	72%	28%			
Lower Court Published	95%	5%			
Criteria: Lower Court Published	57%	43%			
Ideologically Split Panel	28%	72%			
Gender Diverse Panel	45%	55%			
Race Diverse Panel	56%	44%			
Issue Area					
Criminal	33.3%				
Prisoner Petitions	12.8%				
Administrative	16.0%				
Civil, Civil Rights	19.0%				

(*continued*)

Table 3.B.1 Continued

Issue Area		
Civil, Torts	2.9%	
Civil, Other	14.8%	
Bankruptcy	1.2%	
Litigant Type	**Appellant**	**Appellee**
Indigent/Pro Se Person	30.0%	0.5%
Person	62.4%	26.0%
Organization	5.2%	12.4%
State/Local Government	0.9%	4.9%
National Government	1.5%	56.2%

Appendix 3.C: Regression Results

Table 3.C.1 Publication Model: Probit regression model of the probability each ruling is published. * indicates a p-value < 0.05. (Source: Rachael K. Hinkle 2024)

	Coef.	**(S.E.)**
Circuit Prefers Published	0.459*	(0.034)
Circuit Prefers Unpublished	0.047*	(0.014)
Number of Publication Criteria	−0.070*	(0.003)
Citing Unpublished Prohibited	−0.082*	(0.012)
Legal Novelty	1.182*	(0.016)
Oral Argument	1.392*	(0.011)
Criteria: Public Importance	−0.173*	(0.023)
Oral Argument x Criteria: Public Importance	0.224*	(0.017)
Amicus Participation	0.939*	(0.033)
Amicus Participation x Criteria: Public Importance	−0.190*	(0.050)
Reversed	0.468*	(0.014)
Criteria: Reversal	0.297*	(0.022)
Reversed x Criteria: Reversal	0.057*	(0.024)
Lower Court Published	−0.039	(0.027)
Criteria: Lower Court Published	−0.013	(0.013)

(continued)

Table 3.C.1 Continued

	Coef.	(S.E.)
Lower Court Published x Criteria: Lower Court Published	0.083*	(0.040)
Panel Alignment with Outcome	0.056*	(0.015)
Ideologically Split Panel	–0.084*	(0.009)
Gender Diverse Panel	–0.082*	(0.008)
Race Diverse Panel	–0.051*	(0.008)
Ideological Distance: Panel to Circuit	–0.146*	(0.018)
Ideological Distance: Panel to Supreme Court	–0.292*	(0.031)
Issue Area		
Prisoner Petitions	–0.059*	(0.018)
Administrative	–0.134*	(0.013)
Civil, Civil Rights	–0.195*	(0.018)
Civil, Torts	–0.228*	(0.024)
Civil, Other	–0.142*	(0.016)
Bankruptcy	0.162*	(0.034)
Appellant Type		
Person	0.336*	(0.012)
Organization	0.489*	(0.019)
State/Local Government	0.719*	(0.035)
United States	0.674*	(0.030)
Appellee Type		
Person	0.039	(0.058)
Organization	–0.066	(0.058)
State/Local Government	0.016	(0.060)
United States	–0.048	(0.059)
Cases per Judge (in hundreds)	0.060*	(0.005)
Year	–0.026*	(0.002)
Yearly Circuit Publication Rate	2.092*	(0.039)
Intercept	49.592*	(3.775)
N	231,168	
BIC	135842.5	
AIC	135428.5	

4
Invisible Losers
The Fate of "Have-nots" in Unpublished Cases

Introduction

Chapter 2 began with two examples of cases that had unusual characteristics given their publication status. Fuzzy, Junior, and Tatoo Billy had their case resolved by a lengthy unpublished opinion, while Michael McKinzy had his case disposed of with a two-sentence published opinion. Yet these individuals had something in common: they faced opponents with greater resources and litigation experience. Fuzzy and his compatriots' case was a federal criminal proceeding, which means they were going up against the U.S. government. While McKinzy's case was civil, his opponent was the Union Pacific Railroad. To further exacerbate the gap in litigation experience, McKinzy represented himself pro se in the appeal. Both the United States and the Union Pacific Railroad prevailed. The circuit courts upheld the convictions of the meth-dealing bikers and the lower court's summary judgment in favor of the railroad. While the publication decisions in these cases were unusual, the outcomes were not. Such patterns are all too familiar.

In 1974, Galanter famously theorized that society's "haves" are more likely to be successful in litigation than "have-nots" due to both their greater resources and familiarity with the legal system resulting from repeated participation. Others have argued that judicial bias or a normative tilt in the law could also explain such a pattern (see, e.g., Wheeler et al. 1987). Scholars have found evidence that have-nots are more likely to lose than haves in a wide variety of courts. Included among these are the federal circuit courts (Cross 2007; Songer and Sheehan 1992; Songer et al. 1999, 2000; Szmer et al. 2016). Litigants such as government actors who have more resources and experience are more likely to be successful in the U.S. Courts of Appeals than litigants with fewer resources and less experience, such as private individuals (Songer and Sheehan 1992; Songer et al. 1999; Szmer et al. 2016). This is known as the "resource advantage" or "repeat player advantage." The bulk of the existing work focuses on this dynamic within circuit cases resolved by published opinions (Cross 2007; Songer et al. 1999; Songer, Sheehan, and Haire 2000; Szmer et al. 2016, but see Songer and Sheehan 1992).

Selective Publication in the U.S. Courts of Appeals. Rachael K. Hinkle, Oxford University Press.
 DOI: 10.1093/oso/9780197770085.003.0004

In this chapter, I examine the difference in how haves and have-nots fare in the unpublished cases that often go unexamined. This has two important benefits. The first is that understanding the dynamics of judicial decision-making within unpublished cases is important for its own sake since each of those cases matters a great deal to its participants. Second, comparing the resource advantage across published and unpublished cases can shed important light on the underlying mechanism or mechanisms that drive that advantage. For example, if the law itself plainly favors businesses and government actors, then we should observe a relatively large advantage for such litigants in the unpublished cases that often involve clear-cut legal issues. On the other hand, if the resource advantage is primarily based on haves being able to afford more persuasive lawyers, that difference in persuasive ability should emerge more clearly in published cases where the legal issues tend to be closer to fifty-fifty. These are just two examples of how we might expect Galanter's repeat player theory to manifest differently in published and unpublished cases.

Throughout this chapter, I elaborate on a range of theoretical expectations and test them by comparing the size of the repeat player advantage across cases with both published and unpublished opinions. I begin by discussing the tapestry of existing work on the link between resources and litigation outcomes. Next, I apply the insights of existing work to the context of unpublished cases and discuss the theoretical expectations for how resources are likely to matter in that context compared to in published cases. From there, I move on to describe the research design I use to test my theory and present the results of the empirical analysis. The data reveal that the resource advantage, while present in unpublished cases, is notably smaller than it is in published cases. The chapter comes to a close with some concluding thoughts.

The Impact of Resource Advantage on Case Outcomes

Existing scholarship indicates that parties with greater resources who are more familiar with court processes enjoy an advantage in court. In 1974, Marc Galanter first suggested a distinction between repeat player litigants and one-shot litigants and argued that repeat players tend to obtain more favorable judicial decisions (Galanter 1974). One reason for this is that repeat players (i.e., haves) typically have greater resources than one-shotters (who are typically have-nots). Greater resources allow haves to hire more expensive attorneys who presumably have greater experience and expertise, which, in turn, contributes to the higher likelihood of securing favorable litigation outcomes (Wanner 1975; Wheeler et al. 1987; Atkins 1991; Songer and Sheehan 1992; McCormick 1993; Albiston 1999; Farole Jr. 1999; Songer et al. 1999; Szmer et al. 2016). Litigants like governments and corporations also have an advantage in court because they tend to be engaged in litigation frequently. Their repeat player status provides both familiarity with the legal context and the ability to make strategic decisions across multiple cases that can provide long-term benefits. For example, an individual harmed by a faulty product has only one shot in court to win their case and receive compensation. But manufacturers are more likely to be engaged in litigation repeatedly. This puts them in a position to settle cases that might establish unfavorable precedent and only litigate the cases that they are most likely to win.

While Galanter initially proposed his theory of repeat player advantage in the context of trial litigation, his general expectation that courtroom participants who enjoy greater resources and higher status in society tend to enjoy higher rates of success in courts has proved to describe empirical realities in a variety of contexts. Scholars have demonstrated that status and resources carry an advantage in a wide variety of courts, including immigration courts (Miller et al. 2015), the U.S. Supreme Court (Sheehan et al. 1992; Szmer and Ginn 2014), the Supreme Court of Canada (McCormick 1993), appellate courts in the United Kingdom (Atkins 1991; Hanretty 2014), the High Court of Australia (Sheehan and Randazzo 2012), federal appellate courts (Songer, Sheehan and Haire 2000, 1999; Songer and Sheehan 1992; Szmer et al. 2016), and state supreme courts (Farole Jr. 1999; Wheeler et al. 1987; Gibson and Nelson 2021). There are some exceptions to the pattern (see, e.g., Haynie 1994), but the majority of the large amount of research devoted to exploring Galanter's theory reveals the expected pattern.

In addition to broad evidence of a repeat player advantage across a variety of institutions, there are also intriguing indications that different contexts shape the size of that advantage. In appeals courts with agenda control, such as the U.S. Supreme Court and many state high courts, the repeat player advantage is relatively modest (Gibson and Nelson 2021; Sheehan et al. 1992; Szmer and Ginn 2014; Wheeler et al. 1987). When a court can choose which cases it will hear, that power mitigates the impact of litigant selection effects. For example, if a poorly resourced one-shotter seeks discretionary review in a case they are likely to lose, the high court is unlikely to select the case for review because their time is better spent resolving close cases and unsettled questions of law. Consequently, the findings of a smaller resource advantage in courts with agenda control suggest that part of that advantage may be due to litigant selection effects. That is, repeat players are better than one-shotters at choosing to litigate cases they are likely to win. When a high court has discretion over which cases to hear, their decisions about which cases are worthy of consideration eliminate (or at least reduce) any litigant selection effects.

The discretion that goes along with agenda control is not the only feature of such courts that might explain the smaller repeat player advantage. Amicus participation in the U.S. Supreme Court and state apex courts is much more frequent and extensive than in lower courts. Such amicus involvement is likely to mitigate the repeat player advantage since amici can bring resources to bear to buttress otherwise underresourced litigants. In fact, the repeat player advantage extends to amici as well. Research shows that amici who are repeat players are also more likely to achieve their desired outcome compared to amici who are not (Buckler 2015; Hazelton and Hinkle 2022).

Since federal circuit courts have neither formal agenda control nor extensive amicus participation, it is unsurprising that the repeat player advantage is substantially larger in size than that observed in the U.S. Supreme Court or in state high courts (Songer et al. 1999; Songer, Sheehan and Haire 2000; Songer and Sheehan 1992). Songer and Sheehan (1992) estimate a multivariate model that predicts individuals win 34% of the appeals they bring (in published cases) compared to 87% for the U.S. government. The size of the repeat player advantage in circuit courts was also quite consistent from 1925 to 1988 (Songer et al. 1999; Songer, Sheehan, and Haire 2000).

What to Expect in Unpublished Cases

Much of the work applying Galanter's theory to appellate courts has focused on published opinions. However, there are indications that repeat players also enjoy an advantage in unpublished cases. Atkins (1991) finds evidence of a repeat player advantage in the English Court of Appeal using a dataset in which 85% of cases were not included in the law reports. However, that finding is only suggestive as the institutional context is quite distinct from that found in intermediate federal appellate courts in the United States. More informative for circuit courts is the groundwork laid by Songer and Sheehan (1992), who considered both published and unpublished opinions in their study of the repeat player advantage in circuit courts, including examining those types of opinions separately. Although that study examined opinions from only three circuits (Fourth, Seventh, and Eleventh) in a single year (1986), it provides a key starting point (Songer and Sheehan 1992).

Songer and Sheehan (1992) found some evidence of a repeat player advantage in unpublished circuit cases. Their models incorporated separate explanatory variables for the strength of the appellant and appellee. The litigant type of the appellee was not statistically significant in the model of unpublished opinions (although it was for published opinions) (Songer and Sheehan 1992). The evidence regarding the relative size of the effect of appellant strength in published and unpublished cases is ambiguous. Although the coefficient is almost twice as large in the model of unpublished opinions, comparing coefficients across logit models can be misleading (Allison 1999). The predicted probability of an appellant win for each type of appellant shows that the effect varies.[1] A shift from an underdog individual appellant to the United States being an appellant increased the probability of winning by 0.63 in both published and unpublished cases. Moving from an average individual to a business increased the chance of the appellant winning by 0.13 in published cases and 0.20 in unpublished cases. But the opposite pattern was evident when comparing a business to the United States. Under those circumstances, the increase was 0.40 in published cases and 0.20 in unpublished cases. In short, existing empirical work provides the basis to expect that there is a repeat player advantage in unpublished circuit cases, but no clear basis to predict the size of that effect relative to published cases.

While empirical data from unpublished cases is extremely thin, understanding the mechanisms that drive the repeat player advantage can generate expectations for this context. The explanations for the greater success of haves in litigation can generally be sorted into three categories: litigant selection effects, legal inequality, and persuasion (Galanter 1974). Importantly, these explanations all have very different normative implications. If underdogs lose because they insist upon bringing terrible cases, that does not necessarily raise any concerns about structural injustice in the legal system. Conversely, if underdogs lose because the law systematically favors more advantaged members of society, that suggests fundamental unfairness. If resources can purchase more persuasive and effective representation, the specter of inequality is also raised, but in a way that could be mitigated through amicus participation, greater judicial staffing, or more support for legal aid to indigent litigants. In short, these explanations serve two purposes. First, they help provide the basis for theorizing about how the repeat player advantage might be different in published and unpublished cases. Second, upon observing how that advantage does differ in these two contexts, these explanations help us understand what that means for our understanding of the fairness of the legal system.

Litigant Selection Effects

The repeat player advantage is often attributed to the fact that underdogs make worse decisions about which cases to litigate. Due to their lack of knowledge and experience, they are more likely to sue or appeal under circumstances where the facts and law are not on their side. As mentioned previously, agenda control can mitigate the effects of repeat player status. The reason for this is linked to the litigant selection effects mechanism. When there is agenda control, a

[1] These estimates are provided by Songer and Sheehan (1992) in Table 9 of their article.

court's decision about whether to take a case attenuates the effect of the litigants' decisions. There is an analogous attenuation of litigant decisions in published cases. While federal circuit courts have no formal agenda control, the practice of designating only some opinions as binding precedent operates as an informal method of agenda control. Circuit courts cannot decide which cases to resolve, but they can determine which ones will have an impact on circuit law.

The reason scholars posit that agenda control reduces the repeat player advantage is because the court selects cases with legal issues where the law is not already clear. Disputes with legal ambiguity are naturally cases in which both sides have some realistic chance of winning. Conversely, in cases where the law is quite clear, one side has a substantially better chance of winning. More powerful litigants with more resources and experience are likely to be better at assessing their chances of winning a case. That is, they are likely to bring strong cases, while one-shot litigants with few resources are more likely to bring weak cases. When agenda control is not in play, this discrepancy in case selection naturally leads to weaker appellants losing more frequently and stronger appellants winning more frequently.

Selective publication likely sorts cases such that any advantage from litigant selection effects is more pronounced when a ruling is unpublished. Published cases are selected by judges. Moreover, the criteria circuit judges use to determine cases suitable for publication are quite similar to those that apex courts employ for discretionary review. While circuit rules with respect to publication vary as to particulars, they agree that rulings establishing new legal principles should be published. In other words, the kinds of close cases with novel legal issues that are likely to be reviewed by high courts are also likely to be chosen for publication. Therefore, the body of published cases is likely to contain the close cases where both sides have a reasonable chance to win. Conversely, unpublished cases include all remaining appeals that litigants choose to bring. Without any judicial filtering mechanism, the resource advantage in unpublished cases should be larger if it is due to the varied ability of litigants to select high-quality cases for appeal. Consequently, I theorize that to the extent the repeat player advantage is due to have-nots overestimating the strength of their case, the repeat player advantage should be larger among unpublished cases.

Litigants' decisions regarding which cases to argue in court are not always solely driven by the assessment of their chances of winning the particular case in question. Galanter (1974) also points out that litigants such as a product manufacturer who anticipate repeated litigation may make long-term strategic decisions over a series of cases compared to a one-shot litigant like a plaintiff harmed by a faulty product. An experienced repeat player will understand that losing in a case with a published decision is more detrimental to their interests (compared to an unpublished ruling), because it will be binding precedent in future cases in that circuit. Litigants must decide whether to settle an appeal before the court reveals the decision and its publication status,[2] but experienced court observers will often be able to anticipate the kinds of cases that are more likely to culminate in publication. Of course, a repeat player stands to gain from a published decision in their favor. Overall, the stakes are higher for a repeat player in such cases. As a result, in cases where they anticipate publication, repeat players might have additional motivation to act strategically by settling appeals that they are unlikely to win. The effect of this type of litigant selection effect would manifest in repeat players winning more frequently in published cases. Therefore, I theorize that to the extent the repeat player advantage is due to strategic settlement by litigants with long-term interests, it should be strongest among published cases.

Inequality in the Law

A second explanation for the greater success of haves in litigation is that the law has been developed over time to inherently favor them. This explanation, while intuitive, is difficult to test. It follows logically from the fact that the individuals who make both statutory and judicial law are often elite individuals with extensive resources themselves. It is also a natural extension of the explanation in the previous section that repeat players make strategic litigation decisions that allow them to shape the law in their favor over time. But judges do not necessarily always identify the "correct" legal answer in each case. This makes it difficult to disentangle inequality in the underlying law from inequality in how judges treat different litigants. Research partially accounts for this by controlling for the ideological preferences of judges.

As Songer and Sheehan (1992, 254) note: "[I]n the U.S. political system at large, support for business interests against individuals and states versus the federal government is usually related to the differences in the ideological centers of the two major parties." It is also possible that particular types of litigants might be more likely to bring particular types of claims that are conservative or liberal in nature (Sheehan et al. 1992). To address these concerns, most studies of the repeat player hypothesis control for judicial ideology. For example, the work in this area focused on federal circuit courts indicates that judicial ideology (as well as litigant type) influences when the appellant wins (Songer and Sheehan 1992; Songer et al. 1999). The fact that both are significant suggests that the law

[2] Prior to 1994, parties did have the option to settle after an opinion was issued and agree to vacate that decision and render it nonprecedential (Slavitt 1995). But in 1994, the Supreme Court severely curtailed this practice, only allowing vacatur under extraordinary circumstances (see *U.S. Bancorp Mortgage Co. v. Bonner Mall*, 513 U.S. 18 (1994)).

might treat different types of litigants differently, even after controlling for extralegal considerations such as ideological preferences. However, examining the impact of litigant resources in unpublished cases provides an especially good test of whether inequality in the law could be the specific mechanism underlying the repeat player advantage. One of the most prominent features of unpublished cases in that they predominantly involve disputes with a high level of legal clarity. The higher level of "obviousness" of what the law requires to resolve such cases should minimize (or at least reduce) the impact of nonlegal factors on case outcomes. Of course, it is still important to control for the effects of known sources of impact on judicial decision-making such as ideology. But in the aggregate, more unpublished cases should be resolved strictly according to the law compared to published cases. The result of this is that to the extent the repeat player advantage reflects underlying inequality in the law, the advantage should be greater in unpublished cases compared to published cases.[3]

Inequality in Persuasive Ability

A final explanation for why greater resources can lead to greater success in court is that money can purchase more effective advocacy. This is the individual mechanism that has obtained the most empirical support in its own right. A variety of studies show that attorneys with greater experience and expertise are more likely to secure wins for their clients (e.g., Haire et al. 1999; Szmer and Ginn 2014). Resources can buy better attorneys who are better at persuasion. Repeated experience in court can also teach repeat litigants and litigators what types of arguments are most likely to be successful (Hazelton and Hinkle 2022). This mechanism would manifest differently in published and unpublished cases in two ways. First, legal ambiguity is likely to be an important precondition for variable persuasive abilities to result in different case outcomes. Since the law is typically clear in unpublished cases, this would mean resources would have a greater opportunity to help win the day in published cases, where there are typically plausible legal arguments on both sides. So, to the extent that the repeat player advantage is due to the ability to convert money and experience into more persuasive arguments, the advantage should be larger in published cases compared to unpublished ones.

Second, there is a more nuanced way in which the importance of effective persuasion might emerge. Human psychology is such that it is easier to persuade someone who is ideologically predisposed to agree (Braman and Nelson 2007;

[3] As discussed previously, such a pattern could also indicate that one-shot litigants make poor decisions about which cases to litigate at the appellate level.

Taber and Lodge 2006). Confirmation bias smooths the way for convincing a friendly judge, while persuading a hostile judge can be an uphill battle (Hinkle and Nelson 2016; Sunstein et al. 2004). As a result, I theorize that attorneys who are more skilled and effective at persuading judges will see the benefits of their efforts vary according to the nature of the judges they are facing. The most persuasive and expert attorney will find it easier to convince a conservative judge to issue a conservative ruling than a liberal one. I extend this line of thought to also theorize that inexperienced and underresourced litigants will tend to hire attorneys who have a harder time convincing a conservative judge to issue a conservative ruling compared to attorneys hired by highly experienced and expert litigants. To the extent that the repeat player advantage is attributable to one side's greater ability to persuade, I expect the size of the advantage to be smaller when the stronger side faces an ideologically distant panel and greater when they face an aligned panel. Since I also hypothesize that persuasion plays a larger role in published cases, I expect this interactive effect to be larger in published cases compared to unpublished cases.

Table 4.1 provides a summary of the hypotheses. The overall answer to the question of whether the repeat player advantage should be larger in unpublished cases is very much "it depends." The different mechanisms, which may operate individually or in concert, suggest quite different answers to that question. As a result, the empirical findings will shed light on the mechanisms underlying the repeat player advantage, a topic that is often left rather murky. As Table 4.1 shows, there are two explanations that suggest the haves will do even better in published cases and two that indicate they will enjoy enhanced success in unpublished cases. As a result, I will not be able to definitively identify a sole mechanism with this observational study. However, it will be possible to narrow down the possibilities.

Table 4.1 Summary of Hypotheses (Source: Rachael K. Hinkle 2024)

	Repeat Player Advantage	
Mechanism	**Published**	**Unpublished**
Litigant Selection Effects		
"Have-nots" Bringing Weak Appeals	Smaller	Larger
"Haves" Using Long-Term Strategy	Larger	Smaller
Inequality in the Law	Smaller	Larger
Inequality in Persuasive Ability	Larger	Smaller

Research Design

Most of the existing work on the repeat player advantage in the U.S. Courts of Appeals relies on the Songer dataset, which, while an excellent resource, only contains published opinions (Songer et al. 1999; Songer, Sheehan, and Haire 2000; Szmer et al. 2016). Songer and Sheehan (1992) broke important ground by looking at unpublished cases as well, but the resource-intense nature of collecting data from unpublished opinions limited the scope of that work to three circuits over the span of a single year. The C^3PO database includes over two hundred thousand cases from all twelve geographic-based circuits from 2002 to 2012. This provides a unique opportunity to better understand both how and why the types of litigants affect outcomes in circuit courts.

The most central variable for an analysis of repeat player advantage involves the types of litigants involved in each case. Classifying both the appellant and appellee for over two hundred thousand cases requires a streamlined approach. I use the following categories: national government, subnational government, organization, person, and indigent/pro se person. Each appellant and appellee is coded as only one category. The "organization" category includes both for-profit businesses and interest groups. Differentiating organizations to a greater degree would require substantial additional resources. Moreover, organizational entities of any type are composed of multiple people and involve pooled resources in ways that are likely to reflect greater collective resources and litigation experience compared to private individuals. Following the approach of other scholars, individuals listed in their official capacity are coded based on the entity they represent (Songer and Sheehan 1992; Songer et al. 1999).

Wheeler et al. (1987) created an "index of net advantage" to summarize the litigation success for each type of litigant while taking into account the frequency with which they appeared on each side of appellate litigation. This index offers a way to provide an overall summary of the repeat player advantage in a descriptive way. It is calculated by starting with the win rate for a type of litigant as appellant and then subtracting their loss rate when appellee (see also Songer and Sheehan 1992; Songer et al. 1999). This provides a more accurate picture than just a win rate by type because it accounts for the courts' tendency to affirm and variation by litigant type in how frequently they appear on each side of the litigation (Songer and Sheehan 1992). Because this index has been deployed in previous research, it provides a useful way to compare the size of the repeat player advantage in the C^3PO database to previous work on the circuit courts. Therefore, before describing my research design and testing my hypotheses, I first explore the index of net advantage. Table 4.2 shows the net advantage for each type of litigant within unpublished cases and published cases in the C^3PO database alongside

Table 4.2 Index of Net Advantage: Index of net advantage for four types of litigants in published and unpublished cases from 2002 to 2012, as well as comparable numbers reported by Songer and Sheehan (1992) and Songer, Sheehan, and Haire (1999) for comparison. Net advantage is the average win rate of each litigant type when appellant minus their loss rate when appellee. The "organization" category includes only businesses in the comparison articles, but includes all nongovernmental group entities (including nonprofits) in the main datasets. (Source: Rachael K. Hinkle 2024)

Litigant Type	Net Advantage Published	Net Advantage Unpublished	Net Advantage Songer and Sheehan (1992)	Net Advantage Songer, Sheehan and Haire (1999)
Person	-11.9	-3.0	-18.2	-12.6
Organization	3.5	7.3	1.6	-2.8
State/Local Govt.	10.8	11.2	29.9	15.6
U.S. Government	46.6	38.6	45.1	25.6

comparable numbers reported in Songer and Sheehan (1992), which includes both unpublished and published cases together, and Songer et al. (1999), which includes only published cases. For purposes of this comparison, I collapse my category of indigent and pro se persons into the broader category of persons to correspond to the coding in the comparable research. The first interesting thing to note is that for both published and unpublished cases in my dataset, the litigant types sort as expected: individuals fare the worst followed by organizations, state and local governments, and the federal government in turn. Second, this first cut at the data reveals that for two of the four litigant types, the absolute value of the index of net advantage is smaller for unpublished cases compared to published cases. This suggests there might be a smaller resource advantage in unpublished cases.

While the index of net advantage is a useful summary measure, rigorous examination of the repeat player advantage requires multivariate analysis that accounts for potential confounders. Following previous work in the circuit court context, I conduct such analysis using the outcome variable of whether the appellant wins the appeal (Songer and Sheehan 1992; Songer et al. 1999). Looking at appellant success accounts for the fact that who won at the trial level has a very real impact on who wins the appeal. Circuit courts usually affirm which means that appellants typically lose (Songer and Sheehan 1992; Songer et al. 1999). The winner of each case was coded using the text of the opinion to determine whether the circuit court affirmed or reversed.[4] Since this outcome is binary, I estimate probit models. Furthermore, since litigant types may be distributed very differently across opinion type, I estimate two separate models—one for published cases and one for unpublished cases.

The primary explanatory variables must capture the litigants' type, the panel's ideology, and their interaction. To build a single metric to capture repeat player advantage, I use a difference measure that summarizes the gap between the resources and experience of the appellant and the appellee. Past work on the repeat player advantage in the circuit courts has used separate measures of litigant type for appellant and appellee. These are typically numerical scales with the litigant type ordered according to assumptions about the ordering of their resources (Songer and Sheehan 1992; Songer et al. 1999, see also McCormick 1993; Wheeler et al. 1987). For example, with the five categories employed here, indigent or pro se individuals are assigned a value of zero, other individuals a value of one, organizations a value of two, state and local governments equal three, and the national government equals four. Rather than employ these *Appellant Type* and *Appellee Type* variables separately, I build a variable named *Difference in Litigant Type* that equals *Appellant Type* minus *Appellee Type*. This kind of difference measure has gained popularity in more recent research (e.g., Collins 2004, 2007; Szmer et al. 2007). A key benefit of looking at the relative experience and resources of the appellant and appellee is that it better tracks the theoretical expectations regarding the repeat player advantage. The outcome of the appeal is a zero-sum game; one side cannot win without the other side losing. If both sides have extensive resources, we cannot expect them both to be more likely to win. The mechanisms of the hypothesized advantage lie in being in a better position than one's opponent. The difference measure captures this dynamic. Positive values indicate that the appellant has the advantage over the appellee and negative values indicate that the appellee has the relative advantage. Figure 4.1 shows the overall distribution of this measure for unpublished and published cases. Appellees are much more likely to be in a position of strength, and that discrepancy is even greater in unpublished cases.

The next key explanatory variable is panel ideology. Since the outcome is whether the appellant wins, the relevant ideology measure must capture the panel's ideological congruence with the appellant. Past work on the circuit courts has controlled for ideology by using a binary measure that codes a panel as liberal or conservative based on whether the majority of the panel was appointed by Democratic or Republican presidents and then comparing the panel coding to whether the appellant is seeking a liberal or conservative outcome (Songer

[4] Less than 5% of cases have split decisions. Following previous work (Songer and Sheehan 1992; Wheeler et al. 1987), I exclude those from the analysis.

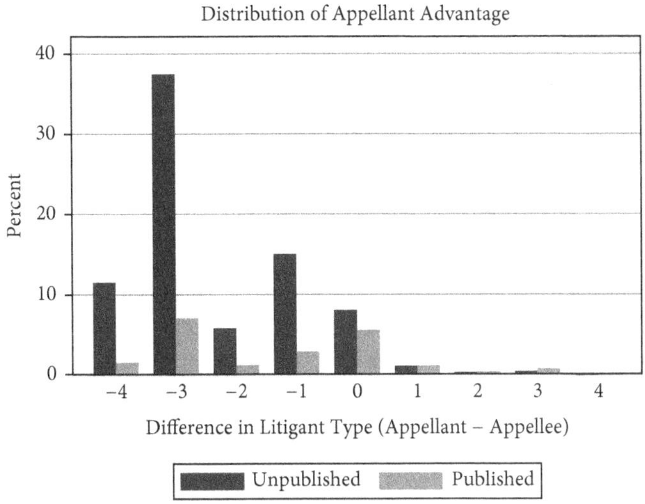

Figure 4.1 Distribution of *Difference in Litigant Type* by Publication Status (Source: Rachael K. Hinkle 2024)

and Sheehan 1992; Songer et al. 1999). For example, a Republican-majority panel is aligned with an appellant who is seeking a conservative ruling (Songer and Sheehan 1992; Songer et al. 1999). I take a similar approach, but employ a continuous measure of panel median ideology, JCS scores. I construct the variable, *Panel Alignment with Appellant*, using the same method employed to calculate *Panel Alignment with Outcome* in Chapter 3. For this analysis, the relevant reference point is *Appellant Ideological Direction*, which equals −1 if the appellant is seeking a liberal ruling, 1 if they are seeking a conservative ruling, and zero if the ideological direction could not be clearly classified. *Panel Alignment with Appellant* is the panel median JCS score multiplied by *Appellant Ideological Direction* (Szmer et al. 2016). Since I expect the effects of *Difference in Litigant Type* and *Panel Alignment with Appellant* to interact with each other, I also include an interaction term in both models.

Finally, I control for other factors that are also likely to influence the probability that the appellant will win and may be correlated with the primary explanatory variables. First, the ideology of potential reviewing courts might shape the panel's willingness to rule in favor of the appellant. In order to account for this possibility, I control for both the full circuit's and Supreme Court's ideological alignment with the appellant. As with panel alignment, these measures are calculated by multiplying the full circuit median JCS score and the Supreme Court median JCS score by *Appellant Ideological Direction*. Next, I control for amicus participation in a case, as the presence of outside groups that bring resources and experience to the court can play a role (Songer and Sheehan 1992). Amici can also indicate that a case presents a difficult legal issue. Other indicators of such legal novelty include the circuit hearing oral arguments in a case and the district judge having decided to publish the ruling in the trial court below. Conversely, issuing a per curiam opinion that does not name an authoring judge suggests that a panel views a case as less important. I control for all these factors. Finally, legal issue areas can present different dynamics (Songer and Sheehan 1992; Songer et al. 1999). I control for issue area with criminal cases composing the baseline category. Because I am interested in variation both within and across circuits, I do not include dummy variables for each circuit. However, it is worth noting that the substantive conclusions regarding litigant type and panel ideology are robust to the inclusion of circuit fixed effects.[5] Summary statistics for all variables are provided in Appendix 4.A in Table 4.A.1.

Results

Figure 4.2 illustrates the results by showing the predicted change in probability of an appellant winning the case when moving a variable from a low to a high value (from its 25th to 75th percentile or from zero to one) and holding other variables at their median or mode as applicable. Because the difference in litigant type and panel ideology variables are interacted, I show the changes in predicted probability for each at low and high values of the other.[6] I begin by analyzing the separate effects of litigant resources and judicial ideology before turning to examine their joint impact. As expected, there is evidence of a repeat player advantage in both published and unpublished cases. When the appellant has greater resources and experience relative to their opponent, the appellant is more likely to win, and that effect is statistically significant in both models. However, the size of that effect does differ in the two models. Whether the panel's ideology is aligned with the appellant or not, the advantage enjoyed by the side with the greater resources and experience is larger in published cases compared to unpublished ones.

Figure 4.3 provides a more comprehensive illustration of the size of the repeat player advantage by showing the predicted probability of an appellant win at every value of *Difference in Litigant Type* for each model. When the appellant is at maximum disadvantage, which means a pro se or indigent individual appealing a ruling in favor of the federal government, they have a 9.2% chance of winning if the ruling is published. When the situation is reversed

[5] The results are also largely robust to excluding all criminal cases and prisoner petitions.
[6] The full regression results are available in Appendix 4.B in Table 4.B.1.

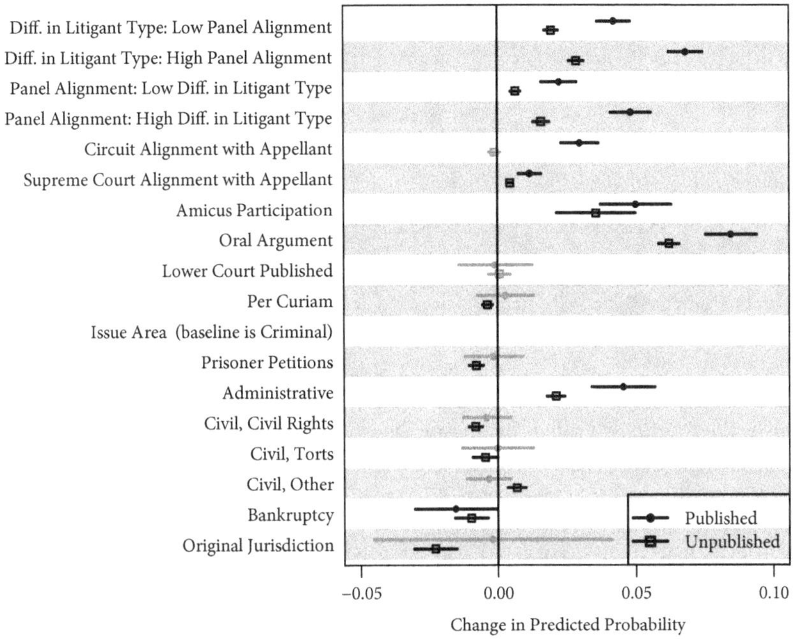

Figure 4.2 Changes in Predicted Probability of Appellant Win: Estimates (and associated 95% confidence intervals) of the change in the predicted probability of the appellant winning generated by moving each variable from a low to high value while holding other variables at their median or mode. Changes produced by *Difference in Litigant Type* and *Panel Alignment with Appellant* are presented at low and high values of the other to illustrate interactive effects. Low and high values are 25th and 75th percentile for continuous variables, and zero and one for binary variables. Estimates from the model of published opinions are solid dots, and estimates from the model of unpublished opinions are empty squares. Estimates and confidence intervals in gray (instead of black) indicate that the confidence interval includes zero. Full regression estimates are available in Appendix 4.B in Table 4.B.1. (Source: Rachael K. Hinkle 2024)

and the federal government is appealing a ruling in favor of such an individual, the chance of the appellant winning the same kind of case rises all the way to 37.5%. That is 28.3% higher than for a maximally disadvantaged appellant. For unpublished cases, the increase is less dramatic. In those cases, the disadvantaged appellant wins an estimated 2.7% of the time compared to 17.5% for the appellant with the maximum advantage. The difference here is 14.8%, just over half of what it is for published cases. This finding provides support for the two hypotheses that anticipate a smaller repeat player advantage in unpublished cases. The first of these is that repeat players use long-term strategy to

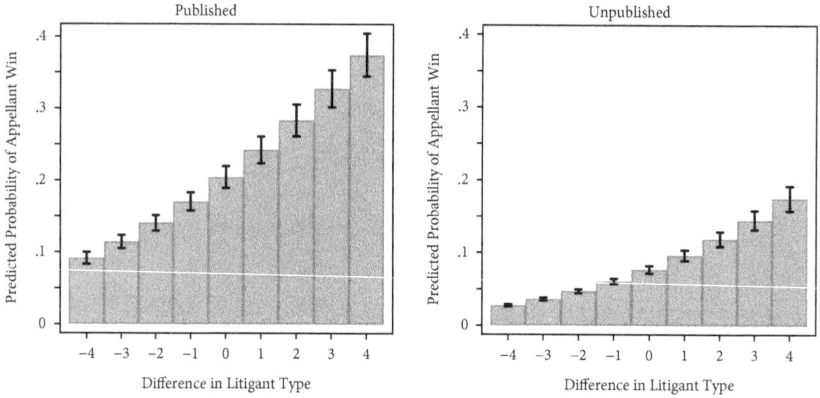

Figure 4.3 Predicted Probability of Appellant Win Across *Difference in Litigant Type*: This graph provides the predicted probability that the appellant will win for each possible value of *Difference in Litigant Type*. Other variables are held at their median or mode in the full dataset. Predicted probabilities from the model of published opinions are shown in the left panel, and those from the model of unpublished opinions are shown on the right. The whiskers for each bar depict the 95% confidence interval around the estimate. (Source: Rachael K. Hinkle 2024)

settle cases differently if they anticipate a ruling being published. The second supported hypothesis is that resources can be used to hire more persuasive lawyers.

As expected, appellants are also more likely to win when the panel's ideology is more closely aligned with the result the appellant is seeking. This statistically significant effect emerges in both models. Figure 4.4 shows how the predicted probability increases in both models as the panel becomes increasingly aligned with the appellant. The steeper slope of the line in the left panel indicates that the effect of judicial ideology is larger in published cases. In fact, the marginal effect of *Panel Alignment with Appellant* is 0.044 in published cases and 0.013 in unpublished cases. This difference in effect is statistically as well as substantively significant.[7] Since unpublished opinions are specifically designed to deal with well-settled legal issues, it is unsurprising that judicial ideology has a smaller effect on who wins and loses in such cases. While law is not sufficiently determinative to eliminate the effect of judges' ideological predispositions in unpublished cases, its effect is less than a third the size of the effect on published cases (where the law is less well-established).

[7] The z-test statistic of the difference in marginal effects is 4.6, which has a p-value less than 0.001.

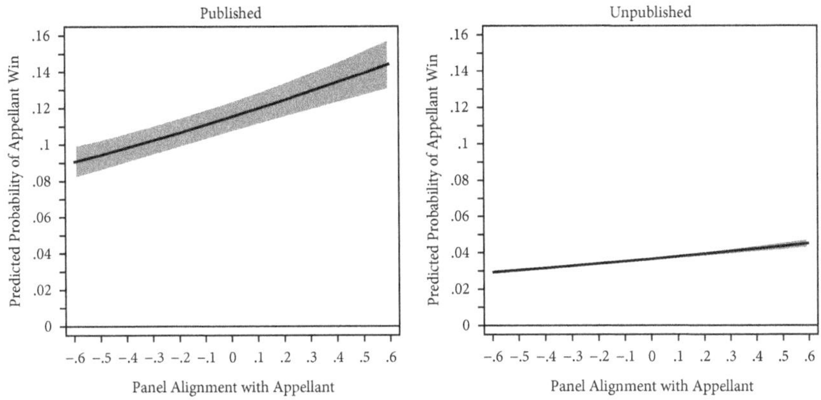

Figure 4.4 Predicted Probability of Appellant Win Across *Panel Alignment with Appellant*: This graph provides the predicted probability that the appellant will win across the range of *Panel Alignment with Appellant.* Other variables are held at their median or mode in the full dataset. Predicted probabilities from the model of published opinions are shown in the left panel, and those from the model of unpublished opinions are shown on the right. The shaded regions depict the 95% confidence intervals. (Source: Rachael K. Hinkle 2024)

Next, I examine the combined effects of litigant type and judicial ideology. Figure 4.2 provides some initial insight. As anticipated, the advantage appellants enjoy when they have more resources and experience than the opposing side is even greater when the panel is also more closely aligned with the appellant. Figure 4.5 provides a more detailed look at this interaction by showing how the marginal effect of *Difference in Litigant Type* changes over the range of all values of *Panel Alignment with Appellant.* There is only a small interactive effect for unpublished opinions, which supports the expectation that greater persuasive ability can only benefit a well-resourced litigant a fairly small amount in cases where the legal issues are often clear. Conversely, and as expected, the interaction is much more notable within published cases, where the law is often more ambiguous. In published cases, the marginal effect of *Difference in Litigant Type* is 0.03 when the panel's ideology is held at its median value. But it varies from 0.017 when the panel is furthest from the appellant to 0.05 when the panel is most closely aligned with the appellant. The baseline predicted probability of an appellant victory when all variables are held at their median or mode is only 0.10. In this context, the fact that the marginal effect of relative litigant strength can be as large as 0.05 is remarkable. Moreover, the range of the effect of litigant strength is also substantial. The marginal effect of the litigant variable is 0.033 higher for the most ideologically

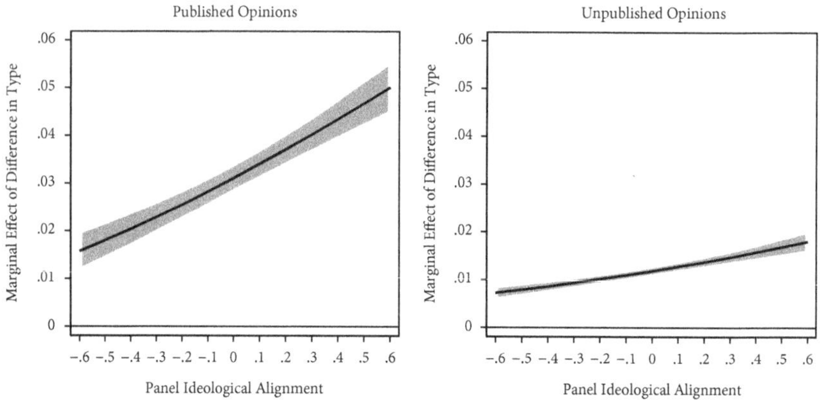

Figure 4.5 Marginal Effects of *Difference in Litigant Type*: This graph provides the marginal effect of the *Difference in Litigant Type* at different values of *Panel Alignment with Appellant* from the minimum to the maximum observed in the data. Other variables are held at their median or mode in the full dataset. Marginal effects from the model of published opinions are shown in the left panel, and those from the model of unpublished opinions are shown on the right. The shaded regions depict the 95% confidence interval around the marginal effects. (Source: Rachael K. Hinkle 2024)

aligned panels compared to those that are the most ideologically distant. This indicates that in cases where the law is not clearly settled, parties with superior resources and experience are more persuasive in ways that are especially effective for ideologically sympathetic judges.

Figure 4.2 shows that the control variables operate largely as expected and often in similar ways across the two models. There is some evidence that concerns about possible review weigh on the panel's decision of whether the appellant wins the case. Both the full circuit's and Supreme Court's alignment with the appellant significantly increase the probability the appellant will win the case at the panel level in published cases. The same pattern holds with respect to the Supreme Court in unpublished cases. The probability of the appellant winning is also linked to features of the case itself. In both models, appellants do better in more important and interesting cases as signaled by amicus participation or the circuit scheduling oral argument. Interestingly, there is no evidence that the district court judge signaling case importance by publishing the trial court ruling is related to the appellant winning on appeal. Appellants are less successful in unpublished cases where the panel issues an unsigned per curiam opinion. Finally, the issue fixed effects show that appellants do better in some types of cases than others.

Conclusions

This chapter provides two types of insights. First, it illuminates the role of litigant type in unpublished cases in the federal circuits. Second, it sheds light on how we understand the mechanisms underlying the repeat player advantage. The first topic is far from trivial. For most litigants in the federal judicial system, their only experience with appeals, if any, will be in a case disposed of in an unpublished decision. These cases are virtually invisible to outside observers because of their sheer volume and the fact that they don't create a binding legal precedent. Yet the lack of policy impact does not diminish the very real impact of those opinions on the litigants involved. As such, understanding how the characteristics of litigants impact the outcomes of such cases carries important significance. The resource advantage is relatively small for these unpublished cases, which is good news in terms of social justice since the resources of a litigant are not legitimate grounds for resolving legal disputes. However, the effect is not negligible. When an individual appeals a case against another individual, their predicted probability of winning is 0.064, but that falls to 0.032 if the federal government is on the other side of the appeal. In other words, the resources and experience on the opposing side can cut the probability of success in half—a sobering reality.

The poor performance of have-nots in litigation is often linked to their poor choices regarding when to settle and when to litigate. If this was a key mechanism driving the repeat player advantage, then unpublished cases in the circuit courts should be an institutional context where this dynamic would clearly emerge. All losing litigants in federal trial court cases have a right to appeal to the circuit courts. It is solely up to the appellant to make that decision. If have-nots were significantly less competent than haves when deciding whether to appeal, then have-nots should also be more likely to lose. This discrepancy is present in unpublished cases, but its effect size is rather small, both in absolute terms and relative to published cases. This suggests that litigant case selection might not be a predominant force behind the repeat player advantage. Along similar lines, fundamental inequality in the law does not appear to play a substantial role in the resource advantage either. Unpublished cases often involve clear-cut legal issues, indicating that widespread inequality in the law based on litigant type should manifest in a notable repeat player advantage in cases resolved primarily on legal grounds. Instead, we see the opposite pattern with a greater advantage in published cases.

The patterns revealed by the data suggest one of two possible explanations. The first is that experienced litigants are substantially more strategic and selective about settling cases that are likely to be resolved with published opinions, while they are less concerned about the nuances of legal development when litigating cases likely to result in unpublished opinions. The second plausible explanation is that in circuit courts, the resource advantage is primarily due to more experienced and resourced litigants being capable of mustering more persuasive arguments. The greater legal clarity in unpublished cases dulls the effect of this advantage. This interpretation of the evidence is further strengthened by the observed interaction between litigant type and judicial ideology. There is only a modest interaction in unpublished cases, which is precisely where persuasion should have less impact. More importantly, there is a substantial interactive effect in published cases. This supports the conclusion that variable persuasive ability is driving the resource advantage because persuasion is the only mechanism that has reason to vary in size based on the ideological alignment between litigant and judge. Overall, the picture that emerges with respect to unpublished cases is that while the law is supposed to be quite clear, there is still room for both relative litigant resources and judicial ideology to affect outcomes, at least to some degree.

While the primary task here is to learn about unpublished opinions by comparing them to cases with published opinions, the results also shed interesting light on previous findings regarding the repeat player advantage more broadly. Past work finding a smaller repeat player advantage in courts of last resort posit that agenda control was a key reason for that difference since it took litigant case selection out of the equation. However, the finding here of a smaller repeat player advantage in unpublished circuit cases calls that conclusion into question. Judges have even less control over the content and legal quality of unpublished circuit cases than they do in published ones. Yet the repeat player advantage does not grow, but actually shrinks. In light of this finding, it seems more plausible that the extensive amicus participation in courts of last resort is the reason for the attenuation of the repeat player advantage in that context. While amicus participation is more likely in published than unpublished circuit cases, the likelihood and extent of amicus participation is vanishingly small in circuit cases compared to courts of last resort.

Appendix 4.A: Summary Statistics

Table 4.A.1 Summary Statistics (Source: Rachael K. Hinkle 2024)

	Min.	25%	50%	75%	Max
Continuous Variables					
Difference in Litigant Type	−4	−3	−3	−1	4
Panel Alignment with Appellant	−0.57	−0.31	−0.02	0.19	0.60
Circuit Alignment with Appellant	−0.49	−0.28	0	0.21	0.49
Supreme Court Alignment with Appellant	−0.14	−0.07	−0.03	0	0.13
Dichotomous Variables	**0**	**1**			
Published	80%	20%			
Appellant Wins	90%	10%			
Amicus Participation	98%	2%			
Oral Argument	67%	33%			
Lower Court Published	95%	5%			
Per Curiam	57%	43%			
Issue Area					
Criminal	34.1%				
Prisoner Petitions	13.5%				
Administrative	14.5%				
Civil, Civil Rights	18.9%				
Civil, Torts	2.9%				
Civil, Other	14.5%				
Bankruptcy	1.3%				
Original Jurisdiction	0.4%				

Appendix 4.B: Regression Results

Table 4.B.1 Appellant Victory Models: Probit regression models of the probability appellant wins in published cases (left columns) and unpublished cases (right columns). * indicates a p-value < 0.05. (Source: Rachael K. Hinkle 2024)

	Published		Unpublished	
	Coef.	(S.E.)	Coef.	(S.E.)
Difference in Litigant Type	0.128*	(0.005)	0.124*	(0.004)
Panel Alignment with Appellant	0.463*	(0.035)	0.315*	(0.033)
Difference in Litigant Type x Panel Alignment	0.077*	(0.014)	0.050*	(0.012)
Circuit Alignment with Appellant	0.318*	(0.035)	−0.027	(0.026)
Supreme Court Alignment with Appellant	0.857*	(0.147)	0.813*	(0.101)
Amicus Participation	0.227*	(0.026)	0.333*	(0.053)
Oral Argument	0.359*	(0.022)	0.505*	(0.012)
Lower Court Published	−0.005	(0.035)	0.008	(0.024)
Per Curiam	0.014	(0.026)	−0.049*	(0.012)
Issue Area				
Prisoner Petitions	−0.008	(0.028)	−0.108*	(0.018)
Administrative	0.208*	(0.025)	0.216*	(0.016)
Civil, Civil Rights	−0.021	(0.023)	−0.113*	(0.017)
Civil, Torts	−0.001	(0.034)	−0.061	(0.032)
Civil, Other	−0.017	(0.021)	0.079*	(0.018)
Bankruptcy	−0.084	(0.043)	−0.138*	(0.049)
Original Jurisdiction	−0.011	(0.116)	−0.421*	(0.114)
Intercept	−0.790*	(0.027)	−1.397*	(0.018)
N	43,272		169,136	
BIC	46502.7		71392.1	
AIC	46355.3		71221.4	

5
Invisible Work
The Role of Privilege in Making Policy

Introduction

Chapter 4 explores the intersection of selective publication and the frequently observed phenomenon of the repeat player advantage. This chapter turns from the distributional consequences for litigants to focus on disparities created for judges themselves. While litigants are the most obvious winners and losers in appellate litigation, the people who decide who wins and loses a case experience varied costs and benefits in different types of cases as well. Just as the rules of the game affect which party goes home victorious, they also impact the power and prestige that individual judges enjoy.

Starting with President Jimmy Carter, several presidents have placed particular focus on diversifying the federal bench. Thanks to these efforts, there is substantial gender and racial diversity among federal circuit judges today. As of October 2020, 34% of active federal circuit judges were women, and 23% had a race or ethnicity other than white.[1] Occupying a circuit seat is a prestigious position that carries with it substantial power. But simply bringing more women and minorities to the bench does not guarantee that they experience the same level of power as their historically privileged white, male counterparts. The practice of publishing only some opinions, while conceived for the necessary goals of managing a tremendous workload and controlling the amount of precedent, provides an opportunity for the kind of differential experiences that permeate our society.

The selective publication norm divides the work product of circuit courts into two kinds. In unpublished cases, the judicial task is unglamorous but necessary to perform the error correction function that crucially supports perceptions of procedural fairness. The ability to appeal at least one time provides losers in federal court with the assurance that there is a forum to get a second legal opinion. This possibility, whether used by an individual litigant or not, is a key reason losing litigants perceive the process to be fair (and, therefore, accept

[1] The 2019 U.S. Census reported that 51% of people in the United States are women and 24% have a race or ethnicity other than white.

Selective Publication in the U.S. Courts of Appeals. Rachael K. Hinkle, Oxford University Press.
 DOI: 10.1093/oso/9780197770085.003.0005

adverse rulings). Although incredibly important, providing an appeal as of right generates a tremendous workload. And many of these cases involve the application of clear legal rules that were properly applied by the trial court judge. As a result, their resolution at the appellate level is routine and quite rote. While these cases are vital to their participants and the integrity of the federal court system, they do not offer the opportunity to shape legal policy. This work, although extensive and crucial, often fades into invisibility, unacknowledged and underappreciated by observers. The second type of work the circuit courts perform is resolving cases that result in published opinions. Such cases perform the previous two functions of error correction and providing an appeal as of right, plus they contain the important added element of shaping the interpretation of law in a way that is binding throughout the circuit.

The impact of diversifying the federal circuits is diminished if judges from historically excluded demographic groups enjoy less power to shape legal policy than their white, male peers. This chapter investigates whether, and why, that power is disproportionately allocated. First, I examine overall case participation at the judge level. Female and minority judges are more likely to engage in the invisible work of dispatching with cases via unpublished decisions when compared to their white male colleagues. Conversely, white men are more likely to engage in the policymaking work of issuing published opinions. Second, I examine the authorship of majority opinions. The judge tasked with writing an opinion exerts considerable control, as the other panel judges are often too busy to request extensive revisions. A similar pattern appears as with case participation. Female and minority judges are more likely to be assigned to draft unpublished rulings than white male judges. Judges of color are less likely to be assigned published opinions. These patterns indicate that the two types of work circuit judges do are disproportionately distributed by race and gender. Even though the federal judiciary has achieved some diversity, women and minorities are doing less policymaking.

Finally, I examine a third aspect of case participation to see how race and gender affect judges' willingness to record their disagreement. While dissenting opinions do not shape current law, they have the potential to trigger review or shape future law by giving voice to an alternative perspective (Hazelton et al. 2016; Hinkle and Nelson 2017). Furthermore, individual judges are entirely responsible for the decision to write separately, so this provides insight into whether disparities in policymaking arise from culturally or institutionally generated reticence of women and minorities. The data on dissents suggest this is not the case. Both women and minorities are more likely than their white male counterparts to write dissenting opinions even after controlling for ideology, panel composition, and a range of other relevant factors.

The picture that emerges is clear. Judges from demographic groups that have been historically excluded from the federal judiciary (as well as many other aspects of society) are clamoring for a voice. They write dissenting opinions despite the effort and time that requires above and beyond their other duties. Yet those same voices are muted when the court pronounces law. Diversity of personnel is only part of the story. The selective publication norm perpetuates lingering inequalities in power even while inequalities in representation are being addressed. This indicates that diversifying the federal bench, while a laudable first step, is not alone sufficient to wipe out race and gender-based discrepancies in judicial power.

A Seat at the Table: Who Participates in Shaping Policy?

Just like litigants, judges can experience cases differently based on whether they ultimately result in published or unpublished decisions. Being in the room where decisions are made is not always the same as having a seat at the table. And having a seat on a federal circuit court does not necessarily guarantee an equal role in shaping legal policy. Only published opinions are binding precedent within the circuit and, therefore, impact the law (Serfass and Cranford 2001; Reagan 2007). Rulings that are left unpublished resolve the dispute at hand but have no further effect. Consequently, if some judges participate in published cases less frequently, that translates into reduced policymaking power. This is yet another reason that the decision to publish has considerable significance.

Chapter 3 establishes that the characteristics of judges on a circuit panel can have an impact on whether an opinion is published. There is substantial variation in the composition of these panels because assignments rotate on a regular basis (Levy 2017). Some panels are composed of three judges with similar ideology and the same gender and race, while others are composed of three judges with varying levels of diversity on such dimensions. Research has demonstrated that both the ideological and demographic composition of panels has important implications for case outcomes within published cases (see, e.g., Boyd et al. 2010; Cross and Tiller 1998; Kastellec 2013). The median voter theorem would predict that the median member of a three-judge panel would control the outcome of a case regardless of whether one or two colleagues agree with their assessment. But this pattern is not what data reveal (Kastellec 2007). Rather, scholars have routinely found that one's peers matter. Split panels resolve cases differently than unified panels. For cases that implicate gender and race issues, there is similar evidence that panels with one woman or minority resolve cases differently compared to all-male or all-white panels (Boyd et al. 2010; Farhang and

Wawro 2004; Kastellec 2013; Peresie 2005). In short, panel diversity influences outcomes.

There is also reason to expect the homogeneity or diversity of the group of judges hearing the case to shape the important determination of whether an opinion is published. A wide variety of research shows that diversity in decision-making groups produces both a wider range of ideas and more deliberation. This dynamic can lead to higher quality policy outputs. For example, Sommers (2006) demonstrates that racially diverse juries make fewer legal errors than homogeneous juries. But the same patterns may also inadvertently depress the ability of diverse groups of judges to shape legal policy, resulting in law disproportionately crafted by homogeneous groups of judges. Hinkle (2021) demonstrates that both demographic and ideological diversity on panels decreases the probability of publication. In the circuit courts, most demographically homogeneous panels are made up of white men. The logical result is that female and minority judges may well exercise less policymaking power than their white male colleagues.

Why would circuit judges not share equally in decision-making? Modern randomization techniques are used to make case assignments. Why go looking for trouble? There is theoretical reason to expect that such inequalities may exist even if "boring" and "exciting" cases are distributed evenly among judges. This reason arises out of the reality that the publication decision can be used as a tool of compromise. Circuit judges resolve cases in a small-group context (Bowie et al. 2014). Such group decision-making generates a need for compromise when the three judges on the panel do not come to the case with identical viewpoints. One of the often observed correlates of diversity within a group setting is that differences in background, perspective, and experiences often generate a wider range of ideas than in a homogeneous group. For example, a panel with greater ideological similarity among the three judges is able to achieve quicker agreement about the proper resolution of a case than a group of three judges with more diverse ideological viewpoints (Bowie et al. 2014, 110). This suggests more deliberation and negotiation are taking place. There is reason to believe diversity of race and gender may similarly generate a range of perspectives on a case. Men and women experience society differently and, therefore, may bring different information and priorities to case deliberations (Boyd et al. 2010; Tillman and Hinkle 2018). A person's race can also shape their view of society and the role of law within that society (Cox and Miles 2008; Gibson and Nelson 2018).

When the three judges on a panel do not agree about how to resolve a case, the publication decision takes on an additional dimension. As well as being a tool of time management, it becomes a vehicle of compromise as well. Consider, for the sake of explication, a case that presents an important and novel legal issue. If all three judges agree on the resolution, they can easily agree to publish their mutually preferred outcome. Each individual judge gains utility from obtaining their desired result and substantial additional utility from publishing the opinion and, therefore, establishing their preferred approach as binding law in the circuit. Figure 5.1 illustrates this on the left-hand side, with the solid black portion of the bar representing the utility from the case outcome and the cross-hatched portion representing the utility from publication.

But what happens when all three judges do not agree on the proper outcome for such a case? In that scenario, the three judges often negotiate to avoid a single judge experiencing the substantial negative utility associated with a published ruling supporting an outcome the judge opposes (illustrated by the far-right bar in Figure 5.1). The publication decision offers a key point of compromise. Each judge's ideal result would be their preferred outcome with a published opinion that constitutes the law of the circuit. However, in the face of divergent views, two judges may be willing to agree to the opinion being unpublished as long as they obtain their desired outcome. This decreases their overall utility, but they still experience positive utility from the outcome. And a lone judge may be willing to go along with an outcome they oppose if the ruling is not published. While such a compromise would still result in negative utility, it would be minimized by limiting it to the negative utility resulting from the opposed outcome without the added negative utility from publication. A panel may also reach a compromise on the outcome of the case itself. For example, if two of the panel judges believe a case should be affirmed and one favors reversal, a compromise may be struck in which the case is affirmed in part and reversed in part. In such a situation, both

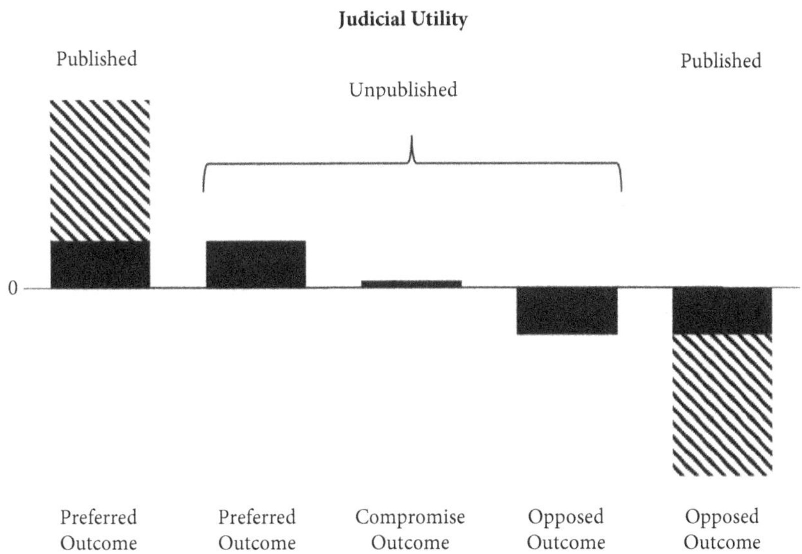

Figure 5.1 Illustration of Individual Judge Utility (Source: Rachael K. Hinkle 2024)

sides likely prefer an unpublished decision since neither is fully comfortable with the resolution and, therefore, may not want to make it binding precedent.

Many factors doubtless influence which precise type of compromise is more or less likely in any given case. Here, I focus not on that nuanced dynamic but on the large-scale implications the need for compromise have for how policymaking power is distributed among judges. If all panel members agree on how the case should be resolved, they can all increase their utility by publishing the opinion and shaping the future law of the circuit.[2] Conversely, if a panel is forging a compromise, the most logical options involve leaving a ruling unpublished. While a panel could technically compromise regarding the outcome and still publish, in most cases it would be unlikely that either side would want to establish a suboptimal result as the law of the circuit. We know from empirical research that even in published cases, a two-judge majority sometimes allows the lone minority judge to secure their preferred outcome (Beim et al. 2014; Boyd et al. 2010; Kastellec 2013; Kim 2009). But logic would suggest that more balanced forms of compromise are considerably more common. As a result, in the aggregate, panels that must compromise during their deliberations should be less likely to publish the ultimate opinion.

So how does the use of nonpublication as a tool of compromise translate into how individual judges have the opportunity to shape policy? The answer is simple. Some judges are more likely than others to serve on the diverse panels that often need to compromise. Women and minorities have been consistently outnumbered by their white, male counterparts on the federal circuit courts. As a result, when three-judge panels are iteratively assembled in a random fashion, white male judges are most likely to experience serving on a homogeneous panel. There are some all-female and all-minority circuit panels, but they are quite rare. Thanks to efforts at diversifying the federal bench, in the C^{3}PO database, only 26% of judge-case observations involve demographically homogeneous panels where all three judges share the same race and gender. But 98% of judges serving on those homogeneous panels were white men, while only 1.5% were white women, and only 0.08% were men of color. There were no instances of three women of color serving together on a panel.

In summary, female and non-white judges are virtually guaranteed to sit on diverse panels. Those panels are more likely to generate a need for compromise than homogeneous panels. A key method of compromise is to leave the opinion unpublished. These three things taken together suggest that participation in cases with published opinions is distributed unequally by race and

[2] Publication decisions will also be shaped by other factors such as the legal novelty of the case, but the overall point holds that if a case is the type that would generally be considered for publication, a panel that agrees on the case outcome has an incentive to publish.

gender. Consequently, I theorize that female and minority judges are less likely to participate in cases with published opinions compared to their male and white colleagues.

Empirical Analysis of Participation

As in previous chapters, all hypothesis tests utilize the C^3PO database. Since the focus here is on how individual judges are impacted by the selective publication norm, the unit of analysis throughout this chapter is the judge-case. There are three observations for each case, one for each member of the panel. To test the participation hypothesis, I model the probability that the case results in a published opinion. Since this outcome variable is binary, I estimate a probit regression model. The data structure includes multiple observations for each case, so I use robust standard errors clustered on the case. The key explanatory variables capture the demographic characteristics of the judge in question. To account for race and gender together, I use indicator variables for whether a judge is a white woman, man of color, or woman of color. The excluded baseline category is a white man.

Of course, it is also important to control for characteristics that might be correlated with both the outcome variable and the main explanatory variables of interest. Judicial ideology is always an important concept to account for in any model of judicial behavior. In this context, the relevant consideration is whether a panel is ideologically diverse. Demographic diversity will often be accompanied by ideological diversity, so it is key to disentangle these two concepts. I do so by including an indicator for whether a panel is ideologically split based on the party of the president who appointed each judge on the panel. This variable equals zero if all three judges share the same party affiliation and equals one otherwise. As discussed in Chapter 3, strategic anticipation of subsequent review may lead panels to publish less frequently when they are more distant from the full circuit or from the Supreme Court. The relationship between demographic characteristics and judicial ideology means that the distance of a panel to potential reviewing courts may be correlated with a single panel judge's race or gender. Therefore, I control for *Ideological Distance: Panel to Circuit* and *Ideological Distance: Panel to Supreme Court.*

Next, because the diversification of the federal bench has occurred relatively recently in history, the race and gender of judges may be correlated with their experience on the bench. A range of judge-level variables capture important elements of that experience. The variable *New Judge* equals one for judges who have served less than two full years at the time of the case in question. *Years on Bench* is a continuous variable that captures exactly how long the judge has served. Because the length of service can have nonmonotonic effects, a squared term is included as well. After circuit judges formally retire and take senior status, they typically continue to work but may play a different role, so I account for such status. Circuits sometimes utilize judges from other circuits to sit by designation. I control for this type of temporary service.[3]

Few of the case-level features that drive the publication decision are likely to be correlated with the race and gender of the judges on the panel. Circuit administrators do not handpick cases and assign them to particular panels based on the features of the panel members. Rather, groups of three judges are assembled mostly randomly, with some attention paid to features like planned vacation time and making sure everyone has an opportunity to serve with all their colleagues. After panels are formed, cases are randomly assigned to panels (Bowie et al. 2014). There is some debate over whether pure randomization is achieved by this process, but it is unlikely to perpetuate systematic differences in the kinds of cases different judges hear. Nevertheless, out an abundance of caution, I control for some key case characteristics that play a role in the publication decision.

The most frequently referenced justification for publishing an opinion is that it addresses a novel legal issue. Therefore, I include my measure of *Legal Novelty*. Next, I control for whether the appellant appeared pro se, since the absence of an attorney may indicate a lower probability of interesting legal issues being raised. The participation of amici, oral argument being heard in the case, and the lower court ruling being published are all indicators of the importance of a case that can increase the probability of publication. Circumstances can vary by circuit as well. To estimate the effects of gender and race across circuits as well as within them, I control for relevant circuit-level features rather than including circuit fixed effects.[4] Specifically, I account for the caseload per active judge and the overall publication rate in the applicable year and circuit. Finally, I control for issue area. Summary statistics for these variables, and all others used in this chapter, are provided in Table 5.A.1 in Appendix 5.A.

The model of which judges participate in published cases contains almost seven hundred thousand observations. Such a large amount of data creates the possibility that very small effects can be estimated with statistical significance. Therefore, it is especially important to focus on substantive significance as well. I do so by illustrating the changes in predicted probabilities that occur when each variable is moved from a low to high value. These quantities and their 95% confidence intervals are plotted in Figure 5.2. As hypothesized, women and

[3] Since the object of this chapter is to evaluate the power wielded by circuit judges, I exclude district court judges sitting by designation from all analyses.

[4] The results are robust to this decision. Using circuit fixed effects instead leads to very similar findings.

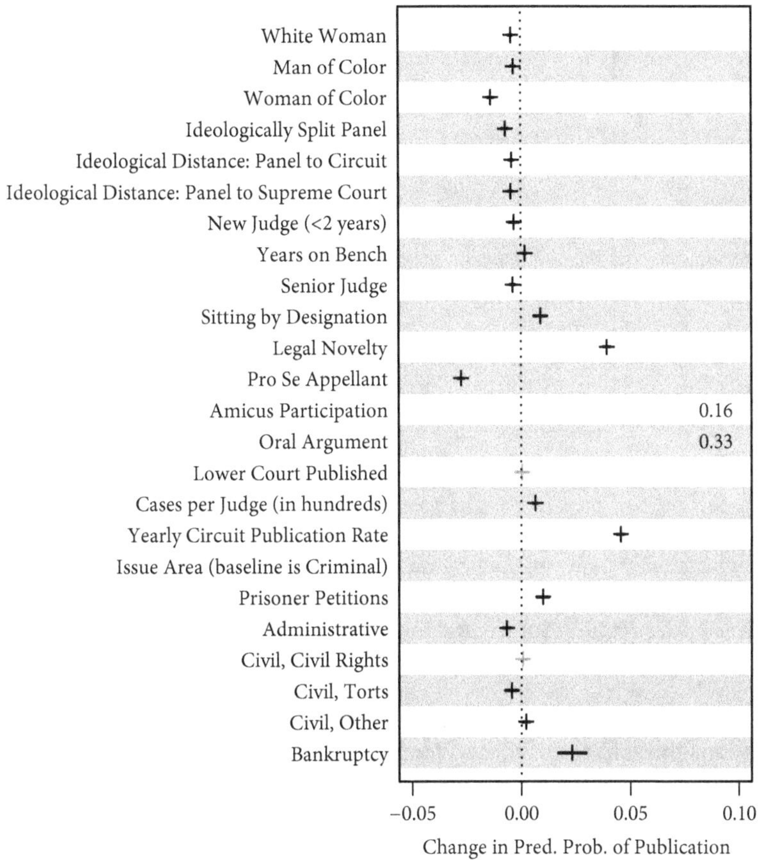

Figure 5.2 Changes in Predicted Probability of Publication: Estimates (and associated 95% confidence intervals) of the change in the predicted probability of publication generated by moving each variable from a low to high value while holding other variables at their median or mode. Low and high values are 25th and 75th percentile for continuous variables, and zero and one for binary variables. Categorical variables are compared to their baseline value. Estimates and confidence intervals in gray (instead of black) indicate that the confidence interval includes zero. Full regression estimates are available in Appendix 5.B in Table 5.B.1. (Source: Rachael K. Hinkle 2024)

minorities are significantly less likely to participate in published cases compared to white men.

While there is support for the participation hypothesis, at first glance the size of the effect appears somewhat modest. White women and men of color are 0.4% and 0.3%, respectively, less likely to participate in a published case compared to

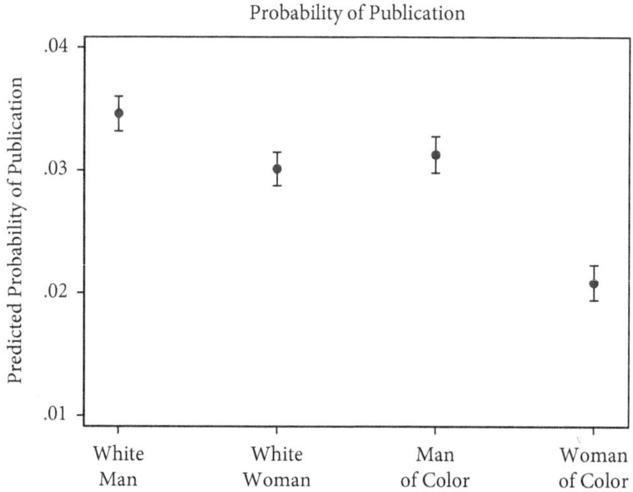

Figure 5.3 Predicted Probability of Publication by Judge Type: This graph provides the predicted probability of publication for each type of judge. Other variables are held at their median. The whiskers depict the 95% confidence interval around the predicted probabilities. (Source: Rachael K. Hinkle 2024)

white men. However, the intersectional impact of being both female and a minority roughly triples the effect. Women of color are 1.4% less likely than white men to be involved in published cases. Figure 5.3 provides context for the size of these differences by showing the predicted probability of publication for each type of judge (while holding all other variables at their median or mode as appropriate). The modal case in the dataset is one in which there was no oral argument and no amicus activity. As Figure 5.2 shows, those two variables have the largest impact on publication. The result is that in the modal case (without either factor) only 3.5% of cases are published even for white male judges. Against this background, the fact that the estimate is 1.4% lower for female judges of color (i.e., 2.1%) is quite notable. In relative terms, the rate of publication for white men is 1.7 times the rate for minority women. Consider how this discrepancy would accumulate over a judge's career. Even in just the time frame from 2002 to 2012, the average judge participated in 2,040 cases (and 10% of judges heard more than four thousand cases). Using the calculations from this model, the average judge would participate in seventy-one published cases if a white man compared to forty-three if they were a woman of color, sixty-one if they were a white woman, and sixty-three if a man of color. Since circuit judges generally serve for multiple decades, these estimated discrepancies are conservative and can likely be doubled or tripled.

Driving the Bus: Who Crafts Policy?

The kind of differences in overall case participation demonstrated in the preceding discussion are not the only place where disproportionate influence may emerge. There is a similar possibility even within individual cases. One of the key duties of circuit judges is opinion writing. Being assigned to write the majority opinion for a case carries with it both responsibilities and opportunities. These vary markedly based on whether the decision is intended for publication. Authorship of a published opinion takes a great deal of time and effort, but also gives a judge the opportunity to influence legal development and shape policy (Boyd 2015b; Bowie et al. 2014; Lax 2007). Unlike the Supreme Court, where justices frequently request detailed revisions from the author of a draft opinion, circuit judges are often too busy to request any changes at all, let alone extensive revisions. As a result, the author of a published opinion plays an especially important role in influencing the contours of law compared to the other judges who participate in the case. The previous analysis demonstrates that female and minority judges are less likely to participate in cases with published opinions. But when they do participate in such cases, are they also less likely to be entrusted with the task of crafting the opinion? Conversely, are they saddled with more opinion-drafting work than their peers in cases with unpublished opinions?

The fact that unpublished rulings do not constitute binding precedent suggests judges may not be as eager to undertake authorship duties in such cases. Such decisions have no impact beyond the disputants in the case at bar. Although they must be written to carry out the error correction and legitimacy enhancing function of an appellate court, they are not glamorous. Working on such cases can be banal, repetitious, and tedious, while offering no opportunity to influence legal development. Although the process of authoring an unpublished decision generally takes less time, the diminished cost does not necessarily outweigh the much steeper drop in the benefit a judge receives compared to drafting published opinions (Robel 1989; Wasby 2001). In short, authoring a larger number of published opinions indicates greater influence over legal development, and authoring a larger number of unpublished decisions simply reflects shouldering a larger, and more tedious, portion of the workload.

In the circuit courts, there is a strong norm to divide opinion drafting duties equally (Bowie et al. 2014). For example, if a panel hears oral arguments in six cases, they will typically each draft the opinion for two of those cases. However, even if every circuit judge wrote the opinion in exactly one-third of their cases, there is still room for power disparities because of the important difference between published and unpublished decisions. Even if circuit judges sought to divide each type of ruling equally, that would frequently prove infeasible, as the number of published opinions will often not be evenly divisible by three. Panel assignments rotate on a regular basis, meaning that each constituted panel resolves a modest number of cases together. This prevents keeping a long-term tally of who has authored published opinions to facilitate equal sharing of those duties. Nevertheless, it is still entirely possible that such duties are equally distributed in the aggregate. However, research indicates that such equality is not always obtained. For example, there is evidence that circuit judges of color author fewer published opinions (Bowie et al. 2014) and that white, male circuit judges write more published, and fewer unpublished, decisions than their peers (Tillman and Hinkle 2018).

Why might female and minority judges have disproportionately fewer opportunities to shape the law through opinion-drafting? There are three theoretical mechanisms that might lead to such discrepancies in how the power of writing published opinions is distributed according to race and gender-based privilege (Tillman and Hinkle 2018). The first two theories focus on the judge who assigns opinion-writing duties, and the third focuses how other judges might request such duties. In the following sections, I explore each theory and discuss their empirical implications in turn before proceeding to test those implications.

The Motivations of the Assigner

On each panel, the longest-serving active judge from the circuit where the case is heard holds the opinion-assigning power (Bowie et al. 2014). Judges from another circuit or from a district court who are sitting by designation are not ever in charge of assigning opinions. Neither are judges who have taken on senior status; that is, they have formally retired and are drawing their pension rather than a paycheck while continuing to work essentially as volunteers. Opinion assignments are typically made when the panel meets in conference after hearing oral arguments in a set of cases (Bowie et al. 2014). After the panelists reach a consensus (or not) on how each case will be resolved, the assigning judge splits up the cases among the panel judges so that the opinion-drafting duties are shared. Cases in which oral arguments are not heard may be similarly addressed, and opinions assigned, during these in-person conferences. Alternatively, cases that are not argued may be dealt with via electronic communications. The publication decision is typically made at approximately the same time (Bowie et al. 2014). This is the overall landscape within which authorship assignments are made in federal circuit courts.

A variety of factors can influence how opinion assigners make their decisions. Much of what we know about how opinions are assigned on collegial appellate courts is based on the particular institutional context of the U.S. Supreme Court. Considerable empirical evidence suggests that chief justices exercise their opinion-assigning power in an ideological and strategic fashion (Brenner and Spaeth 1986; Maltzman and Wahlbeck 1996). The power of assignment is valuable because the opinion author possesses a first-mover advantage in framing the scope and content of the legal rule (Lax 2007; Maltzman et al. 2000; Murphy 1964). We currently know less about the politics of opinion assignment at the circuit level, but what we know suggests the process is different from the Supreme Court (Bowie et al. 2014; Cheng 2008; Farhang et al. 2015; Tillman and Hinkle 2018). For example, evidence indicates that collaboration and issue specialization play more of a role, while seeking out an ideological ally for assignment duties does not appear to drive the process (Farhang et al. 2015).

In-group Favoritism

Tajfel (1969, 1970) famously theorized and demonstrated that individuals tend to favor members of their in-groups. Group membership is a psychological state that confers a social identity to an individual (Hogg and Abrams 1988). Scholars suggest that self-esteem provides a mechanism that accounts for this in-group bias: individuals tend to favor members of their in-groups to enhance the image of that group. There is evidence of this type of bias affecting both elites in general and judges in particular. For example, both female and minority judges are significantly less likely to negatively cite an opinion written by a judge who shares their gender or race compared to an opinion written by an out-group judge (Hinkle and Nelson 2018). Minority judges are also more likely to positively cite a precedent written by a judge of the same race or ethnicity (Hinkle and Nelson 2018). These results make sense since in-group favoritism is typically stronger where the groups are more salient and important to the individual members (Ellemers and Haslam 2011; Hinkle and Nelson 2018). There is also some evidence that circuit judges assign more published than unpublished opinions to be written by members of their racial in-group (Tillman and Hinkle 2018). The same pattern also emerges for gender, but only when men are assigning opinions (Tillman and Hinkle 2018).

Overall, previous research indicates that there is good reason to look for the effects of in-group favoritism on how opinion-writing duties are distributed. Such assignments in published cases carry prestige and power. Therefore, Tajfel's theory suggests that assigners should be more likely to assign such drafting duties to members of their in-group, that is, judges who share the same gender or race or both. But for unpublished cases, in-group bias would most likely manifest in the opposite direction. The unglamorous drudgery of preparing such rulings is more likely to be shunted off on members of the out-group. Consequently, I expect that if in-group bias shapes opinion assignment, judges of the same race and gender as the assigner will draft more published and fewer unpublished decisions compared to out-group judges.

A further note is in order with respect to the in-group favoritism theory. The operation of such bias will not balance out overall if all judges favor those who look like them. The demographic composition of the circuit courts and the role of seniority in exercising the opinion assignment power mean that white and male judges are disproportionately well represented among opinion assigners. In fact, from 2002 to 2012, the judge with the power to assign opinion-writing duties was a white man in 62% of the cases. Only 14% of cases had an assigner who was a judge of color.[5] If all groups were equally represented among those making assignments, in-group favoritism would not necessarily lead to an unequal distribution of power. But given the imbalance in opinion assigners, any in-group favoritism in the assignment process would likely undermine women and minorities' ability to craft legal policy.

Biased Task Assignment

The next mechanism through which policymaking power may end up being correlated with demographics is biased task assignment. Scholars have documented many ways in which gender and racial biases impact employment. For example, African Americans and women are more likely to receive tasks with little variety or decision authority, and they are more likely to be assigned heavier workloads (Hughes and Dodge 1997). Within academia, female faculty members on average teach more classes and publish fewer articles compared to male faculty (Seaberg 1998). Minority faculty members advise more minority students, suggesting they perform more service than white faculty members (García 2000; Jarmon 2001; Seaberg 1998). On average, women spent 62.1% of their time teaching and 11.8% doing research, compared to men who spent only 54.9% teaching and 18.1% researching (Toutkoushian and Bellas 1999). Minorities spent 7.9% of their time doing service, compared to 6% for white faculty members. Lawyers also face biases in task assignments. Szmer et al. (2021) report that female attorneys are underrepresented in presenting oral arguments to the Supreme Court, and when they do get the chance, it is in less complex cases or when the content is linked to stereotypical women's issues.

There is also evidence suggestive of biased task assignment within courts. Christensen et al. (2012) find that in state high courts with assignment procedures analogous to circuit courts, Black male justices are less likely than white male justices to be assigned opinion-writing duties. However, in state high courts with assignment by fixed rotation, no such race-based distinction was in evidence (Christensen et al. 2012). In the circuit courts, white men write more

[5] During this time frame, 17% of all judges participating in cases were judges of color.

published opinions (Bowie et al. 2014). This suggests the possibility that women and minorities are given a disproportionately large amount of the scut work of unpublished rulings to draft. In fact, Tillman and Hinkle (2018) find just such a pattern in the circuit courts for the year 2012. Other work suggests that female and minority circuit judges operate in the context of norms that require them to work harder than their white male counterparts (Moyer et al. 2021). Taken together, this research indicates a possibility that underlying norms, stereotypes, or habits may lead (even if only subconsciously) to assigning the task of writing unpublished decisions to women and minorities more frequently than to white men.

The Motivations of the Assignee

There is a third theoretical mechanism that might lead to discrepancies in how the opportunity to shape legal policy is distributed. Although the power to assign opinions is important, evidence suggests that the process is far from autocratic in the circuit courts. On the contrary, research indicates the assigner will often weigh and grant requests from their peers to write particular opinions (Cheng 2008; Cohen 2002; Farhang et al. 2015; Oakes 1990). Since circuit judges can influence the assignment process through making requests, it is also possible that the characteristics of the potential assignee could shape who writes opinions.

Crafting legal policy, like fortune, favors the bold. Those who ask for such assignments more frequently may well secure more power than their colleagues. So, who is more likely to ask? To answer this question, one must consider the potential downside of the task. Writing published opinions does carry an additional risk that almost never exists for unpublished decisions—the risk of reversal. Because published opinions make binding legal doctrine, they are considerably more likely than unpublished decisions to be reviewed (and potentially reversed) by the full circuit en banc or by the Supreme Court (Black and Owens 2009; Hazelton et al. 2016; Wald 1995; Wasby 2001). Even in cases with published opinions, the probability of review, let alone reversal, is quite low. However, even though reversal is unlikely, it does pose a risk of diminishing the reputation of the panel in general and the opinion author in particular (Westerland et al. 2010).

Research suggests that gender and race can affect how people perceive and assess risk (see, e.g., Finucane et al. 2000; Slovic et al. 1997; Tillman and Hinkle 2018). Flynn et al. (1994) found that women and minorities were more likely to identify a behavior as risky and express an intention to avoid it compared to white men. Such differences in risk perception have also been found among highly educated scientists (Barke et al. 1997). These differences may appear because "the world seems safer" for members of groups that do not have a history of being subjected to widespread discrimination (Finucane et al. 2000). In terms of the risk of reversal, minorities may have an additional reason to estimate the risk of reversal as higher than their white counterparts do. Sen (2015) provides evidence that federal trial judges of color are reversed at a higher rate than white judges. Since circuit judges are the ones issuing those rulings and many circuit judges have previous experience as district judges as well, the reality faced by non-white district judges could plausibly contribute to race-based differences in the perceived probability of reversal among circuit judges.

A difference between judges in risk perception could come in two forms. Women and minorities might believe that the risk of reversal is higher across the board than white men believe it to be. Alternatively, women and minorities might estimate that opinions written by judges who look like them are more likely to be reversed. Whether that higher risk perception is individual or general, it would have the same effect. Believing the risk of reversal is higher might decrease a judge's willingness to request authorship duties in a case with a published opinion where review is possible. To the extent that assigning judges defer to requests, this could ultimately lead to women and minorities crafting less legal policy.

Empirical Analysis of Authorship

The foregoing discussion sets forth three hypotheses with respect to opinion assignment, which are summarized in Table 5.1. The outcome variable is whether an individual judge writes the majority opinion in a given case. Since theory suggests authorship dynamics will vary by publication status, I estimate two models: one for published cases and one for unpublished cases. Both are probit regression models with standard errors clustered on the case. In the circuit courts, many decisions do not list an author, and I necessarily exclude such cases from consideration in this analysis. Also excluded are dissenting judges since they are almost never assigned to write the majority opinion.

The primary explanatory variables for the authorship models are listed in Table 5.1. First, I account for whether the judge and assigner share demographic characteristics. The baseline category is when the two judges are a different gender and race. Included in the model are three indicator variables for whether the judge and assigner are the same gender (but different race), the same race (but different gender), or share both the same race and gender. Next, I account jointly for the race and gender of the judge using the same three binary variables used in the participation model: *White Woman*, *Man of Color*, and *Woman of Color*. The excluded baseline category is white men.

Table 5.1 Summary of Authorship Hypotheses (Source: Rachael K. Hinkle 2024)

	Expected Effect	
Mechanism	**Published**	**Unpublished**
In-group Favoritism		
In-group Judge	+	–
Out-group Judge	–	+
Biased Task Assignment		
White Woman		+
Minority Man		+
Minority Woman		+
Differential Request		
White Woman	–	
Minority Man	–	
Minority Woman	–	

The control variables in these models are focused on judge-level factors because when an assigner is making the decision about opinion-drafting duties, all case and circuit-level characteristics are inherently held constant. As always, ideology is a foremost consideration. Assigners may prefer to assign their ideologically proximate colleagues to write, especially published opinions. I measure the ideological distance between a judge and the opinion assigner using Judicial Common Space scores (Boyd 2010; Epstein et al. 2007; Giles et al. 2001; Poole 1998). Research shows that circuit judges are more likely to assign opinions to themselves (Farhang et al. 2015), so I control for whether the judge in question is also the assigner. Finally, I control for a variety of judicial characteristics that may reflect a judge's level of experience and, therefore, suitability for opinion drafting. This set of variables is the same as those used in the participation model. I account for whether a judge is new on the bench, how long they have served, whether they have taken senior status, and if they are a circuit judge sitting by designation.

Figure 5.4 presents the results of the authorship models. First, I will evaluate the in-group favoritism hypothesis. This hypothesis posits that judges assign more published, and fewer unpublished, decisions to colleagues who are members of the same demographic groups. There is no support for this hypothesis. Rather, the opposite pattern emerges. When it comes to unpublished rulings, judges are significantly *more* likely to assign them to members of their

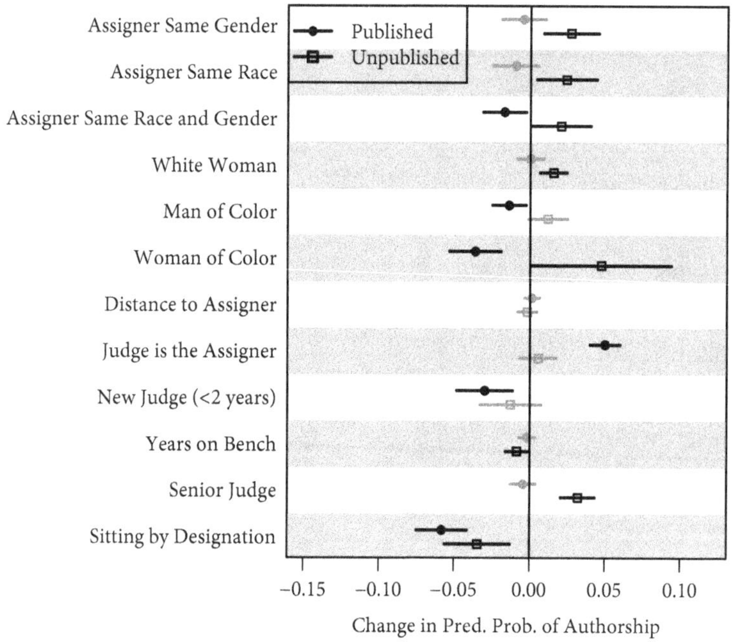

Figure 5.4 Changes in Predicted Probability of Authorship: Estimates (and associated 95% confidence intervals) of the change in the predicted probability of authorship generated by moving each variable from a low to high value while holding other variables at their median. Low and high values are 25th and 75th percentile for continuous variables, and zero and one for binary variables. Estimates from the model of published opinions are dots, and estimates from the model of unpublished opinions are squares. Estimates and confidence intervals in gray (instead of black) indicate that the confidence interval includes zero. Full regression estimates are available in Appendix 5.B in Table 5.B.2. (Source: Rachael K. Hinkle 2024)

in-group. When an assigner shares both the same race and gender with a judge, they are also significantly *less* likely to assign that judge to draft a published opinion. These results are rather puzzling and suggest the need for further work on the topic of how shared group identity plays a role in circuit courts. However, one thing appears clear: there is no indication that in-group favoritism leads judges to shift greater policymaking power to their peers who look like them.

The biased task assignment hypothesis predicts women and minorities will shoulder a greater burden when it comes to drafting unpublished opinions, while the differential request hypothesis predicts the opposite pattern for published opinions. These two are difficult to disentangle because the strong norm of equal opinion writing on circuit panels usually means that being assigned less of one type of opinion will mean getting more of the other. For the moment, I consider these two hypotheses alongside one another. The next section takes on the task of distinguishing between them.

Unlike the lack of evidence of in-group favoritism, Figure 5.4 provides some evidence both of biased assignment and differential requests. White and minority female judges are significantly more likely to be assigned to write unpublished decisions compared to white male judges. While the estimate for women of color is imprecisely estimated (due to relatively sparse data), the effect is triple the size for white women. Minority judges, both male and female, are less likely to author published opinions, potentially because they are more hesitant to request such responsibility. While no gender effects appear for white judges, women of color are significantly less likely than men of color to write published majority opinions ($p = 0.03$).

Kicking Up Dust: Who Dissents?

Circuit judges are primarily able to shape the law through participation in cases with published opinions and by drafting those opinions. However, the ability to write a dissenting opinion in any case also provides a means through which some power, albeit a much smaller amount, can be wielded. Dissenting opinions can make legal arguments that are persuasive to future legal actors and thus they have the potential for long-term impact on the law (Hinkle and Nelson 2017). Dissents can also serve an important whistle-blowing function on intermediate courts of appeals. They can signal the need to review to the full circuit or to the Supreme Court. Research shows that both petitions for review en banc and petitions for certiorari are more likely to be granted to review cases in which there is a dissenting opinion.

Although the influence of a dissent is far from guaranteed, examining the exercise of this type of power provides a special kind of insight because the decision to dissent is solely within the purview of a single judge. The results regarding authorship of majority opinions are somewhat ambiguous. Minorities draft fewer published opinions, and women write more unpublished decisions than white men, and those patterns are exacerbated for women of color. But such evidence could indicate either biased task assignment or differences in how judges request authorship duties. Evaluating the frequency of dissent is a way to adjudicate between these two explanations. If women or minorities avoid the risk of being declared wrong publicly after review of a published opinion, it would also make sense that they might avoid the risk of publicly expressing that their views diverge from those of their colleagues. In other words, the differential request hypothesis implies that women and minorities will dissent less frequently than their white male colleagues.

Empirical Analysis of Dissent

The model of dissenting behavior in many ways tracks the first model in this chapter of whether each case a judge participates in is published, although a few additional control variables are needed in this context. Here the outcome is whether a judge dissents, and once again I estimate a probit regression model with standard errors clustered on the case. My key explanatory variables continue to reflect judge demographics with binary variables that equal one if a judge is a white woman, man of color, or woman of color (and zero otherwise).

The control variables are the same as those in the publication model with the exceptions discussed here. First, the decision to dissent is affected by judicial ideology differently than the decision to publish, so I take a different approach. Dissent is more likely when a judge is prone to disagree with the other members of the panel; in other words, when they are more ideologically distant. Consequently, I use JCS scores to measure the distance from the judge to the panel median. The larger the distance, the more likely dissent should be. Judges can also be empowered to make their disagreement public when they can serve as a whistle-blower to signal an ideologically allied higher court to grant discretionary review (Cross and Tiller 1998). I measure distance to the full circuit, which can grant en banc review, as well as the Supreme Court. These variables should be negatively correlated with dissent; the judge should be more likely to dissent the closer they are to potential reviewing courts. Next, the ultimate decision to dissent is generally finalized relatively late in the process of adjudication and will be made in light of whether the majority opinion is going to be published and whether the majority is reversing the lower court. Since both factors may shape a judge's determination of whether to invest the time and effort required by dissent, they are included in the model as well. Finally, rather than controlling for the rate of publication in the relevant circuit, I control for the rate of dissent.

Figure 5.5 shows that gender and race are related to dissenting behavior. However, the picture that emerges is the opposite from what is predicted by the differential request hypothesis. Rather than avoiding risk, conflict, and potentially negative attention, the data reveal that minorities are significantly *more* likely to dissent compared to white men. Women of color are also significantly more likely to dissent than men of color ($p = 0.04$). Notably, these differences emerge even after accounting for the effect of ideology. Moreover, the race or

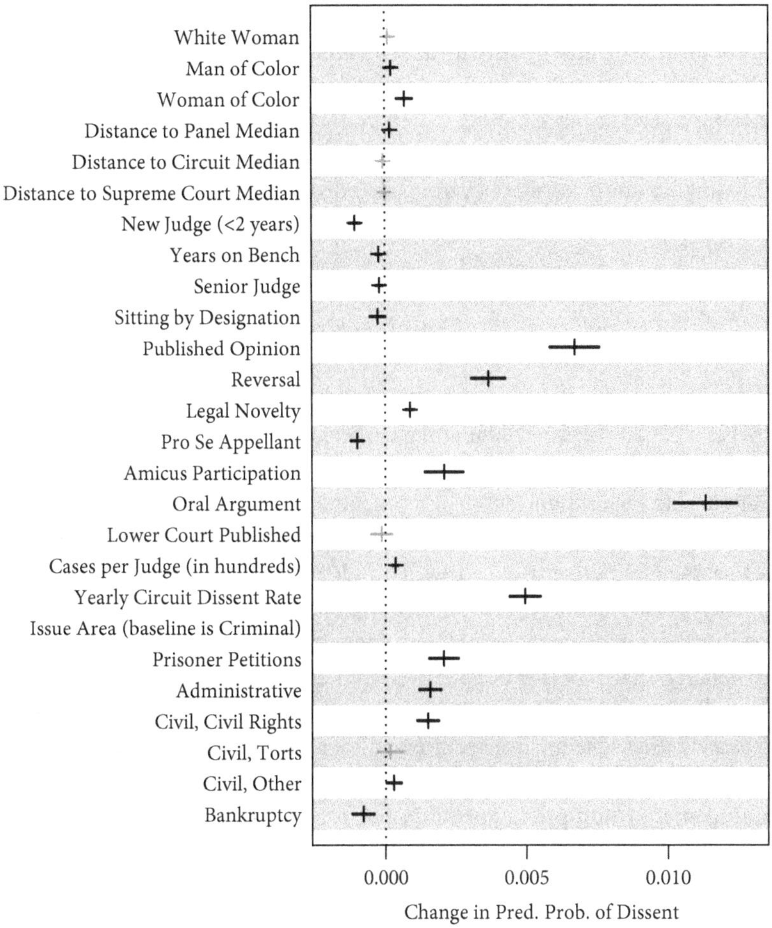

Figure 5.5 Changes in Predicted Probability of Dissent: Estimates (and associated 95% confidence intervals) of the change in the predicted probability of dissent generated by moving each variable from a low to high value while holding other variables at their median. Low and high values are 25th and 75th percentile for continuous variables, and zero and one for binary variables. Categorical variables are compared to their baseline value. Estimates and confidence intervals in gray (instead of black) indicate that the confidence interval includes zero. Full regression estimates are available in Appendix 5.B in Table 5.B.3. (Source: Rachael K. Hinkle 2024)

ethnicity of a judge has a larger impact on their propensity to dissent than ideology does. These findings call into question the theory that women or minorities are less likely to ask the opinion assigner to let them draft published decisions. Those requests take place behind closed doors where only the judges themselves know what happens. But we can observe when judges choose to invest effort and seek to impact future legal policy by writing dissenting opinions. Surely the same judges who are bold in the public eye are unlikely to be shy or reticent in private.

Conclusions

Scholars have shown that gender and race can impact judicial decision-making (Boyd et al. 2010; Peresie 2005; Songer, Sheehan, and Haire 2000; Christensen et al. 2012). However, we know less about how judge demographics effect judicial outputs beyond voting on the outcome of a case. This chapter explores how both participation and authorship vary across published and unpublished cases in ways that are correlated with a judge's race and gender and examines why discrepancies emerge. The importance of such questions is underscored by the reality that circuit court judges have considerable power to shape legal policy.

In general, diversity is praised and sought as a desirable feature of group dynamics. In the context of a policymaking task like judging, having a variety of perspectives that reflects those of citizens has an important function. Moreover, just as multiple judges are used to increase the probability of reaching the correct outcome, so multiple perspectives may be valuable to achieve the same goal. However, in spite of these normatively positive goals, it is possible that the very diversity that can strengthen the deliberative process and make it more robust may also have the counterintuitive result of producing more law shaped by white male judges. Since more diverse decision-making groups tend to be more likely to produce a wider range of perspectives, they are also more likely to generate divergent viewpoints about a case and, thus, a need to compromise. Many forms of compromise are available to circuit judges who do not initially see eye to eye about the resolution of a case. A key way to compromise is to leave the opinion unpublished so that the judge unhappy with the result can be assured it will at least not shape the law of the circuit (Hazelton et al. 2016). Unsurprisingly, cases where there is more likely to be disagreement among judges are also more likely to result in unpublished opinions. This, in turn, means that female and minority judges have relatively less power over the policy that is shaped by published opinions.

The potential for differential power extends to authoring published opinions as well as participating in those cases. Social psychologists have long recognized the importance of shared group membership to human behavior and demonstrated that individuals show favoritism to others who share their group memberships (Tajfel 1970). Such in-group favoritism could be expected to manifest on courts as assigners being more likely to assign the plum, policy-shaping assignments of published opinions to colleagues who share their gender or race. Yet the data reveal no such pattern. In fact, in-group favoritism appears to have the opposite of the expected effect. Rather than shielding in-group members from the drudgery of cranking out unpublished opinions, circuit judges are actually more likely to assign those like them to author such rulings.

Although in-group favoritism does not appear as theorized, women are overall more likely to be assigned to write unpublished opinions, and judges of color are less likely to write the published opinions that declare law. These pattern are consistent with two theories. The first is that like many workplaces, in the federal courts work is distributed in a way that favors white men when it comes to consequential tasks and overburdens women and minorities when it comes to more boring, rote, unglamorous tasks. The second theory is that women and minorities are socialized in a way that leads to them being more hesitant to request to write published opinions. Looking at dissenting behavior is a useful way to distinguish between these two theories because judges who are reluctant to insert themselves proactively into a discussion of precedent are unlikely to dissent frequently. However, white women dissent at similar rates as their white male counterparts, and minorities are even *more* likely to dissent than white men. Therefore, I conclude that the most likely explanation for the discrepancies in authorship of majority opinions is biased task assignment.

All-white and all-male panels are no longer the most typical type of panel litigants face. But power discrepancies between white male judges and their colleagues appear to persist. Looking at the aggregate distribution of workload and influence in the federal circuit courts reveals that gender and race play a role even in an increasingly diverse judiciary. The privilege that accompanies being white and male carries with it an enhanced ability to shape policy. This indicates that diversifying the federal bench, while a laudable first step, is not alone sufficient to wipe out racial and gender discrepancies in power.

Appendix 5.A: Summary Statistics

Table 5.A.1 Judge-Case Level Summary Statistics (Source: Rachael K. Hinkle 2024)

Continuous Variables	**Min.**	**25%**	**50%**	**75%**	**Max**
Ideological Distance: Panel to Circuit	0.00	0.05	0.13	0.39	0.97
Ideological Distance: Panel to Supreme Court	0.00	0.19	0.29	0.38	0.66
Years on Bench	0	9	17	24	49
Legal Novelty	0.00	0.00	0.20	0.41	1.00
Cases per Judge (in hundreds)	1.16	3.39	4.40	5.04	7.40
Yearly Circuit Publication Rate	0.07	0.14	0.18	0.32	0.81
Distance to Assigner	0.00	0.00	0.09	0.48	1.14
Distance to Panel Median	0.00	0.00	0.06	0.34	1.12
Distance to Circuit Median	0.00	0.08	0.20	0.49	1.02
Distance to Supreme Court Median	0.00	0.23	0.34	0.43	0.73
Yearly Circuit Dissent Rate	0.01	0.01	0.02	0.05	0.07
Dichotomous Variables	**0**	**1**			
Published	79%	21%			
Dissent or Dissent in Part	97%	3%			
Ideologically Split Panel	28%	72%			
New Judge (< 2 years)	97%	3%			
Senior Judge	80%	20%			
Sitting by Designation	99%	1%			
Pro Se Appellant	73%	27%			
Amicus Participation	98%	2%			
Oral Argument	66%	34%			
Lower Court Published	95%	5%			
Judge Is the Assigner	65%	35%			
Reversed	91%	9%			

Table 5.A.1 Continued

Categorical Variables	
Judge Demographics	
White Man	64%
White Woman	19%
Man of Color	13%
Woman of Color	4%
Judge-Assigner Relationship	
Out-group	7%
Same Gender (only)	12%
Same Race (only)	18%
Same Race and Gender	63%
Issue Area	
Criminal	33.4%
Prisoner Petitions	12.9%
Administrative	16.1%
Civil, Civil Rights	18.9%
Civil, Torts	2.9%
Civil, Other	14.4%
Bankruptcy	1.5%

Appendix 5.B: Regression Results

Table 5.B.1 Participation Model: Probit regression model of the probability each case a panel judge participates in results in a published decision. Standard errors are clustered on the case and * indicates a p-value < 0.05. (Source: Rachael K. Hinkle 2024)

	Coef.	(S.E.)
White Woman	−0.062*	(0.006)
Man of Color	−0.045*	(0.007)
Woman of Color	−0.219*	(0.012)
Ideologically Split Panel	−0.085*	(0.009)
Ideological Distance: Panel to Circuit	−0.165*	(0.018)
Ideological Distance: Panel to Supreme Court	−0.316*	(0.030)
Citing Unpublished Prohibited	0.019*	(0.008)
New Judge (< 2 years)	−0.042*	(0.016)
Years on Bench	0.001	(0.001)
Years on Bench^2	0.00003	(0.00002)
Senior Judge	−0.050*	(0.007)
Sitting by Designation	0.106*	(0.016)
Legal Novelty	1.212*	(0.015)
Pro Se Appellant	−0.640*	(0.015)
Amicus Participation	0.888*	(0.025)
Oral Argument	1.453*	(0.009)
Lower Court Published	0.007	(0.020)
Cases per Judge (in hundreds)	0.052*	(0.004)
Yearly Circuit Publication Rate	2.593*	(0.025)
Issue Area		
Prisoner Petitions	0.117*	(0.015)
Administrative	−0.095*	(0.012)
Civil, Civil Rights	0.009	(0.012)
Civil, Torts	−0.062*	(0.021)
Civil, Other	0.027*	(0.011)
Bankruptcy	0.244*	(0.028)
Intercept	−2.584*	(0.028)
N	673,172	
BIC	394927.3	
AIC	394630.4	

Table 5.B.2 Authorship Models: Probit regression models of the probability a panel judge will write the opinion in published cases (left columns) and unpublished cases (right columns). Standard errors are clustered on the case and * indicates a p-value < 0.05. (Source: Rachael K. Hinkle 2024)

	Published		Unpublished	
	Coef.	(S.E.)	Coef.	(S.E.)
Same Gender	−0.012	(0.020)	0.078*	(0.027)
Same Race	−0.026	(0.020)	0.069*	(0.030)
Same Race and Gender	−0.047*	(0.020)	0.059*	(0.029)
White Woman	0.001	(0.012)	0.045*	(0.013)
Man of Color	−0.038*	(0.016)	0.034	(0.019)
Woman of Color	−0.100*	(0.024)	0.134*	(0.065)
Distance to Assigner	0.008	(0.014)	−0.011	(0.019)
Judge Is the Assigner	0.132*	(0.013)	0.016	(0.018)
New Judge (< 2 years)	−0.082*	(0.027)	−0.038	(0.031)
Years on Bench	0.005*	(0.001)	−0.007*	(0.002)
Years on Bench^2	−0.0002*	(0.000)	0.0002*	(0.000)
Senior Judge	−0.012	(0.012)	0.091*	(0.016)
Sitting by Designation	−0.163*	(0.025)	−0.104*	(0.034)
Intercept	−0.430*	(0.023)	−0.478*	(0.032)
N	118,576		75,445	
BIC	151707.6		95986.3	
AIC	151572.0		95857.1	

Table 5.B.3 Dissent Model: Probit regression model of the probability a panel judge will write a dissenting opinion (in whole or in part). Standard errors are clustered on the case and * indicates a p-value < 0.05. (Source: Rachael K. Hinkle 2024)

	Coef.	(S.E.)
White Woman	0.017	(0.009)
Man of Color	0.034*	(0.011)
Woman of Color	0.098*	(0.017)
Distance to Panel Median	0.083*	(0.008)
Distance to Circuit Median	−0.027	(0.014)
Distance to Supreme Court Median	−0.002	(0.028)
New Judge (< 2 years)	−0.245*	(0.027)
Years on Bench	−0.016*	(0.001)
Years on Bench^2	0.0004*	(0.000)
Senior Judge	−0.034*	(0.011)
Sitting by Designation	−0.045	(0.024)
Published Opinion	0.508*	(0.015)
Reversal	0.352*	(0.015)
Legal Novelty	0.343*	(0.024)
Pro Se Appellant	−0.221*	(0.026)
Amicus Participation	0.238*	(0.027)
Oral Argument	0.671*	(0.019)
Lower Court Published	−0.023	(0.032)
Cases per Judge (in hundreds)	0.035*	(0.005)
Yearly Circuit Dissent Rate	12.988*	(0.300)
Issue Area		
Prisoner Petitions	0.236*	(0.023)
Administrative	0.193*	(0.020)
Civil, Civil Rights	0.186*	(0.019)
Civil, Torts	0.026	(0.033)
Civil, Other	0.044*	(0.019)
Bankruptcy	−0.164*	(0.049)
Intercept	−3.216*	(0.036)
N	673,172	
BIC	136321.3	
AIC	136013.0	

6
What Comes Next? Publication and Further Review

Introduction

In 2002, an inmate named Timothy Williams sued prison employees, alleging that he had been improperly denied surgery and a handicap cell that suitably accommodated his medical condition. The trial court dismissed the lawsuit on procedural grounds, and the Sixth Circuit upheld that ruling in an unpublished opinion.[1] Williams sought further review in the Supreme Court, which took up his case alongside two other unpublished Sixth Circuit rulings that presented the same legal issue.[2] In a unanimous ruling, the Supreme Court overruled the Sixth Circuit, and Williams was allowed to pursue his claims against the correctional officers.[3] While Williams ultimately lost on the merits,[4] getting a second chance at his appeal after an unpublished ruling was an incredibly rare opportunity. From 2002 to 2012, the Supreme Court agreed to review only 121 unpublished circuit rulings—0.07% of all such decisions during that time.

As Williams's case illustrates, a ruling by a three-judge circuit panel is not always the end of the road. The litigant on the losing side may request review en banc by the full circuit, or they may request the Supreme Court to grant a writ of certiorari. Such review is a rare prize, and it is particularly rare when the panel ruling is unpublished. Critics of the selective publication norm frequently point to the lack of accountability for such unpublished decisions due to the infrequency with which they are reviewed (Hannon 2001; Martineau 1994; Richman and Reynolds 2013). Research shows that panels give less heed to the preferences of the potential reviewing courts in unpublished cases compared to published ones (Hinkle 2023). The results in Chapter 3 also provide evidence that panels are less likely to publish when they are more ideologically distant from the full circuit and the Supreme Court, a pattern that is consistent with actively seeking to avoid accountability.

[1] *Williams v. Overton*, 136 Fed. Appx. 859 (6th Cir., 2005).
[2] *Williams v. Overton*, 547 U.S. 1002 (2006).
[3] *Jones v. Bock*, 549 U.S. 199 (2007).
[4] *Williams v. Overton*, 2010 U.S. Dist. LEXIS 103046 (E.D. Mich. 2010).

Selective Publication in the U.S. Courts of Appeals. Rachael K. Hinkle, Oxford University Press.
 DOI: 10.1093/oso/9780197770085.003.0006

While lack of judicial accountability is a matter of concern itself, that concern is compounded when different types of litigants have unequal opportunities to ensure panels are accountable. This inequality of opportunity for review is the focus here. In addition to showing strategy in publication decisions, Chapter 3 also documents that appellants with fewer resources and less experience are less likely to have the opinion in their case published. Chapter 4 demonstrates that such "have-nots" are also less likely to win when going up against stronger and more capable opponents. This pattern emerges when rulings are unpublished as well as published. In this chapter, I weave these threads together to examine their implications for how selective publication can also create downstream disparities in who is able to obtain further review of their appeal. Disadvantaged members of society are both more likely to lose and more likely to have an unpublished opinion. En banc and Supreme Court review are much more difficult to obtain when a ruling is unpublished. Taken together, these patterns suggest the likelihood that inequalities in how resources are allocated during the first appeal continue to affect who gets a chance to hold the judges from their panel ruling accountable.

Considering how disparities generated by selective publication manifest at the next stage of litigation is not a simple matter. There are two possible sources of review and two steps in the process of securing discretionary review. First, the losing litigant must request review. Only after a request is made will the relevant court determine whether they will grant the request (Giles et al. 2006; Mak et al. 2013).[5] I examine both of these stages for both en banc and certiorari requests. There is evidence of selective publication affecting both litigant and judicial decisions in ways that vary across litigant type. The failure to publish a ruling has a greater deterrent effect on requests for review made by individuals and organizations than by government actors. Conversely, publication enhances the possibility of cert being granted most for the federal government and least for indigent persons or those without an attorney. Once discretionary review is granted, there is little theoretical reason to expect publication status to continue to have any kind of impact. Nevertheless, I examine whether publication does affect who wins and loses en banc and Supreme Court cases (and, if so, whether that effect varies by litigant type) as a sort of placebo test to examine what happens when there is little reason to expect the selective publication norm to have an effect. Interestingly, those who obtain Supreme Court review of an unpublished opinion are *more* likely to experience success on the merits than those who obtain review of a published one. Most likely, this reflects the difficulty of

[5] Circuits do have the power to initiate en banc proceedings without a petition, but that step is quite unusual (Giles, Walker, and Zorn 2006).

getting an unpublished ruling reviewed; it must be exceptionally terrible to justify such an unusual step.

Next Steps: After the Panel

Circuit panels have the last word in the vast majority of federal appeals (Dragich 1994). Subsequent review of their rulings is the exception rather than the rule (Wald 1995). Cross (2005, 379) describes the probability of review and reversal of a circuit ruling as "vanishingly low." Howard (1977) reports that the percentage of circuit cases reviewed by the Supreme Court is less than 2%. George and Solimine (2001) observe that circuits conduct en banc review of about eighty to ninety cases per year, while Giles et al. (2007) estimate that about 1% of circuit cases are reheard en banc. These numbers are so low because en banc monitoring is costly (Kim 2009). This observation is borne out by evidence from the Ninth Circuit, which began granting en banc review in a larger number of cases after they changed their rules to streamline the en banc process, making it less costly in terms of judicial resources (Giles et al. 2007).

The rarity of review does not render the question of which cases get reviewed any less important. Scholars have long recognized the pivotal role of the decision to review (see, e.g., George 1999; Perry 1991). One key factor in such decisions is the publication status of a panel ruling. Vladeck and Gulati (2005) assert that unpublished rulings are almost never reviewed. Brown et al. (2021) report that from 2018 to 2021, the Supreme Court granted cert petitions to review only thirty-one unpublished opinions. Several others have similarly noted that published opinions are more likely to be reviewed than those that are not published (e.g., Black and Owens 2009; Beske 2018; Vladeck and Gulati 2005). This pattern is hardly a surprise. While the costs of reviewing published and unpublished opinions are similar, the benefits are much lower in the case of unpublished opinions (Hazelton et al. 2016; Hinkle 2023). As Black and Owens (2009, 1069) note, "Supreme Court Justices are hesitant to review such [unpublished] decisions because of their nonprecedential nature." In short, because unpublished opinions do not establish binding precedent, there is less reason to expend the cost necessary to review (Law 2004).

Scholars have not stopped at simply observing that selective publication leads to variation in accountability; they have also worked to estimate the size of this effect. Berdejó (2013), using data from the Ninth Circuit from 1991 to 2006, finds that 0.1% of all cases are reviewed, but 3.4% of published cases are reviewed. Hannon (2001) reports that based on documents in Westlaw's SCT database,

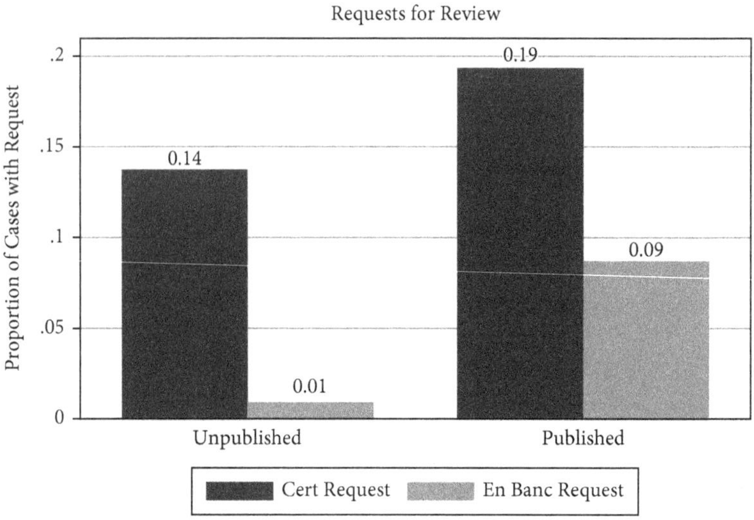

Figure 6.1 Summary of Requests for Discretionary Review by Publication Status (Source: Rachael K. Hinkle 2024)

the Supreme Court first saw a cert petition from an unpublished circuit opinion in 1974 and since then has resolved cert petitions in at least seventy-one such cases, fifty-seven of which were granted. Finally, Hazelton et al. (2016) examine search and seizure cases from 2005 to 2008 and determine that among unpublished cases none were reviewed en banc and 0.03% were granted cert, while among published cases 0.8% were reviewed en banc and 1.8% were granted cert. As noted in the introduction to this chapter, in the C^3PO database, the Supreme Court granted cert in only 0.07% of all unpublished opinions. During that same time, they granted cert in 0.86% of all published cases. For en banc petitions, these numbers are 0.01% and 0.57%, respectively.

It is clear what happens after a panel issues an unpublished opinion; for all practical purposes it is game over. But the two-stage nature of this process is often ignored (but see Giles et al. 2006; Mak et al. 2013). For a case to be reviewed, the losing side must first decide to request review and the court must next decide to grant that request (Hettinger et al. 2006). Figure 6.1 shows the percentage of cases by publication status in which requests are made, and Figure 6.2 shows the percentage of those requests that are granted. Even these simple summary statistics reveal that publication matters to litigants as well as to judges. In the next sections, I take up the decision of litigants to request review and the decision of judges whether to grant such requests in turn before examining what happens on the merits when discretionary review is granted.

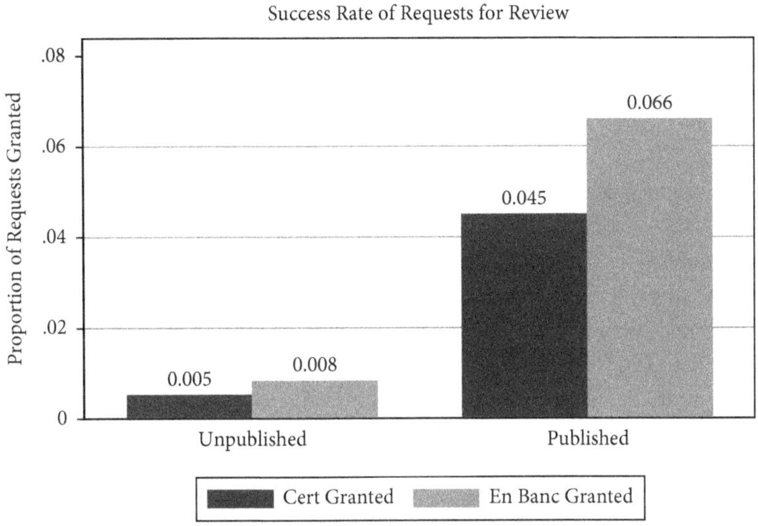

Figure 6.2 Summary of Granting of Requests for Discretionary Review by Publication Status (Source: Rachael K. Hinkle 2024)

Asking for Review: The Role of Litigants

As Figure 6.1 illustrates, a substantial majority of panel decisions go unchallenged. Even when the ruling is published, the litigant on the losing side seeks further review in the Supreme Court in 19% of cases and en banc review 9% of the time. Along similar lines, Bowie et al. (2014) find that in a sample of circuit cases, litigants requested a cert petition from the Supreme Court 25% of the time. When a panel does not publish, requests for review drop even further. In total, from 2002 to 2012, 84% of all circuit cases were final after the panel disposition; no request for discretionary review was made.[6] These decisions litigants make prevent courts from having the opportunity to reconsider a wide swath of cases (Mak et al. 2013). Yet, despite such an impact, the reasons for those decisions have gone largely unexamined.[7]

There are multiple reasons to expect publication status of the panel opinion to influence litigants' decisions with respect to requesting further review. If this is the case, the selective publication norm can continue to have effects beyond the

[6] This pattern is not unusual. For example, Boyd (2015a) reports that less than 20% of losing litigants in federal trial courts exercise their right to appeal to the circuit courts.

[7] Two notable exceptions are one study on litigant decisions to petition for en banc review (Giles, Walker, and Zorn 2006) and one on the decision to request cert (Mak, Sidman, and Sommer 2013).

opinion itself. The first reason defeated parties may be less likely to further pursue a case after the ruling is left unpublished is simply due to the reality that such review is highly unlikely. To the extent scholars do discuss the role of litigants in discretionary review, they suggest that their decisions will often anticipate how such requests are likely to fare (Giles et al. 2006; Mak et al. 2013; Songer et al. 1994). This form of strategy can help litigants conserve their own scarce resources (Boyd 2015a). Perhaps the best example is the very sophisticated strategy the Department of Justice uses to determine which cases they ask the Supreme Court to review; they are very concerned about the likelihood of review and winning the case and are quite good at estimating both (Zorn 2002). It is no secret that review is much less likely to be granted when the ruling is unpublished. As a result, litigants might be hesitant to request review if they estimate the resources needed to ask are not worth the minuscule probability of success. In a study of federal circuit free exercise cases from 1968 to 2006, Mak et al. (2013) find precisely this pattern in losing litigants' willingness to file cert petitions.

Even if courts were equally willing to re-examine all cases, litigants might still be less likely to request review of unpublished rulings because they do not constitute binding precedent. Why do litigants invest the resources necessary to request review? Some do so because they are simply concerned that they lost the dispute at hand, and they would like a different resolution. Such motivation is equally weighty whether the ruling was published or not. However, motivations may also be related to the long-term development of the law (Boyd 2015a). For example, Boyd (2015a, 298) argues that in the context of the original decision to appeal, "status-advantaged litigants are likely to filter their potential appeals, moving forward with a purposefully chosen few and declining to advance all others." A similar dynamic may operate with respect to discretionary review, but with a twist generated by selective publication. Consider a losing litigant who expects to encounter similar legal issues in the future. If the opinion ruling against them is published, not only do they lose the case at hand but the opinion also shapes law in a way that may detrimentally affect them in the future. Because they stand to lose in the future as well as the present, such a litigant would have a substantial motivation to seek review to overturn such a ruling. However, if the same litigant lost in an unpublished ruling that did not affect the law, their losses are confined to the present. As a result, it is possible that litigants with long-term interests in the state of the law might request review of unpublished rulings less frequently than published ones.

There is also a third possible reason for publication to affect requests for review. Commentators have criticized the selective publication norm on the grounds that it sends the message that some cases, issues, and litigants are inferior (Brown et al. 2021; Cleveland 2010; Slavitt 1995). Such feelings of inferiority are typically viewed as normatively undesirable in their own right and for the impact they can have on courts' legitimacy (Dragich 1994; Vladeck and Gulati 2005). It is also possible they could affect litigant decisions about requesting review. Defeated litigants whose opinions are unpublished may infer their case is of little value and that they are unlikely to be treated with more care at a later stage of an appeal. This may discourage them from requesting review.

There are several reasons to expect litigants to request review less in unpublished cases. This raises the question of how we might begin to disentangle these mechanisms. Each explanation also suggests related behavior, and these are distinct from one another. First, we know from previous research that review is more likely to be granted when an opinion addresses a novel legal issue, contains a dissent, reverses the trial court, or reaches an outcome that is contrary to the ideological preferences of the potential reviewing court (e.g., Black and Boyd 2012; Giles et al. 2006). If these factors increase the probability litigants request review, that is evidence of strategic anticipation of which requests for review will be granted. Second, some litigants are more likely to have long-term interests in the law (Boyd 2015a). The most likely to be focused on future litigation are government actors. If government actors are more likely to appeal published rulings in a way that is noticeably different from private individuals or organizations, that would be suggestive that the nonprecedential status of unpublished opinions is an important factor.

Finally, if private litigants are more likely to be deterred from requesting review by nonpublication compared to governments, that pattern would be suggestive that signals of inferiority may be driving that decision, as government representatives are often frequent participants in the court system and should be less likely to take a single opinion as a personal affront. There are also other features of litigation that a litigant may interpret as signals that their case was not taken very seriously, such as a short opinion, sparing use of caselaw, or failure to schedule oral argument. If these features reduce requests for review alongside nonpublication, this collective pattern could suggest that litigants' impressions regarding the importance with which they are viewed by the court system plays a role in their decisions regarding continued participation. Nevertheless, a caveat is in order. Such factors could also indicate a case does not involve any novel or interesting points of law, which would also be reason for a litigant to avoid the cost of a request for review that is unlikely to be granted.

Empirical Analysis of Requesting Discretionary Review

For the first stage of empirical analysis in this chapter, I begin with the full C^3PO database of all circuit court decisions from 2002 to 2012.[8] The unit of analysis

[8] Because the type of the losing litigant must be identified, the analysis here necessarily requires dropping cases in which the winner could not be clearly coded.

throughout this chapter is the case. To examine the determinants of the decision to request review, I model two outcomes: whether the losing party requested Supreme Court review and whether they requested en banc review. There is no bar to requesting both types of review, so each is evaluated in a separate model. Since the outcomes are binary, I estimate probit regression models.

The key explanatory variables capture both publication status and a range of factors that may help disentangle underlying motivations. The first explanatory variable is simply whether the panel opinion was published. The second is the litigant type of the party that lost and, therefore, must decide whether to request review. Two of the three reasons publication status might affect requests for review suggest that some types of litigants would be affected by publication more than others. Therefore, I interact each of the litigant type categories with *Published*. Another set of variables reflects signals litigants may perceive as indicators of how much the court values a case. These include the length of the panel opinion (using the log of the word count), the total number of citations to caselaw it contains, and whether oral argument was held in the case. Next, I account for factors known to be associated with a higher probability of review: the legal novelty of the claims involved (Giles et al. 2006), the presence of a dissent in the panel case (Caldeira and Wright 1988), whether the trial court was reversed (George 1999), and the potential reviewing court's ideological compatibility with the panel's ruling (Black and Boyd 2012; Mak et al. 2013). Most of these variables have been described and used in previous chapters. The reviewing court's alignment with the panel outcome is calculated by multiplying the median JCS score of the relevant court by the *Direction of Case Outcome* variable described in Chapter 3.

Finally, I control for other potentially relevant factors. In both models, I account for the issue and year in case of chronological or topic-based variation. In the model of en banc requests, I also control for two additional circuit-level features that may affect the process. These are the number of judges on the circuit and the average caseload per judge. Both more judges and a heavier caseload may affect litigants' willingness to request review from the full circuit.

Analysis of both models shows that, as expected, the marginal effect of publication is positive and statistically significant.[9] When holding all other variables at their median or modal value, the predicted probability of filing a cert petition is 0.21 for unpublished cases and 0.22 for published cases.[10] The difference of 0.01 is statistically significant ($p < 0.001$). En banc petitions are much rarer but exhibit the same pattern. The predicted probability of a request for en banc review

[9] Full regression results are provided in Table 6.A.1 in Appendix 6.A.

[10] All reported predicted probabilities throughout this chapter are calculated holding all other variables at their median or mode as applicable.

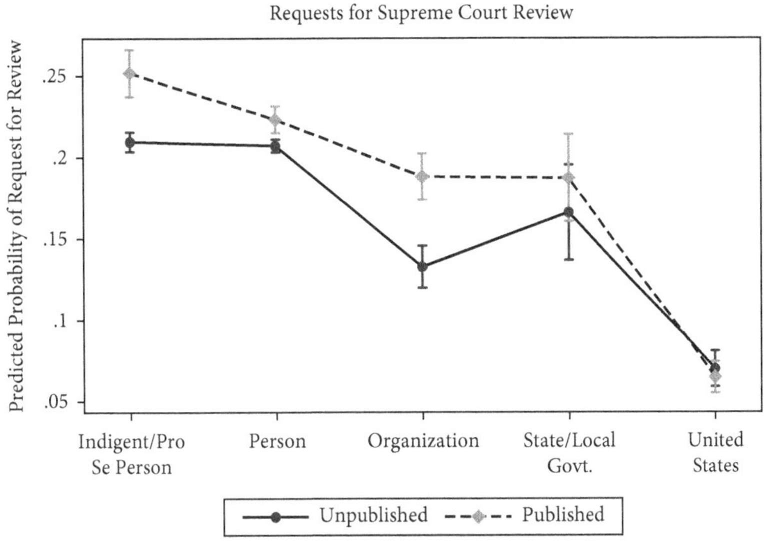

Figure 6.3 Predicted Probability of Cert Petition: This graph provides the predicted probability of a petition for cert being filed by publication status and the type of litigant who lost the panel case. Other variables are held at their median or mode. The whiskers depict the 95% confidence intervals around the predicted probabilities. (Source: Rachael K. Hinkle 2024)

is 0.006 for unpublished cases and 0.041 for published cases with a difference of 0.035 ($p < 0.001$). These findings that nonpublication suppresses requests for review is not surprising. The more interesting question is *why* this pattern emerges.

To seek to disentangle the various possible ways in which selective publication might affect requests for review, I begin by exploring how publication impacts different types of litigants. Figures 6.3 and 6.4 show the predicted probability of requests for review in both published and unpublished cases for each type of litigant. First, consider Supreme Court review. Figure 6.3 indicates that when government entities lose a case, their decision to request cert is not affected by publication status to a statistically significant degree. However, requests for cert are significantly more likely in published cases for indigent and pro se individuals, other individuals, and private organizations. This pattern suggests that a loss of confidence in the courts' willingness to treat a case with care may be a better explanation for why publication matters than concerns about long-term legal development.

The potential benefits of en banc review are more modest compared to Supreme Court review since a circuit can only make law within its own borders. This may lead to different dynamics in litigants' requests. Figure 6.4 suggests this

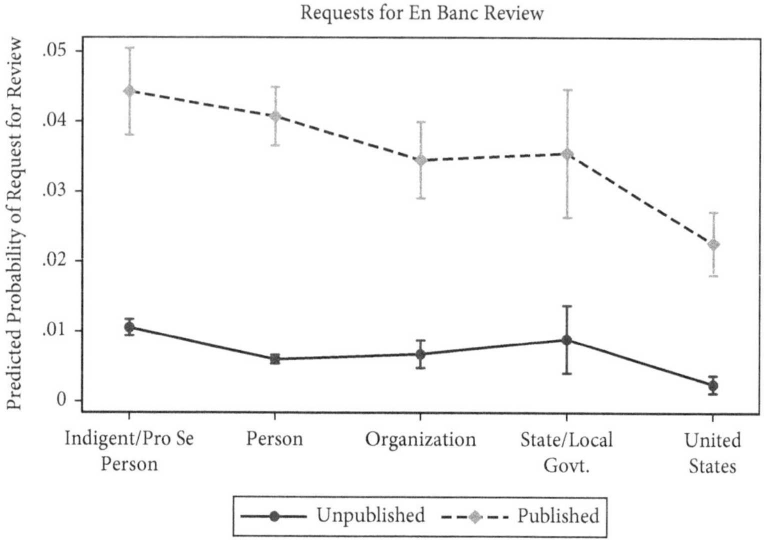

Figure 6.4 Predicted Probability of En Banc Petition: This graph provides the predicted probability of a petition for en banc review being filed by publication status and the type of litigant who lost the panel case. Other variables are held at their median or mode. The whiskers depict the 95% confidence intervals around the predicted probabilities. (Source: Rachael K. Hinkle 2024)

is the case, as a new pattern emerges for en banc petitions. In this context, the publication effect is significant and notable for all litigant types. However, the effect of publication does decrease gradually as litigant sophistication and resources increase. This trend, while less stark than among cert petitions, is generally consistent with the loss-of-confidence mechanism operating in addition to the long-term-legal-development explanation.

Now I turn to consider the other variables that can shed more light on why publication matters to litigants. To consider the effect of these factors, Figure 6.5 presents the changes in predicted probabilities that occur when each variable is moved from a low to high value while holding *Published* equal to one and all others at the median or mode. To the extent that longer and more thorough opinions and oral argument signal willingness to invest resources in a case, higher values of these variables should also increase the probability of requests for review if litigants care about such things. All three of these factors significantly increase the probability of en banc requests, and both the number of citations and oral argument significantly increase the likelihood of cert petitions. These results, taken together with the variation in how publication affects different kinds of litigants, provide some indication that litigants might

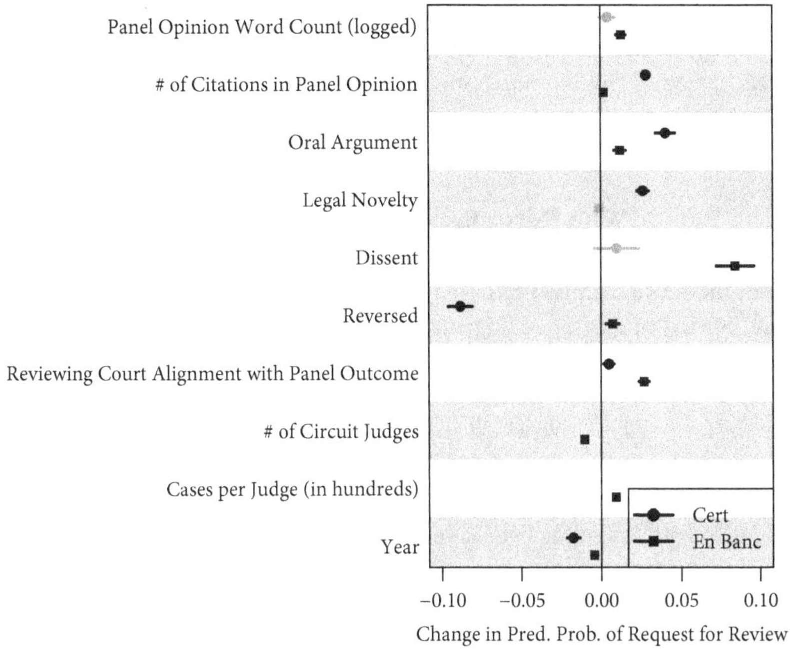

Figure 6.5 Changes in Predicted Probability of Requests for Review: Estimates (and associated 95% confidence intervals) of the change in the predicted probability of a request for review generated by moving each variable from a low to high value while holding other variables at their median or mode. Low and high values are 25th and 75th percentile for continuous variables, and zero and one for binary variables. Estimates from the model of cert petitions are dots, and estimates from the model of request for en banc review are squares. Estimates and confidence intervals in gray (instead of black) indicate that the confidence interval includes zero. Full regression estimates are available in Appendix 6.A in Table 6.A.1. (Source: Rachael K. Hinkle 2024)

well be more willing to give up on cases where they have been made to feel inferior or unimportant.

Of course, publication may affect review requests for multiple reasons. The models also provide support for the received wisdom that litigants estimate the likelihood of success and are more likely to ask for things they are more likely to get. For example, litigants are more likely to file cert petitions when the circuit panel opinion relies more heavily on out-of-circuit and other nonbinding precedent. En banc petitions are more likely when there was a dissent or the trial court was reversed. However, there are some findings at odds with the expectation that litigants strategically anticipate how courts will react to their requests. Cert petitions are actually *less* likely when the trial court was reversed. Perhaps most perplexing is the finding that both cert and en banc petitions are more likely when the potential reviewing court is more closely aligned ideologically with the panel's outcome. This is quite counterintuitive, as review is more likely when the reviewing court disapproves of a ruling than when it agrees with it.[11]

Who Gets a Second Bite at the Apple?

Out of the more than two hundred thousand cases circuit panels disposed of from 2002 to 2012, defeated litigants requested review from the Supreme Court in under thirty-two thousand cases and from the full circuit in less than six thousand cases. Having discussed which requests are made, I now turn to consider the factors that drive which requests are granted. There are several known factors that shape the probability of discretionary review. The Supreme Court is more likely to grant certiorari when there is inter-circuit conflict, ideological disagreement with the ruling being appealed, a request from the Solicitor General, or a request from a repeat player (Black and Boyd 2012; Caldeira and Wright 1988; George and Solimine 2001). Elements such as strategy and ideology play a role in how frequently circuit judges grant en banc review (Giles et al. 2006; Giles et al. 2007; George 1999). Such review is more likely when there is a dissent or the panel reversed the trial court (Giles et al. 2007; George 1999). There are a variety of reasons each of these elements is important. For example, dissents can be used strategically to signal the need for review (e.g., Cross and Tiller 1998).

As discussed previously, it is well established that leaving an opinion unpublished decreases the likelihood of review (Black and Owens 2009; Beske 2018; Berdejó 2013; Hazelton et al. 2016; Vladeck and Gulati 2005). Reasons for this pattern often focus on the relative benefits of review (Hazelton et al. 2016). Since unpublished opinions do not establish binding precedent, there is less reason to expend the cost necessary to review (Mak et al. 2013; Law 2004). If the difference in precedential status is the primary reason unpublished opinions are not reviewed, then the characteristics of the panel opinion should have little impact on the decision to grant review. Indeed, there have been anecdotal accusations that the Supreme Court cert process operates in precisely this way (much to the consternation of some justices). In 2015, the Supreme Court refused to review a well-written forty-page opinion that the Fourth Circuit designated as unpublished, over the vociferous objections of Justice Thomas (and joined by Justice Scalia) that nonpublication should not be a de facto veto of

[11] Indeed, the analysis in the next section shows that these same variables that have a significant positive effect on whether review is requested have a significant negative effect on whether such requests are granted.

the certiorari process (Hazelton et al. 2016; Liptak 2015; Weiss 2015). This is not the only time the issue has been raised by Supreme Court justices. In a 1991 dissent, Justice Harry A. Blackmun wrote, "Nonpublication must not be a convenient means to prevent review" (Liptak 2015). Justice Stevens raised the same concerns, and he was actually *more* likely to vote for cert in unpublished cases (Cleveland 2009).

There is another possible reason why review is granted less frequently in unpublished cases. Discretionary review is intended to address important and novel legal issues, and they are more likely to appear in published opinions (Mak et al. 2013; Zorn 2002). Chapter 3 demonstrates that many of the formal rules regarding publication criteria have a role in publication decisions. This includes the fact that cases with a higher degree of legal novelty are more likely to be published. To the extent that the inherent suitability of a case for review is a factor rather than its publication status, the features of a lower court opinion should impact the decision to grant review. Longer opinions that incorporate more caselaw overall and a higher proportion of persuasive precedent should be more likely to be reviewed. Other features such as dissent and reversal of the trial court that are known to affect the likelihood of review also capture the importance and novelty of the legal issues at hand (and are related to publication through specific criteria in some circuits as well).

Just as different types of litigants make different decisions about when to request review, there is also research that shows this factor can affect whether discretionary review is granted (Black and Boyd 2012). The repeat player advantage theory developed by Galanter (1974) and discussed at length in Chapter 4 applies to grants for review as well as winning and losing cases on the merits (Black and Boyd 2012). However, virtually nothing is known about whether the repeat player advantage operates differently when requesting review of a published opinion compared to an unpublished one. Since review of unpublished opinions is so rare, it is possible that courts equally deny review to all types of litigants in such cases. For example, if courts refuse to review unpublished opinions largely due to their lack of precedential effect, then there would be little reason for such refusals in unpublished cases to vary by litigant type. However, since courts select a quite small number of cases for discretionary review, they choose among a sizable pool of published opinions, which provides the opportunity to select cases they personally deem more important. Judges' assessment of how important or interesting a case is might be affected by who is involved (Pether 2004; Songer et al. 1988). Therefore, it is possible that previous findings of litigant type affecting which cases are reviewed may be mostly driven by published cases. If the repeat player advantage emerges with respect to unpublished rulings too, that would suggest judicial estimations of relative importance of litigants extend across the board.

Empirical Analysis of Granting Discretionary Review

The second stage of empirical analysis examines the subset of the data in which the losing party requested discretionary review. The outcome variable here is whether the court in question granted the request for review. Once again there are separate models for requests for Supreme Court and en banc review. The outcome variables are binary, so I continue to estimate probit models. All of the explanatory and control variables are the same as those in the previous models of litigants' decision to request review. There are two reasons for this approach. First, theory suggests similar determinants drive the decisions to request and grant review. Second, using the same empirical model permits more direct comparison of the two stages of the process.[12]

We know that publication status affects which cases are reviewed, but how big is that effect and how much of it is attributable to judicial decisions after accounting for litigants' actions? The model of when the Supreme Court decides to grant cert petitions estimates that the predicted probability of such a grant is 0.005 when the ruling below is not published and 0.015 when it is. The difference of 0.01 is statistically significant ($p < 0.001$). While a 1% drop in the decision to grant cert may not seem large, in this context it is substantial. The chance a cert request will be granted triples when the panel opinion is published. The effect is even more remarkable for en banc petitions. The predicted probability of granting a request for en banc review is 0.006 for an unpublished ruling, but 0.032 for a published one. The difference of 0.026 is statistically significant ($p = 0.03$) as well as a substantial five times increase.

Next, I examine how litigant type affects the success of requests for review for both published and unpublished cases in Figures 6.6 and 6.7. Figure 6.6 shows that the patterns in the Supreme Court look to be roughly similar for the two kinds of cases. Grants of requests are more likely for published opinions for each litigant type. In both types of cases, requests by indigent or pro se individuals are the least likely to be granted, and those made by the United States are most likely to be granted. The advantage enjoyed by the United States is particularly large in published cases. Cert petitions by the federal government are granted in an estimated 6.4% of such cases, more than triple the next closest litigant category. These estimates indicate that justices' assessment that some kinds of litigants bring more important and interesting cases affect the success of requests for review in all types of cases, but to a somewhat greater degree when the panel ruling is published.

[12] Full regression results are available in Table 6.A.2 in Appendix 6.A.

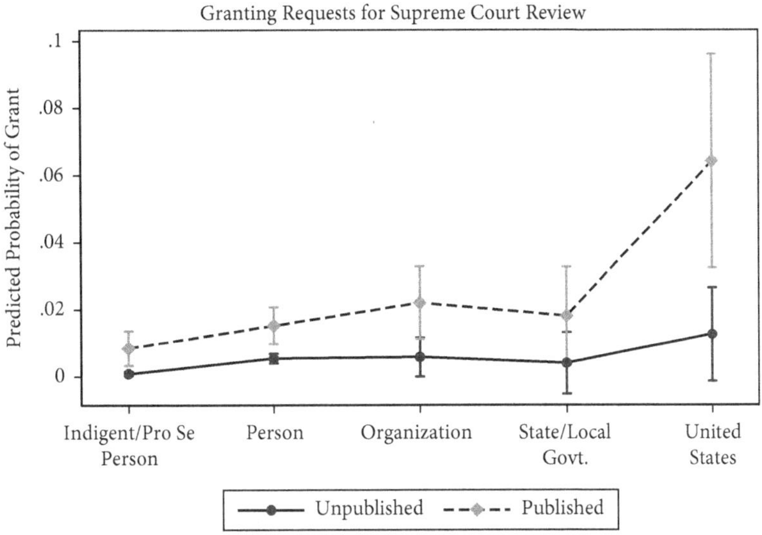

Figure 6.6 Predicted Probability Cert Is Granted: This graph provides the predicted probability that a petition for cert is granted by publication status and the type of litigant who lost the panel case. Other variables are held at their median or mode. The whiskers depict the 95% confidence intervals around the predicted probabilities. (Source: Rachael K. Hinkle 2024)

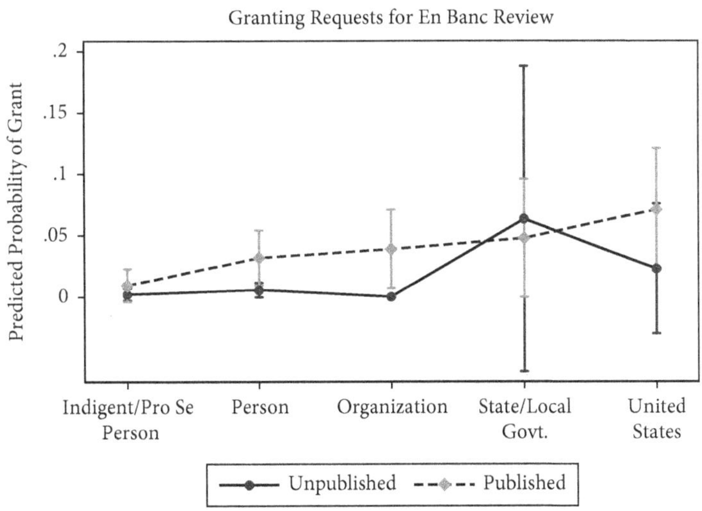

Figure 6.7 Predicted Probability En Banc Is Granted: This graph provides the predicted probability of a petition for en banc review being granted by publication status and the type of litigant who lost the panel case. Other variables are held at their median or mode. The whiskers depict the 95% confidence intervals around the predicted probabilities. (Source: Rachael K. Hinkle 2024)

Figure 6.7 indicates that the process of granting en banc review of unpublished rulings is a bit different than for published ones. In published cases, the expected pattern (and the one that emerges for both types of cases when examining cert) is evident. The probability an en banc petition will be granted is lowest when the request is made by a poor person or one not represented by counsel, highest when made by the federal government, and increases incrementally for each litigant type in between. However, for requests to review unpublished rulings en banc, the key distinction appears to be between private and governmental actors. The probability of review being granted is at similar extremely low level for all types of individuals and private organizations. Both state and local governments and the federal government enjoy a higher level of success in such cases. However, it is worth noting that some of these effects are estimated imprecisely, so these results should be interpreted with some caution.[13]

How do factors beyond publication and litigant type affect which requests for review are granted? Figure 6.8 shows the effect on the predicted probability of a grant when moving each variable from a low to high value. There is only evidence of one element of the text of lower court opinions having an impact on which requests for review are granted. The length of the opinion and its legal novelty are not statistically significant, but both cert and en banc review are more likely to be granted when the panel opinion cites caselaw more extensively.

Other characteristics of the panel proceeding have mixed effects as well. Whether there was oral argument does not appear to matter, but dissent is associated with a higher level of granting requests in both models, and reversal significantly increases the chance of a cert petition being granted. Unsurprisingly, ideology plays a role in judicial decisions to grant review. Both the Supreme Court and circuits are more likely to grant review when they are more ideologically opposed to the outcome below. Finally, granting requests for en banc review is more likely in circuits with more judges and heavier caseloads; a peculiar finding, to say the least.

From Losing to Winning

Very few circuit litigants obtain a second level of appellate review for their case. The previous sections show that publication status is an important factor in both litigant and judicial decisions leading to such review. Moreover, how publication matters varies depending on the type of litigant who lost the panel case. But

[13] While this model has over five thousand data points, the interaction between publication and litigant type and the relatively low level of requests granted combine to result in some imprecision in the estimates.

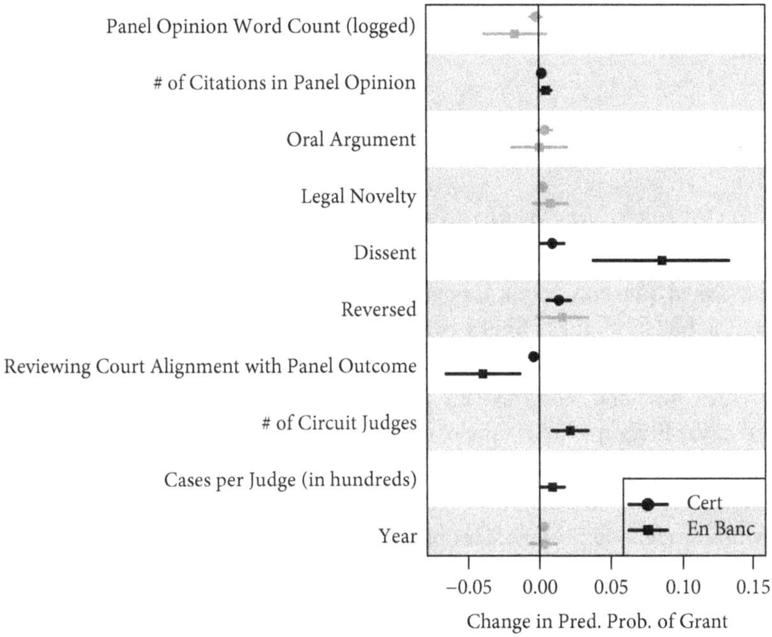

Figure 6.8 Changes in Predicted Probability of Granting a Request for Review: Estimates (and associated 95% confidence intervals) of the change in the predicted probability of a request for review being granted generated by moving each variable from a low to high value while holding other variables at their median or mode. Low and high values are 25th and 75th percentile for continuous variables, and zero and one for binary variables. Estimates from the model of cert petitions are dots, and estimates from the model of request for en banc review are squares. Estimates and confidence intervals in gray (instead of black) indicate that the confidence interval includes zero. Full regression estimates are available in Appendix 6.A in Table 6.A.2. (Source: Rachael K. Hinkle 2024)

what about those rarefied cases where discretionary review is granted? Does the publication status of the panel opinion still matter, and does its effect vary for different kinds of parties? There is little reason to expect either to shape the merits once discretionary review is granted. Publication is a signal regarding the importance of the legal issues in play and an important factor in calculations regarding whether the cost of further review is worthwhile. But once cert or a petition for en banc review has been granted, neither of these is relevant. The focus of the ruling on the merits is how to develop law and apply it to the facts of a given dispute. Whether the previous court to consider the same question published their conclusion has little bearing on whether the reviewing court will agree with the substance of the panel ruling. Since there is little reason to expect publication to shape the merits, there is also no reason to expect variation in such an effect by litigant type.

Empirical Analysis of Winning a Discretionary Review

Although there is little theoretical reason to expect the selective publication norm to influence decisions on the merits during discretionary review, this is an empirical question. I look for evidence of such effects to trace where the impact of publication might finally come to an end. Out of the more than 200,000 circuit cases disposed of from 2002 to 2012, only 482 were taken up by the Supreme Court and only 248 were reheard en banc. The outcome variables are whether the litigant who lost the panel case won in the Supreme Court or the en banc proceeding respectively. Since these are binary variables, I estimate probit models. There is too little data to use all the same explanatory variables as the previous models, so I estimate more parsimonious models. In order to track the continued effect of publication, I include both that variable and litigant type and their interaction. There is little reason to expect characteristics of the panel-level case to shape the merits at the next level, so I safely exclude such explanatory variables. The controls in this model are the reviewing court's ideological alignment with the panel case outcome and the year.[14]

A word of caution is in order before discussing the results. Even with the streamlined models, there is still substantial imprecision in the estimates. However, an interesting and initially counterintuitive finding does emerge. Conditional on asking for review and having it granted, petitioners whose panel cases were unpublished are actually *more* likely to win than if their case was published. In the Supreme Court, the predicted probability of a petitioner victory is 0.91 when the ruling below was unpublished, compared to 0.70 when it was published. This substantively large difference of 0.21 is also statistically significant ($p < 0.001$). A similar pattern is evident in en banc proceedings where the predicted probability of a petitioner win is 0.88 when reviewing an unpublished opinion and 0.73 when reviewing a published one. However, this smaller difference of 0.14 is more imprecisely estimated ($p = 0.25$).

Figures 6.9 and 6.10 show the predicted probability the petitioner (the party who lost the panel case) wins on further review based on the kind of petitioner. In these figures, the lack of a confidence interval indicates the estimate is based on a single data point in that category, and the absence of an estimate indicates there were no data in that category. The only category with a statistically significant publication effect is individual petitioners in the Supreme Court. Nor are

[14] The full regression estimates are available in Table 6.A.3 in Appendix 6.A.

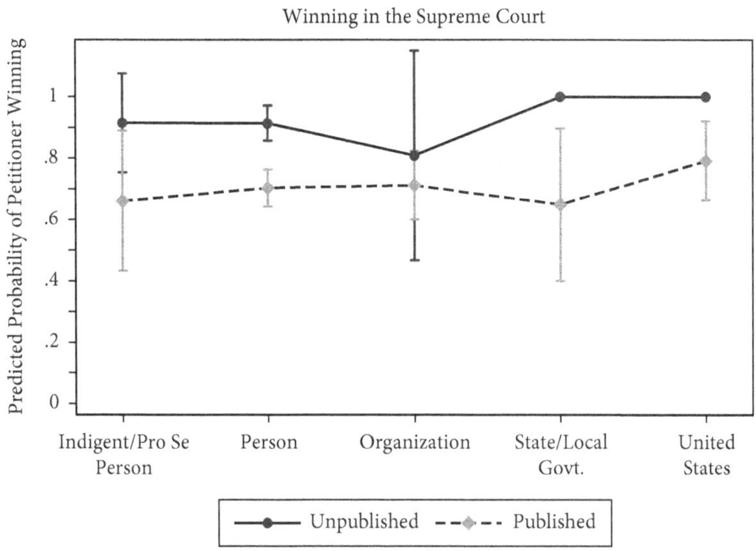

Figure 6.9 Predicted Probability of Petitioner Winning in the Supreme Court: This graph provides the predicted probability the side making a successful request for cert also wins on the merits by publication status and the type of litigant who lost the panel case. Other variables are held at their median or mode. The whiskers depict the 95% confidence intervals around the predicted probabilities. Full regression estimates are available in Appendix 6.A in Table 6.A.3. (Source: Rachael K. Hinkle 2024)

there any significant patterns that indicate some types of litigants are more likely to win than others, but the data are too sparse to draw any conclusions about the lack of such an effect. In fact, the only statistically significant result is that nonpublication leads to a greater win rate in the Supreme Court. This pattern is likely a function of how difficult it is to get an unpublished ruling reviewed. Since both the Supreme Court and full circuits are generally reluctant to grant discretionary review in such cases, it is likely that the nature of the unpublished cases they do review is distinctive. In short, an unpublished opinion must be particularly terrible or problematic to inspire such an unusual step.

Conclusions

Litigants play a key role in agenda setting in federal courts (Boyd 2015a). Yet, previous work largely ignores their significance. Mak et al. (2013, 56) point out that "we know surprisingly little about the decision making of those bringing

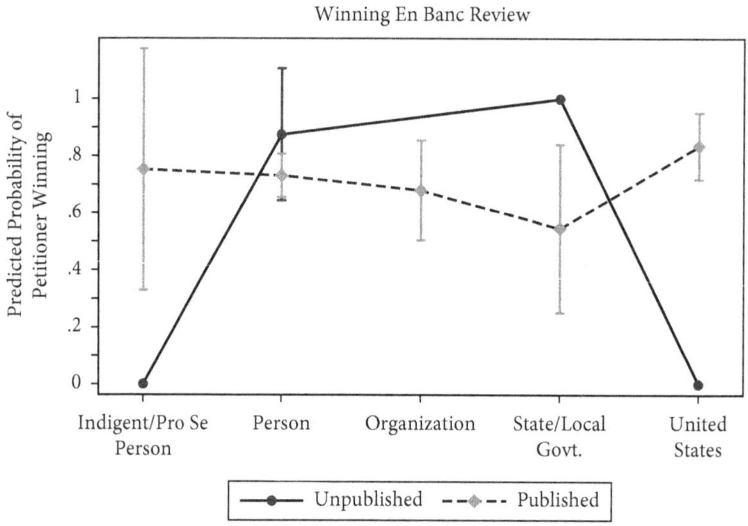

Figure 6.10 Predicted Probability of Petitioner Winning En Banc Review: This graph provides the predicted probability the side making a successful request for en banc review also wins on the merits by publication status and the type of litigant who lost the panel case. Other variables are held at their median or mode. The whiskers depict the 95% confidence interval around the predicted probabilities. Full regression estimates are available in Appendix 6.A in Table 6.A.3. (Source: Rachael K. Hinkle 2024)

cases from the courts of appeals to the highest court in the land." Giles et al. (2006) note a similar shortcoming in the research examining which kinds of cases are reviewed en banc. While these scholars provide key advancement in our understanding of discretionary review, neither is equipped with the data necessary to further consider the implications of selective publication in a comprehensive way. Thus, this chapter advances our knowledge in two dimensions, first by distinguishing litigant and judicial behavior, and second by thoroughly considering the impact of publication on discretionary review.

As Giles et al. (2006) and Mak et al. (2013) both found, litigants not asking for review and judges refusing it are two different things. Nonpublication suppresses requests for review most among have-nots, while it reduces grants of requests most for haves. Judges are understandably more likely to agree to review cases with which they disagree, but litigants are inexplicably more likely to request review of cases more closely aligned with the court they are requesting to review the case. These distinctions highlight the importance of considering both the role litigants and judges play in holding circuit panels accountable.

The fact that unpublished opinions are less likely to be reviewed is well established. However, the analyses in this chapter reveal hitherto unknown discrepancies in how publication matters for different types of parties. When it comes to requesting review, individual and private organizations are more deterred by nonpublication than their government counterparts. Litigants are also less likely to request review based on other indicators that the panel invested relatively little time and effort in their case. Taken together, these patterns suggest that losing parties can take a lack of investment in their case to heart and interpret it as an indication that the court system is likely to continue giving their case short shrift.

Publication also has a differential effect for how requests from different litigants are treated. However, in this situation, the effect is largest for the federal government and decreases as the litigant's resources and experience decrease. This indicates that judges' perceptions of which cases are important and interesting enough to merit discretionary review includes the nature of the party making the request. Such perceptions matter most when the panel opinion was published, but they emerge even when it was not.

How do these findings fit with the results from the previous chapters? Consider some examples. If an indigent or pro se person appeals a district court ruling, there is a 93% chance their case will be resolved in an unpublished opinion. If the case is unpublished, such appellants win only 4% of the time. In the cases they lose, they request cert 14% and en banc review only 1% of the time. Overall, less than one-sixth of a percent of those requests are granted. Compare this to the path of an appeal filed by the United States. First, only 37% of such rulings are unpublished. And among those, the United States wins 43%. In the cases where the federal government loses in an unpublished decision, they seek cert only 3% of the time and en banc review only 0.3%. But those requests are successful 4% and 6% of the time, respectively. There is a clear distinction between the course of an appellant based on their resources and experience.

The pro se appellant's track record is not nearly as dire in the 7% of cases that are published. In those cases, they win 17% of the time, more than four times as frequently as in unpublished cases. When they lose published cases, they are bolder about requesting review, asking for cert in 30% of cases and en banc review in 9%. Those requests are also more successful, being granted 1.4% and 1.1% of the time. While this track record does not come close to how well the federal government fares even in unpublished cases, it illustrates the disparate effects the selective publication norm can create for litigants at multiple stages of the process.

Both litigant and judicial behavior combine to leave unpublished panel opinions with much less accountability than published ones, and the level of accountability depends on who lost in the original circuit proceeding. In this way, disparities generated by selective publication during the initial appeal also create further downstream distributional consequences with respect to review. Quite simply, the "haves" are not only more likely to win, they are also more likely to get a second bite at the apple in the cases where they lose. The only glimmer of light that emerges is for those fortunate few who do secure discretionary review of an unpublished ruling. Once one crosses this formidable hurdle, the odds of winning on the merits are exceedingly favorable.

Appendix 6.A: Regression Results

Table 6.A.1 Request for Review Models: Probit regression models of the probability the losing litigant requests review of the panel decision from the Supreme Court (left columns) or the full circuit en banc (right columns). * indicates a p-value < 0.05. (Source: Rachael K. Hinkle 2024)

	Cert.		En banc	
	Coef.	(S.E.)	Coef.	(S.E.)
Published Opinion	0.139*	(0.024)	0.603*	(0.037)
Litigant Type				
Person	−0.008	(0.010)	−0.206*	(0.023)
Organization	−0.306*	(0.031)	−0.163*	(0.054)
State/Local Government	−0.162*	(0.060)	−0.063	(0.103)
United States	−0.669*	(0.043)	−0.504*	(0.085)
Person x Published	−0.084*	(0.026)	0.167*	(0.038)
Organization x Published	0.090*	(0.043)	0.048	(0.065)
State/Local Government x Published	−0.057	(0.080)	−0.039	(0.119)
United States x Published	−0.179*	(0.057)	0.205*	(0.094)
Panel Opinion Word Count (logged)	0.007	(0.004)	0.076*	(0.009)
Number of Citations in Panel Opinion	0.008*	(0.000)	0.002*	(0.000)
Oral Argument	0.128*	(0.010)	0.123*	(0.020)
Legal Novelty	0.213*	(0.015)	−0.025	(0.029)
Dissent	0.032	(0.023)	0.592*	(0.026)
Reversed	−0.343*	(0.017)	0.079*	(0.021)
Supreme Court Alignment with Outcome	0.235*	(0.080)		
Full Circuit Alignment with Outcome			0.599*	(0.032)

Table 6.A.1 Continued

	Cert.		En banc	
	Coef.	(S.E.)	Coef.	(S.E.)
Issue Area				
Prisoner Petitions	−0.030*	(0.012)	0.121*	(0.023)
Administrative	−1.225*	(0.017)	−0.138*	(0.027)
Civil, Civil Rights	−0.468*	(0.011)	0.121*	(0.019)
Civil, Torts	−0.678*	(0.024)	0.024	(0.036)
Civil, Other	−0.681*	(0.013)	0.058*	(0.022)
Bankruptcy	−0.639*	(0.035)	−0.068	(0.054)
Number of Circuit Judges			−0.025*	(0.002)
Cases per Judge (in hundreds)			0.066*	(0.005)
Year	−0.012*	(0.001)	−0.010*	(0.002)
Intercept	22.956*	(2.801)	17.698*	(4.595)
N	211,806		211,806	
BIC	161414.3		41186.1	
AIC	161168.0		40919.3	

Table 6.A.2 Granting Request for Review Models: Probit regression models of the probability a request for review is granted by the Supreme Court (left columns) or the full circuit en banc (right columns). * indicates a p-value < 0.05. (Source: Rachael K. Hinkle 2024)

	Cert.		En banc	
	Coef.	(S.E.)	Coef.	(S.E.)
Published Opinion	0.750*	(0.148)	0.507	(0.460)
Litigant Type				
Person	0.592*	(0.103)	0.326	(0.412)
Organization	0.611*	(0.198)	−2.798	(121.170)
State/Local Government	0.483	(0.405)	1.330*	(0.625)
United States	0.898*	(0.240)	0.858	(0.621)
Person x Published	−0.368*	(0.147)	0.168	(0.475)
Organization x Published	−0.237	(0.230)	3.382	(121.170)
State/Local Government x Published	−0.191	(0.441)	−0.648	(0.686)

(continued)

Table 6.A.2 Continued

	Cert.		En banc	
	Coef.	(S.E.)	Coef.	(S.E.)
United States x Published	-0.030	(0.274)	0.023	(0.668)
Panel Opinion Word Count (logged)	-0.030	(0.029)	-0.126*	(0.063)
Number of Citations in Panel Opinion	0.004*	(0.001)	0.006*	(0.001)
Oral Argument	0.092	(0.062)	0.004	(0.139)
Legal Novelty	0.153	(0.097)	0.265	(0.194)
Dissent	0.194*	(0.070)	0.667*	(0.080)
Reversed	0.266*	(0.059)	0.189*	(0.081)
Supreme Court Alignment with Outcome	-1.695*	(0.452)		
Full Circuit Alignment with Outcome			-1.181*	(0.158)
Issue Area				
Prisoner Petitions	0.010	(0.066)	-0.162	(0.122)
Administrative	0.287*	(0.115)	-0.147	(0.166)
Civil, Civil Rights	0.217*	(0.067)	-0.142	(0.113)
Civil, Torts	0.374*	(0.113)	-0.402	(0.209)
Civil, Other	0.416*	(0.064)	-0.220	(0.115)
Bankruptcy	0.626*	(0.140)	-0.263	(0.297)
Number of Circuit Judges			0.052*	(0.006)
Cases per Judge (in hundreds)			0.076*	(0.030)
Year	0.012	(0.008)	0.006	(0.012)
Intercept	-27.562	(15.379)	-15.189	(24.703)
N	31,274		5,313	
BIC	4384.4		1675.8	
AIC	4183.9		1504.8	

Table 6.A.3 Winning on Discretionary Review Models: Probit regression models of the probability a successful request for review also results in a victory on the merits in the Supreme Court (left columns) or the full circuit en banc (right columns). * indicates a p-value < 0.05. (Source: Rachael K. Hinkle 2024)

	Cert.		En banc	
	Coef.	**(S.E.)**	**Coef.**	**(S.E.)**
Published Opinion	−0.957	(0.612)	5.808	(471.705)
Litigant Type				
Person	−0.005	(0.557)	6.277	(471.705)
Organization	−0.497	(0.829)	−0.215	(0.724)
State/Local Government	3.572	(299.148)	10.322	(633.115)
United States	3.656	(133.759)	−0.008	(667.091)
Person x Published	0.125	(0.645)	−6.341	(471.705)
Organization x Published	0.641	(0.902)		
State/Local Government x Published	−3.605	(299.149)	−10.889	(633.115)
United States x Published	−3.256	(133.760)	0.300	(667.091)
Supreme Court Alignment with Outcome	0.086	(1.358)		
Full Circuit Alignment with Outcome			−0.046	(0.410)
Year	−0.025	(0.023)	−0.003	(0.029)
Intercept	52.298	(45.684)	0.909	(475.158)
N	482		248	
BIC	574.6		333.7	
AIC	524.5		295.0	

7
The Future of Selective Publication

Introduction

The selective publication norm both generates and reveals disparities in power and privilege. Now what? The most optimistic takeaway is that sometimes becoming consciously aware of discriminatory patterns is sufficient to work toward dismantling those differences (Patton and Smith 2017). It is more likely that this knowledge is only a first step. What should the next steps be? The answer to that question is far from easy. Proposals range from imposing uniform publication criteria to doing away with the concept of publication entirely. Since hard-copy law reporters are no longer part and parcel of everyday legal practice, there is less reason to make hard decisions about what rulings are worthy of sacrificing trees. The circuit courts could, instead, simply make all rulings available without distinction. However, without also addressing staffing levels, this "fix" would likely cause other problems. The most comprehensive solution would also need to include increasing personnel, including the number of circuit judges, to provide a high-quality level of legal analysis to all litigants who come before the circuit courts. Over the years, many reforms such as these and others have been proposed. The empirical evidence presented in this book brings new light to such suggestions, reinforcing some and calling others into question. In this concluding chapter, I provide a summary of the highlights of those findings and then proceed to discuss how they play a role in the discussion of possible reforms going forward. I draw the book to a close with some parting thoughts about which solutions appear most practical and promising.

Highlights of Findings

To begin this final chapter, I present some of my most noteworthy observations for easy reference and further consideration. They are listed by topic to collect findings relevant to various proposed reforms to the selective publication norm.

Selective Publication in the U.S. Courts of Appeals. Rachael K. Hinkle, Oxford University Press.
 DOI: 10.1093/oso/9780197770085.003.0007

Rules/Legal Doctrine

- The highest publication rates occur where the circuit rules state an a priori preference for publishing opinions.
- Publication rates are lowest when the rules give a moderate amount of guidance, and higher when rules are vague or highly specific.
- The variables that have the largest impact on the publication decision are all related to rules and legal doctrine.
- Oral argument, reversal, and lower court publication all have a significantly bigger impact on the publication decision when they are listed as criteria in the circuit rules compared to when they are not.
- In circuits that include dissent as a publication criterion, over 40% of rulings with a dissent are left unpublished, compared to less than 20% in other circuits.

Litigant Characteristics

- Appeals brought by indigent prisoners or people representing themselves pro se make up 36% of unpublished rulings, and only 10% of published ones.
- The percentage of published opinions is four times greater than unpublished when the appellant is an organization, nearly five times greater when they are a subnational government, and more than six times greater for the United States.
- Litigants with more resources and experience than their opponents are more likely to win both published and unpublished cases, but the repeat player advantage is larger in published cases.
- The repeat player advantage is significantly greater when the litigant with the advantage is also ideologically aligned with the panel, and this interactive effect is much larger in published cases.
- Litigants are more likely to ask for discretionary review when the panel ruling was published.
- Nonpublication depresses litigant requests for review more for private actors than for government actors.
- Requests for review are less frequent when the panel opinion contains fewer citations or was decided without oral argument.
- Nonpublication depresses grants of requests for review more for have-nots than for haves.

Judge Characteristics

- Panels are less likely to publish when they have ideological, gender, or racial diversity.
- Female and minority judges are less likely to participate in cases with published opinions compared to male and white judges.
- Female judges are significantly more likely to be assigned to write unpublished decisions compared to white male judges.
- Judges of color are significantly less likely to be assigned to write published decisions compared to white male judges.
- Minority judges are more likely to dissent than white male judges.

Hierarchical Constraints

- Panels are less likely to publish when they are further ideologically from the full circuit or the Supreme Court.
- Courts are more likely to grant requests for discretionary review when the panel ruling was published.
- Requests for review are granted more frequently when the panel opinion has more citations, was accompanied by a dissent, or is further from the reviewing court ideologically.
- When discretionary review is granted, the petitioner is actually more likely to win if the panel ruling was unpublished compared to when it was published.

Miscellaneous

- Criminal cases are 34% of unpublished cases, but they are also 30% of published ones.
- Published opinions are longer, more syntactically complex, cite more caselaw, and cite a higher proportion of persuasive caselaw compared to unpublished opinions.
- Panels are less likely to publish when they are more ideologically opposed to the outcome.

Potential Reforms

Even in the early days when selective publication was initially being discussed to address the caseload explosion, observers noted that the increased pressures on appellate courts were likely to continue increasing over time (Carrington 1968). However, McAlister (2020, 551) argues that "the 'crisis' that led to the creation of unpublished decisions has plateaued, if not receded." Brown et al. (2021) note that caseloads in the circuit courts leveled off between 2005 and 2018. That change in circumstances has not led to a serious reconsideration of the need for selective publication. In fact, the rate of unpublication continues to rise (Bowie et al. 2014; Brown et al. 2021). McAlister (2020) attributes this trend to the fact that pro se appeals continue to increase.

Caseloads are not the only relevant factor that has changed. Morande (2003, 755) has noted that some of the concerns that supported the move to selective publication "have become obsolete with the advent of new technologies." As conditions change, many of the debates remain the same. Baker (1994, 125) points out that "[a]s long as common law courts have decided appeals, debate has persisted concerning limited publication of opinions." In this section, I consider the current state of those debates by discussing proposed reforms in light of findings from the foregoing chapters.

Uniform Publication Rules

The most modest reform to the system of publication that has been suggested addresses the patchwork nature of publication criteria from circuit to circuit. Even when experimentation was originally viewed as a way to efficiently learn about the strengths and weaknesses of different approaches to selective publication, some argued that each circuit making their own publication criteria would be a bad idea (Murrah 1973). As the decades have passed, others have similarly pushed for widespread adoption of a uniform set of rules regarding publication (Baker 1994; Cleveland 2010; Morande 2003). My findings support the intuition that varying rules will lead to varying practices. Both the nature and extent of circuit rules shape the number and types of opinions that are ultimately published. Since selective publication was adopted to solve a common set of problems, it makes sense to implement the norm with at least some degree of uniformity. Experimentation may have had value initially, but the verdict is now in. Chapters 2 and 3 reveal a substantial amount of information about the impact of different rules. If selective publication is to continue unabated, the time has at least come to make a choice among the available options and implement it across the circuits.

There is no shortage of suggestions about important features of any uniform set of publication criteria. For example, Reynolds and Richman (1981) suggested a Model Rule that included a presumption of publication, nine specific criteria for publication, and a requirement that publication be withheld only if there was no oral argument and the case was patently frivolous. Others have emphasized the importance of specific criteria. A frequent point of emphasis is that disagreement among judges is evidence that the law on a point is, in fact, not well-settled. As such, is it often argued that publication should be required when there is a separate opinion or the trial court is reversed (Brown et al. 2021; Dragich 1994; Hoffman 1981; Reynolds and Richman 1981). Beske (2018) asserts that all circuit rules should explicitly say new law must be published. Another proposal is to include an explicit provision that gives the litigants, or even outside observers, the right to petition for publication of any opinion (Hoffman 1981; Martineau 1994). Empirical findings indicate that many of these recommendations could materially alter the shape of selective publication in the circuit courts if implemented across the board. There is evidence that publication criteria matter, but also that even concrete criteria like dissent and reversal do not uniformly determine publication decisions. Requiring publication in such instances rather than merely suggesting it would provide more consistent results.

Alternate Decision Maker

While uniform rules across all circuits would diminish variation in publication practices from circuit to circuit, my findings demonstrate that ideology and strategy play a role in the decision to publish alongside formal rules. The possibility of such extralegal factors has led some to call for a separation of the publication and merits decisions. Concerns regarding judges determining whether a case they are deciding should be published have long been voiced. Sir Francis Bacon advised: "[L]et not the judges themselves meddle with the reports; lest from being too fond of their own opinions, and relying on their own authority, they exceed the province of a reporter" (see Surrency 1981, 48). The Annual Report of the American Bar Association from 1898 similarly noted that judges "ought not to have the power of preventing the publication of their opinions" (American Bar Association 1898, 444).

Nevertheless, when the selective publication norm emerged in federal appellate courts, judges were granted the power to determine publication status (Wald 1995). Murrah (1973, 10) noted that "[t]he use of an outside agency . . . was considered undesirable unless experience should prove that other methods will not work." A middle ground has been suggested whereby circuits establish special panels with the specific task of determining whether an opinion should be published (and sending it back to the merits panel for revision if necessary) (Martineau 1994). This approach would prevent the ideology of the panel members from affecting the determination of publication, but perhaps simply in exchange for the preferences of the publication panel. However, dividing the responsibilities in this way would remove the panel's ability to negotiate and compromise among themselves using nonpublication as a bargaining chip. Chapter 5 reveals that the unintended consequence of such bargaining is to reduce the power of judges from historically excluded groups. This power disparity could well be diminished or eliminated by separating the publication and merits decisions.

Precedential Status for Unpublished Rulings

A third possible reform is directed at neither the publication criteria nor the decision maker, but at the doctrinal implications of unpublished opinions. The original determination that only published opinions constituted precedent was deemed necessary because of the lack of access to unpublished rulings. In the 1970s, continuing to make all opinions precedential imposed a significant logistical burden. Making precedent available to the bench and bar required printing physical copies. Technology has long since rendered exhaustive print resources unnecessary, and continued advances are increasingly changing the face of legal research in ways that are relevant to considering the future of selective publication. Electronic resources make a vast array of opinions not only widely accessible but also easily searchable (Cleveland 2009; Cohen 2002; White 1998). Westlaw has provided the full text of legal documents since 1978, and Lexis at least since the early 1980s (Brenner 1990). While "full text" did not initially include unpublished opinions because of their limited availability, Congress passed the E-Government Act of 2002, which required that the circuits make all unpublished opinions available electronically.[1] Many unpublished circuit opinions have been available in print as well in West's *Federal Appendix*, which was launched in 2001 (Beske 2018). While there is still evidence of some gaps in coverage, the term "unpublished" is clearly a misnomer (Beske 2018; Magrath 2019; McAlister 2020). All circuit opinions are widely available.

Arguably, technology has changed the game. Some scholars argue that precedential status should be clear and consistent and that to achieve this goal it would be optimal if all opinions had equal status as precedent (Cleveland 2010). Brown et al. (2021, 28) note that "most critics of unpublished opinions have focused on their nonprecedential status," and Arnold (1999, 223) argues that "[e]very case has *some* precedential value, maybe not much, but some." Some scholars and jurists go so far as to assert that the current practice of withholding precedential status from unpublished opinions is (or at least should be) unconstitutional (Cleveland 2009). In 2000, the Eighth Circuit issued such a ruling

[1] 44 USC § 3501 et seq.

declaring that all opinions must be regarded as precedent, but it was overturned in short order (Brown et al. 2021; Merritt and Brudney 2001; Schiltz 2005a).

In addition to legal arguments about all opinions being precedent, there are also arguments that uniform precedential status would help the legal system operate better and more efficiently. Unpublished opinions not constituting precedent can create problems, especially when they diverge from or change settled law (Ricks 2006). People expect past rulings to control future cases (Cleveland 2009). However, Ricks (2006, 220) notes, "[T]he risk that district courts will apply non-precedential opinions inconsistently raises serious concerns." This, in turn, creates uncertainty for litigants about whether unpublished opinions will be followed (Ricks 2006). Equal precedential status for all opinions can reduce such uncertainty, thus increasing efficiency (Brown et al. 2021, 90). Greater confidence in anticipating how disputes will be resolved is helpful for future disputants to evaluate the strength of their claims, which can reduce the overall incidence of litigation (Ricks 2006). This suggested reform could also enhance how participants view the courts' fairness since litigants whose cases are resolved by unpublished opinions would know that their case was still part of the legal framework (Cleveland 2009). Along similar lines, patterns that lead to female and minority judges writing more unpublished opinions would not inherently exacerbate existing power disparities, because all opinions would shape the law and all judges would have a more equal voice.

Abolishing Selective Publication

The most extensive reform that has been suggested is to entirely do away with selective publication. For example, Slavitt (1995) argues that it would be better to have universal publication, pointing out that judges cannot always tell in advance which opinions will be important and useful for future litigants. Others question whether the distinction of publication is still relevant in the computer age (Brenner 1990; Magrath 2019). Pether (2004) points to the example of the Texas Supreme Court, which ended unpublication in civil cases in 2003.

Proponents of abandoning selective publication acknowledge that such a move would most likely require an expansion of the judiciary in order to avoid a decrease in the quality of all opinions (Baker 1994; Richman and Reynolds 1995; Slavitt 1995; Vladeck and Gulati 2005). Vladeck and Gulati (2005) point out that federal district courts had a caseload explosion too, and the system of magistrates was expanded to help address this need. They argue that similar creativity in staffing is needed for the courts of appeals too (Vladeck and Gulati 2005). Baker (1994) suggests that an increase in the supply of circuit judges could be partially produced by greater use of senior and visiting judges.

As the most extreme reform proposed, it is not surprising that it has also attracted its share of detractors. For example, Brown et al. (2021, 1081) argue that "[c]ompletely abolishing nonpublication is neither feasible nor desirable." The feasibility certainly seems questionable considering the reluctance circuit judges have displayed over expanding their numbers. Jones (1995) claims that having too many new circuit judgeships is problematic because prestige is a key reason lawyers agree to be judges, and the more judges there are, the less prestigious the job will become. Richman and Reynolds (2013, 221) characterize the many arguments made in favor of keeping a small judiciary as follows: "The themes of power, elitism, status, and image appear with distressing regularity." However, regardless of the motivation, the fact remains that if judges themselves do not ask for more judgeships, the issue never gets on the agenda (Richman and Reynolds 2013). As a result, judicial unwillingness to expand substantially is likely to stymie any coordinated efforts to simultaneously abandon selective publication and increase judicial resources.

Parting Thoughts

Judge Learned Hand once said, "If we are to keep our democracy, there must be one commandment: Thou shalt not ration justice" (Baker 1994, ix). The picture that emerges upon careful examination of the U.S. Courts of Appeals makes it clear that the selective publication norm is something very like rationing of justice. Furthermore, not everyone is given an equal ration. The resources of litigants and identity of judges affect the role they play in legal development. Only published opinions make law, and that increasingly rare resource is distributed based not only on formal rules and legal doctrine but also on judge's ideology, internal and external strategic calculations, and perceptions of which cases and participants are worthy. The norm was originally adopted for two reasons: to allow for the more efficient disposition of a large number of cases and to slow the growth of caselaw. Yet as Slavitt (1995) argues, efficiency should be about what is overall best for "social welfare" not just what saves time or money. And Pether (2004, 1516) points out that technology is making the growth of caselaw argument "potentially irrelevant." The time for change has come. While the circuit courts perform many aspects of their difficult job very well, there is room for important improvements.

Amending the Federal Rules of Appellate Procedure to adopt uniform procedures and criteria with respect to publication is appealing as a first step. While the rule changes with regard to citation bans were only achieved after nearly twenty years of intense debate (Cleveland 2010), many rule changes can be achieved more easily since they are within the direct control of the courts themselves. Pursuing such a goal may be feasible and is an incremental step better than the current state of affairs, but it would still be a matter of tinkering with a system that has some fundamental flaws. In short, to achieve uniformity of inequality would be a rather hollow victory.

In my opinion, the most feasible reform with any real promise of ameliorating inequality is to adopt a new rule that declares all opinions, regardless of publication status, constitute binding precedent. This step would have a relatively small impact on the work process and product of the judiciary while taking a meaningful step toward allowing litigants and judges alike to participate equally in the process of shaping law. The sky did not fall when circuits were required to permit citation to unpublished opinions. Case disposition times did not balloon, and extra judges and staff members were not immediately necessary (Schiltz 2005a). In fact, there was relatively little change to opinions themselves (Brown et al. 2021). A change to granting unpublished opinions precedential status may well have a similar impact. Judges could continue to write unpublished opinions with the same level of care and detail as they did before. Cases without new legal issues could be easily disposed of with quick reference to previous caselaw that resolved the same point. The only major difference would be that judges would not be free to ignore any relevant caselaw that happened to be unpublished. This burden does not seem unreasonable.

One of the key original reasons for adopting selective publication was worry over the burgeoning number of precedents judges and lawyers had to address. Making all opinions precedent would, of course, reduce this benefit of selective publication. Retaining the distinction between published and unpublished would still allow judges to control the costs of physical law libraries by limiting which opinions are published and, therefore, get printed in physical law reporters. But such a rule change would substantially increase the total amount of caselaw judges and lawyers must engage with. However, the current state of technology has largely done away with concerns created by a large amount of precedent. Algorithms, large language models, and generative AI can efficiently point humans to the most relevant caselaw. An increasing amount of caselaw in databases will only mean the most relevant caselaw produced by a search is more directly on point.

While the actual process of deciding circuit cases would change relatively little if unpublished opinions were acknowledged as binding precedent, there would be two significant improvements for how people experience the federal appellate system. The first is that both litigants and judges would know that even cases resolved by means of an unpublished opinion play an equal role in the important process of developing the law. This may well improve perceptions of fairness and equality. Second, the most concrete shift would be to how discretionary review is administered. The fact that unpublished opinions do not make law has long been a major factor in the calculus of both granting cert and en banc review. As I demonstrated in Chapter 6, this results in publication decisions having substantial downstream implications. Making unpublished rulings precedential would mean only the actual underlying importance of the issues in a case would play a role in review decisions. The panel's determination that a ruling should be unpublished would undoubtedly still be a powerful signal regarding the importance of the case. But higher courts would no longer be able to wash their hands of a case on the grounds that they have no reason to waste their time on an opinion that is not law.

Many may not agree with my assessment of the best road forward. But that does not undermine the empirical realities uncovered throughout this book. The problems caused by the selective publication norm are not simple to solve, but they do exist. As a result, we must grapple with the costs and benefits of potential solutions.

Bibliography

Albiston, Catherine. 1999. "The Rule of Law and the Litigation Process: The Paradox of Losing by Winning." *Law & Society Review* 33(4):869–910.

Allison, Paul D. 1999. "Comparing Logit and Probit Coefficients Across Groups." *Sociological Methods & Research* 28(2):186–208.

American Bar Association. 1895. "Report of the 18th Annual Meeting of the American Bar Association." https://hdl.handle.net/2027/njp.32101047032915 (accessed November 19, 2023).

American Bar Association. 1898. "Report of the 21st Annual Meeting of the American Bar Association." https://hdl.handle.net/2027/njp.32101047032923 (accessed November 19, 2023).

Arnold, Richard S. 1999. "Unpublished Opinions: A Comment." *Journal of Appellate Practice & Process* 1(2):219–26.

Atkins, Burton M. 1991. "Party Capability Theory as an Explanation for Intervention Behavior in the English Court of Appeal." *American Journal of Political Science* 35(4):881–903.

Bachrach, Peter and Morton S. Baratz. 1962. "Two Faces of Power." *American Political Science Review* 56(4):947–52.

Baker, Thomas E. 1994. *Rationing Justice on Appeal: The Problems of the U.S. Courts of Appeals*. St. Paul, MN: West Publishing Co.

Barke, Richard P., Hank Jenkins-Smith, and Paul Slovic. 1997. "Risk Perceptions of Men and Women Scientists." *Social Science Quarterly* 78(1):167–76.

Barrow, Deborah J. and Thomas G. Walker. 1988. *A Court Divided: The Fifth Circuit Court of Appeals and the Politics of Judicial Reform*. New Haven, CT: Yale University Press.

Beim, Deborah, Alexander V. Hirsch, and Jonathan P. Kastellec. 2014. "Whistleblowing and Compliance in the Judicial Hierarchy." *American Journal of Political Science* 58(4):904–18.

Beim, Deborah, Alexander V. Hirsch, and Jonathan P. Kastellec. 2016. "Signaling and Counter-Signaling in the Judicial Hierarchy: An Empirical Analysis of En Banc Review." *American Journal of Political Science* 60(2):490–508.

Bell, Griffin B. 1970. "Toward a More Efficient Federal Appeals System." *Judicature* 54(6):237–45.

Berdejó, Carlos. 2013. "It's the Journey, Not the Destination: Judicial Preferences and the Decision-Making Process." *University of Louisville Law Review* 51(2):271–321.

Beske, Elizabeth Earle. 2018. "Rethinking the Nonprecedential Opinion." *UCLA Law Review* 65(4):808–59.

Black, Ryan C. and Christina L. Boyd. 2012. "U.S. Supreme Court Agenda Setting and the Role of Litigant Status." *Journal of Law, Economics, & Organization* 28(2):286–312.

Black, Ryan C. and Ryan J. Owens. 2009. "Agenda Setting in the Supreme Court: The Collision of Policy and Jurisprudence." *Journal of Politics* 71(3):1062–75.

Boucher Jr., Robert L., and Jeffrey A. Segal. 1995. "Supreme Court Justices as Strategic Decision Makers: Aggressive Grants and Defensive Denials on the Vinson Court." *Journal of Politics* 57(3):824–37.

Bowie, Jennifer Barnes, Donald R. Songer, and John Szmer. 2014. *The View from the Bench and Chambers: Examining Judicial Process and Decision Making on the U.S. Courts of Appeals*. Charlottesville, VA: University of Virginia Press.

Boyd, Christina L. 2010. "Federal District Court Judge Ideology Data." http://cLboyd.net/ (accessed November 19, 2023).

Boyd, Christina L. 2015a. "Litigant Status and Trial Court Appeal Mobilization." *Law & Policy* 37(4):294–323.
Boyd, Christina L. 2015b. "The Hierarchical Influence of Courts of Appeals on District Courts." *Journal of Legal Studies* 44(1):113–41.
Boyd, Christina L., Lee Epstein, and Andrew D. Martin. 2010. "Untangling the Causal Effects of Sex on Judging." *American Journal of Political Science* 54(2):389–411.
Braman, Eileen and Thomas E. Nelson. 2007. "Mechanism of Motivated Reasoning? Analogical Perception in Discrimination Disputes." *American Journal of Political Science* 51(4):940–56.
Brenner, Saul and Harold J. Spaeth. 1986. "Issue Specialization in Majority Opinion Assignment on the Burger Court." *Western Political Quarterly* 39(3):520–25.
Brenner, Susan W. 1990. "Of Publication and Precedent: An Inquiry into the Ethnomethodology of Case Reporting in the American Legal System." *DePaul Law Review* 39(3):461–542.
Brown, Rachel, Jade Ford, Sahrula Kubie, Katrin Marquez, Bennett Ostdiek, and Abbe R. Gluck. 2021. "Is Unpublished Unequal? An Empirical Examination of the 87% Nonpublication Rate in Federal Appeals." *Cornell L.aw Review* 107(1):1–150.
Buckler, Kevin G. 2015. "Supreme Court Outcomes in Criminal Justice Cases (1994–2012 Terms): An Examination of Status Differential and Amici Curiae Effects." *Criminal Justice Policy Review* 26(8):773–804.
Caldeira, Gregory A. and John R. Wright. 1988. "Organized Interests and Agenda Setting in the U.S. Supreme Court." *American Political Science Review* 82(4):1109–27.
Cameron, Charles M., Jeffrey A. Segal, and Donald Songer. 2000. "Strategic Auditing in a Political Hierarchy: An Informational Model of the Supreme Court's Certiorari Decisions." *American Political Science Review* 94(1):101–16.
Carlson, Keith, Michael A. Livermore, and Daniel N. Rockmore. 2020. "The Problem of Data Bias in the Pool of Published U.S. Appellate Court Opinions." *Journal of Empirical Legal Studies* 17(2):224–61.
Carrington, Paul D. 1968. "Crowded Dockets and the Courts of Appeals: The Threat to the Function of Review and the National Law." *Harvard Law Review* 82(3):542–617.
Chanin, Leah F. 1974. "A Survey of the Writing and Publication of Opinions in Federal and State Appellate Courts." *Law Library Journal* 67(3):362–79.
Cheng, Edward K. 2008. "The Myth of the Generalist Judge: An Empirical Analysis of Opinion Specialization in the Federal Courts of Appeals." *Stanford Law Review* 61(3):519–72.
Christensen, Robert K., John Szmer, and Justin M. Stritch. 2012. "Race and Gender Bias in Three Administrative Contexts: Impact on Work Assignments in State Supreme Courts." *Journal of Public Administration Research and Theory* 22(4):625–48.
Cleveland, David R. 2009. "Draining the Morass: Ending the Jurisprudentially Unsound Unpublication System." *Marquette Law Review* 92(4):685–748.
Cleveland, David R. 2010. "Local Rules in the Wake of Federal Rule of Appellate Procedure 32.1." *Journal of Appellate Practice & Process* 11(1):19–74.
Cohen, Jonathan M. 2002. *Inside Appellate Courts: The Impacts of Court Organization on Judicial Decision Making in the United States Courts of Appeals*. Ann Arbor, MI: University of Michigan Press.
Collins, Paul M. 2004. "Friends of the Court: Examining the Influence of Amicus Curiae Participation in U.S. Supreme Court Litigation." *Law & Society Review* 38(4):807–32.
Collins, Paul M. 2007. "Lobbyists Before the U.S. Supreme Court: Investigating the Influence of Amicus Curiae Briefs." *Political Research Quarterly* 60(1):55–70.
Cox, Adam B. and Thomas J. Miles. 2008. "Judging the Voting Rights Act." *Columbia Law Review* 108(1):1–54.
Cross, Frank. 2005. "Appellate Court Adherence to Precedent." *Journal of Empirical Legal Studies* 2(2):369–405.
Cross, Frank B. 2007. *Decision Making in the U.S. Courts of Appeals*. Redwood City, CA: Stanford University Press.

Cross, Frank B. and Emerson H. Tiller. 1998. "Judicial Partisanship and Obedience to Legal Doctrine: Whistleblowing on the Federal Courts of Appeals." *Yale Law Journal* 107(7):2155–78.

Cross, Frank, Tonja Jacobi, and Emerson Tiller. 2012. "A Positive Political Theory of Rules and Standards." *University of Illinois Law Review* 2012(1):1–42.

Davies, Thomas Y. 1981. "Gresham's Law Revisited: Expedited Processing Techniques and the Allocation of Appellate Resources." *Justice System Journal* 6(3):372–404.

Dragich, Martha J. 1994. "Will the Federal Courts of Appeals Perish If They Publish? Or Does the Declining Use of Opinions to Explain and Justify Judicial Decisions Pose a Greater Threat?" *American University Law Review* 44(3):757–802.

Ellemers, Naomi and S. Alexander Haslam. 2011. "Social Identity Theory." In *Handbook of Theories of Social Psychology*, edited by Paul A.M. Van Lange, Arie W. Kruglanski, and E. Tory Higgins, 379–98. Los Angeles, CA: Sage.

Epstein, Lee, Andrew D. Martin, Jeffrey A. Segal, and Chad Westerland. 2007. "The Judicial Common Space." *Journal of Law, Economics, & Organization* 23(2):303–25.

Epstein, Lee and Tonja Jacobi. 2010. "The Strategic Analysis of Judicial Decisions." *Annual Review of Law and Social Science* 6(1):341–58.

Epstein, Lee, William M. Landes, and Richard A. Posner. 2013. *The Behavior of Federal Judges.* Cambridge, MA: Harvard University Press.

Farhang, Sean and Gregory Wawro. 2004. "Institutional Dynamics on the U.S. Court of Appeals: Minority Representation under Panel Decision Making." *Journal of Law, Economics, & Organization* 20(2):299–330.

Farhang, Sean, Jonathan P. Kastellec, and Gregory J. Wawro. 2015. "The Politics of Opinion Assignment and Authorship on the U.S. Court of Appeals: Evidence from Sexual Harassment Cases." *Journal of Legal Studies* 44(S1):S59–85.

Farole Jr., Donald J. 1999. "Reexamining Litigant Success in State Supreme Courts." *Law & Society Review* 33(4):1043–58.

Finucane, Melissa L., Paul Slovic, C.K. Mertz, James Flynn, and Theresa A. Satterfield. 2000. "Gender, Race, and Perceived Risk: The 'White Male' Effect." *Health, Risk & Society* 2(2):159–72.

Fischman, Joshua B. 2021. "How Many Cases Are Easy?" *Journal of Legal Analysis* 13(1): 595–656.

Flynn, John, Paul Slovic, and C.K. Mertz. 1994. "Gender, Race, and Perception of Environmental Health Risks." *Risk Analysis* 14(6):1101–08.

Galanter, Marc. 1974. "Why the Haves Come Out Ahead: Speculations on the Limits of Legal Change." *Law & Society Review* 9(1):95–160.

García, Mildred. 2000. *Succeeding in an Academic Career: A Guide for Faculty of Color.* Westport, CT: Greenwood Publishing Group.

George, Tracey E. 1999. "The Dynamics and Determinants of the Decision to Grant En Banc Review." *Washington Law Review* 74(2):213–74.

George, Tracey E. and Michael E. Solimine. 2001. "Supreme Court Monitoring of the United States Courts of Appeals En Banc." *Supreme Court Economic Review* 9(1):171–204.

Gibson, James L. and Michael J. Nelson. 2018. *Black and Blue: How African Americans Judge the U.S. Legal System.* New York, NY: Oxford University Press.

Gibson, James L. and Michael J. Nelson. 2021. *Judging Inequality: State Supreme Courts and the Inequality Crisis.* New York, NY: Russell Sage Foundation.

Gignoux, Edward T. 1978. *Opinion Publication Plans in the United States Courts of Appeals.* Report of the Subcommittee on Federal Jurisdiction of the Committee on Court Administration of the Judicial Conference of the United States.

Giles, Micheal W., Thomas G. Walker, and Christopher Zorn. 2006. "Setting a Judicial Agenda: The Decision to Grant En Banc Review in the U.S. Courts of Appeals." *Journal of Politics* 68(4):852–66.

Giles, Micheal W., Virginia A. Hettinger, Christopher Zorn, and Todd C. Peppers. 2007. "The Etiology of the Occurrence of En Banc Review in the U.S. Court of Appeals." *American Journal of Political Science* 51(3):449–63.

Giles, Micheal W., Virginia A. Hettinger, and Todd Peppers. 2001. "Picking Federal Judges: A Note on Policy and Partisan Selection Agendas." *Political Research Quarterly* 54(3):623–41.

Ginsburg, Ruth Bader. 1985. "The Obligation to Reason Why." *University of Florida Law Review* 37(2):205–24.

Haire, Susan B., Laura P. Moyer, and Shawn Treier. 2013. "Diversity, Deliberation, and Judicial Opinion Writing." *Journal of Law and Courts* 1(2):303–30.

Haire, Susan B., Roger Hartley, and Stefanie A. Lindquist. 1999. "Attorney Expertise, Litigant Success, and Judicial Decisionmaking in the U.S. Courts of Appeals." *Law & Society Review* 33(1):667–85.

Hannon, Michael. 2001. "A Closer Look at Unpublished Opinions in the United States Courts of Appeals." *Journal of Appellate Practice & Process* 3(1):199–250.

Hanretty, Chris. 2014. "Haves and Have-Nots Before the Law Lords." *Political Studies* 62(3):686–97.

Haynie, S.L. 1994. "Resource Inequalities and Litigation Outcomes in the Philippine Supreme Court." *Journal of Politics* 56(3):752–72.

Hazelton, Morgan L.W. and Rachael K. Hinkle. 2022. *Persuading the Supreme Court: The Significance of Briefs in Judicial Decisionmaking.* Lawrence, KS: University of Kansas Press.

Hazelton, Morgan, Rachael K. Hinkle, and Jee Seon Jeon. 2016. "Sound the Alarm? Judicial Decisions Regarding Publication and Dissent." *American Politics Research* 44(4):649–81.

Hellman, Arthur D. 2007. "The Law of the Circuit Revisited: What Role for Majority Rule." *Southern Illinois University Law Journal* 32(3):625–40.

Hettinger, Virginia A., Stefanie A. Lindquist, and Wendy L. Martinek. 2006. *Judging on a Collegial Court.* Charlottesville, VA: University of Virginia Press.

Hinkle, Rachael. 2023. "Publication and Strategy in the U.S. Courts of Appeals." *Journal of Institutional and Theoretical Economics* 179(1):121–45.

Hinkle, Rachael K. 2015. "Legal Constraint in the U.S. Courts of Appeals." *Journal of Politics* 77(3):721–35.

Hinkle, Rachael K. 2016. "Strategic Anticipation of En Banc Review in the U.S. Courts of Appeals." *Law & Society Review* 50(2):383–414.

Hinkle, Rachael K. 2017. "Panel Effects and Opinion Crafting in the U.S. Courts of Appeals." *Journal of Law and Courts* 5(2):313–36.

Hinkle, Rachael K. 2021. "How Policy Influence Varies with Race and Gender in the U.S. Courts of Appeals." *Research & Politics* 8(3):1–7.

Hinkle, Rachael K. and Michael J. Nelson. 2016. "The Transmission of Legal Precedent among State Supreme Courts in the Twenty-First Century." *State Politics & Policy Quarterly* 16(4):391–410.

Hinkle, Rachael K. and Michael J. Nelson. 2017. "How to Lose Cases and Influence People." *Statistics, Politics and Policy* 8(2):195–221.

Hinkle, Rachael K. and Michael J. Nelson. 2018. "The Intergroup Foundations of Policy Influence." *Political Research Quarterly* 71(4):729–42.

Hoffman, Daniel N. 1981. "Nonpublication of Federal Appellate Court Opinions." *Justice System Journal* 6(3):405–34.

Hogg, Michael A. and Dominic Abrams. 1988. *Social Identifications: A Social Psychology of Intergroup Relations and Group Processes.* New York, NY: Routledge.

Howard, J. Woodford. 1977. "Role Perceptions and Behavior in Three U.S. Courts of Appeals." *Journal of Politics* 39(4):916–38.

Hruska, Roman L. 1975. "Report of the Commission on Revision of the Federal Court Appellate System." https://www.ojp.gov/pdffiles1/Digitization/25944NCJRS.pdf (accessed November 19, 2023).

Hughes, Diane and Mark A. Dodge. 1997. "African American Women in the Workplace: Relationships Between Job Conditions, Racial Bias at Work, and Perceived Job Quality." *American Journal of Community Psychology* 25(5):581–99.

Jarmon, B. 2001. "Unwritten Rules of the Game." In *Sisters of the Academy: Emergent Black Women Scholars in Higher Education*, edited by Reitumetse Mabokela and Anna L. Green, 175–82. Sterling, VA: Stylus Publishing.

Jones, Edith H. 1995. "Back to the Future for Federal Appeals Courts: Rationing Federal Justice by Recovering Limited Jurisdiction." *Texas Law Review* 73(6):1485–504.

Kagan, Michael, Rebecca Gill, and Fatma Marouf. 2017. "Invisible Adjudication in the U.S. Courts of Appeals." *Georgetown Law Journal* 106(3):683–720.

Kastellec, Jonathan P. 2007. "Panel Composition and Judicial Compliance on the U.S. Courts of Appeals." *Journal of Law, Economics, & Organization* 23(2):421–41.

Kastellec, Jonathan P. 2013. "Racial Diversity and Judicial Influence on Appellate Courts." *American Journal of Political Science* 57(1):167–83.

Keele, Denise M., Robert W. Malmsheimer, Donald W. Floyd, and Lianjun Zhang. 2009. "An Analysis of Ideological Effects in Published versus Unpublished Judicial Opinions." *Journal of Empirical Legal Studies* 6(1):213–39.

Kim, Pauline T. 2009. "Deliberation and Strategy on the United States Courts of Appeals: An Empirical Exploration of Panel Effects." *University of Pennsylvania Law Review* 157(5):1319–81.

Kirks, Rowland F. 1972. "Report of the Proceedings of the Judicial Conference of the United States." https://www.uscourts.gov/sites/default/files/1972-04_0.pdf (accessed November 19, 2023).

Klein, David E. and Robert J. Hume. 2003. "Fear of Reversal as an Explanation of Lower Court Compliance." *Law & Society Review* 37(3):579–606.

Kuersten, Ashlyn and Donald Songer. 2001. *Decisions on the U.S. Courts of Appeals*. New York, NY: Routledge.

Law, David S. 2004. "Strategic Judicial Lawmaking: Ideology, Publication, and Asylum Law in the Ninth Circuit." *University of Cincinnati Law Review* 73(3):817–66.

Law, David S. 2005. "Judicial Ideology and the Decision to Publish: Voting and Publication Patterns in Ninth Circuit Asylum Cases." *Judicature* 89(4):212–19.

Lax, Jeffrey R. 2007. "Constructing Legal Rules on Appellate Courts." *American Political Science Review* 101(3):591–604.

Levy, Marin K. 2017. "Panel Assignment in the Federal Courts of Appeals." *Cornell Law Review* 103(1):65–116.

Liptak, Adam. 2015. "Courts Write Decisions That Elude Long View." *New York Times*, February 2, 2015. https://perma.cc/7NVM-HZXV (accessed December 1, 2023).

Liu, Zhuang. 2018. "Does Reason Writing Reduce Decision Bias? Experimental Evidence from Judges in China." *Journal of Legal Studies* 47(1):83–118.

Magrath, Paul. 2019. "Law Reporting and Public Access in the Courts: Is Too Much a Good Thing?: Part 1: The English Experience." *Legal Information Management* 19(4):224–29.

Mak, Maxwell, Andrew H. Sidman, and Udi Sommer. 2013. "Is Certiorari Contingent on Litigant Behavior? Petitioners' Role in Strategic Auditing." *Journal of Empirical Legal Studies* 10(1):54–75.

Maltzman, Forrest, James F. Spriggs II, and Paul J. Wahlbeck. 2000. *Crafting Law on the Supreme Court: The Collegial Game*. Cambridge University Press.

Maltzman, Forrest and Paul J. Wahlbeck. 1996. "May It Please the Chief? Opinion Assignments in the Rehnquist Court." *American Journal of Political Science* 40(2):421–43.

Martineau, Robert J. 1994. "Restrictions on Publication and Citation of Judicial Opinions: A Reassessment." *University of Michigan Journal of Law Reform* 28(1):119–50.

McAlister, Merritt E. 2019. "Downright Indifference: Examining Unpublished Decisions in the Federal Courts of Appeals." *Michigan Law Review* 118(4):533–608.

McAlister, Merritt E. 2020. "Missing Decisions." *University of Pennsylvania Law Review* 169(4):1101–80.

McCormick, Peter. 1993. "Party Capability Theory and Appellate Success in the Supreme Court of Canada, 1949–1992." *Canadian Journal of Political Science* 26(3):523–40.

McLaughlin, G. Harry. 1969. "SMOG Grading—A New Readability Formula." *Journal of Reading* 12(8):639–46.

Merritt, Deborah Jones and James J. Brudney. 2001. "Stalking Secret Law: What Predicts Publication in the United States Courts of Appeals." *Vanderbilt Law Review* 54(1):69–122.

Miller, Banks, Linda Camp Keith, and Jennifer S. Holmes. 2015. "Leveling the Odds: The Effect of Quality Legal Representation in Cases of Asymmetrical Capability." *Law & Society Review* 49(1):209–39.

Montgomery, Matthew D., Michael P. Fix, and Justin T. Kingsland. 2021. "Rigid Rules and Slippery Standards: How the Nature of U.S. Supreme Court Precedents Influences Subsequent State Court Treatments." *Social Science Quarterly* 102(6):2894–906.

Morande, Dean A. 2003. "Publication Plans in the United States Courts of Appeals: The Unattainable Paradigm." *Florida State University Law Review* 31(3):751–84.

Moyer, Laura P., John Szmer, Susan Haire, and Robert K. Christensen. 2021. "'All Eyes Are on You': Gender, Race, and Opinion Writing on the U.S. Courts of Appeals." *Law & Society Review* 55(3):452–72.

Murphy, Walter F. 1964. *Elements of Judicial Strategy*. Chicago, IL: University of Chicago Press.

Murrah, Alfred P. 1971. "Federal Judicial Center Annual Report." https://www.uscourts.gov/sites/default/files/1971-10.pdf (accessed November 19, 2023).

Murrah, Alfred P. 1973. "Standards for Publication of Judicial Opinions: A Report of the Committee on Use of Appellate Court Energies of the Advisory Council on Appellate Justice." https://ncsc.contentdm.oclc.org/digital/api/collection/appellate/id/33/download (accessed November 19, 2023).

Oakes, James L. 1990. "In Memoriam: Harold R. Medina." *Columbia Law Review* 90(6):1459–62.

Olney III, Warren. 1964. "Report of the Proceedings of the Judicial Conference of the United States." https://www.uscourts.gov/sites/default/files/1964-03_0.pdf (accessed November 19, 2023).

Patton, Dana and Joseph L. Smith. 2017. "Lawyer, Interrupted: Gender Bias in Oral Arguments at the U.S. Supreme Court." *Journal of Law and Courts* 5(2):337–61.

Peresie, Jennifer L. 2005. "Female Judges Matter: Gender and Collegial Decisionmaking in the Federal Appellate Courts." *Yale Law Journal* 114(7):1759–90.

Perry, H.W. 1991. *Deciding to Decide: Agenda Setting in the United States Supreme Court*. Cambridge, MA: Harvard University Press.

Pether, Penelope. 2004. "Inequitable Injunctions: The Scandal of Private Judging in the U.S. Courts." *Stanford Law Review* 56(6):1435–1580.

Poole, Keith T. 1998. "Recovering a Basic Space from a Set of Issue Scales." *American Journal of Political Science* 42(3):954–93.

Posner, Richard A. 2017. *The Federal Judiciary: Strengths and Weaknesses*. Cambridge, MA: Harvard University Press.

Prince, Eugene M. 1962. "Law Books, Unlimited." *American Bar Association Journal* 48(2):134–37.

Reagan, Robert T. 2007. "Citing Unpublished Federal Appellate Opinions Issued Before 2007." Federal Judicial Center. http://www.fjc.gov/ (accessed December 1, 2023).

Rempell, Scott. 2016. "Unpublished Decisions and Precedent Shaping: A Case Study of Asylum Claims." *Georgetown Immigration Law Journal* 31(1):1–52.

Reynolds, William L. and William M. Richman. 1981. "An Evaluation of Limited Publication in the United States Courts of Appeals: The Price of Reform." *University of Chicago Law Review* 48(3):573–631.

Richman, William M. and William L. Reynolds. 1995. "Elitism, Expediency, and the New Certiorari: Requiem for the Learned Hand Tradition." *Cornell Law Review* 81(2):273–342.

Richman, William M. and William L. Reynolds. 2013. *Injustice on Appeal: The United States Courts of Appeals in Crisis*. New York, NY: Oxford University Press.

Ricks, Sarah E. 2006. "The Perils of Unpublished Non-Precedential Federal Appellate Opinions: A Case Study of the Substantive Due Process State-Created Danger Doctrine in One Circuit." *Washington Law Review* 81(2):217–78.

Robel, Lauren K. 1989. "The Myth of the Disposable Opinion: Unpublished Opinions and Government Litigants in the United States Courts of Appeals." *Michigan Law Review* 87(5):940–62.

Sassman, Wyatt G. 2019. "Introducing the Tenth Circuit Database Project." *Denver Law Review* 97(2):383–94.

Schiltz, Patrick J. 2005a. "Citation of Unpublished Opinions in the Federal Courts of Appeals." *Fordham Law Review* 74(1):23–80.

Schiltz, Patrick J. 2005b. "Much Ado about Little: Explaining the *Sturm und Drang* over the Citation of Unpublished Opinions." *Washington & Lee Law Review* 62(4):1429–90.

Seaberg, James R. 1998. "Faculty Reports of Workload: Results of a National Survey." *Journal of Social Work Education* 34(1):7–19.

Sen, Maya. 2015. "Is Justice Really Blind? Race and Reversal in U.S. Courts." *Journal of Legal Studies* 44(1):187–229.

Serfass, Melissa M. and Jessie L. Cranford. 2001. "Federal and State Court Rules Governing Publication and Citation of Opinions." *Journal of Appellate Practice and Process* 3(1):251–86.

Sheehan, Reginald S. and Kirk A. Randazzo. 2012. "Explaining Litigant Success in the High Court of Australia." *Australian Journal of Political Science* 47(2):239–55.

Sheehan, Reginald S., William Mishler, and Donald R. Songer. 1992. "Ideology, Status, and the Differential Success of Direct Parties Before the Supreme Court." *American Political Science Review* 86(2):464–71.

Siegelman, Peter and John J. Donohue III. 1990. "Studying the Iceberg from Its Tip: A Comparison of Published and Unpublished Employment Discrimination Cases." *Law & Society Review* 24(5):1133–70.

Slavitt, Howard. 1995. "Selling the Integrity of the System of Precedent: Selective Publication, Depublication, and Vacatur." *Harvard Civil Rights–Civil Liberties Law Review* 30(1):109–42.

Slovic, Paul, Torbjörn Malmfors, C.K. Mertz, Nancy Neil, and Iain F.H. Purchase. 1997. "Evaluating Chemical Risks: Results of a Survey of the British Toxicology Society." *Human & Experimental Toxicology* 16(6):289–304.

Sommers, Samuel R. 2006. "On Racial Diversity and Group Decision Making: Identifying Multiple Effects of Racial Composition on Jury Deliberations." *Journal of Personality and Social Psychology* 90(4):597–612.

Songer, Donald, Ashlyn Kuersten, and Erin Kaheny. 2000. "Why the Haves Don't Always Come Out Ahead: Repeat Players Meet Amici Curiae for the Disadvantaged." *Political Research Quarterly* 53(3):537–56.

Songer, Donald R., Danna Smith, and Reginald S. Sheehan. 1988. "Nonpublication in the Eleventh Circuit: An Empirical Analysis." *Florida State University Law Review* 16(4):963–84.

Songer, Donald R., Jeffrey A. Segal, and Charles M. Cameron. 1994. "The Hierarchy of Justice: Testing a Principal-Agent Model of Supreme Court–Circuit Court Interactions." *American Journal of Political Science* 38(3):673–96.

Songer, Donald R. and Reginald S. Sheehan. 1992. "Who Wins on Appeal? Upperdogs and Underdogs in the United States Courts of Appeals." *American Journal of Political Science* 36(1):235–58.

Songer, Donald R., Reginald S. Sheehan, and Susan B. Haire. 1999. "Do the Haves Come Out Ahead over Time—Applying Galanter's Framework to Decisions of the U.S. Courts of Appeals, 1925–1988." *Law & Society Review* 33(4):811–32.

Songer, Donald R., Reginald S. Sheehan, and Susan B. Haire. 2000. *Continuity and Change on the United States Courts of Appeals*. Ann Arbor, MI: University of Michigan Press.

Songer, Donald R. and Sue Davis. 1990. "The Impact of Party and Region on Voting Decisions in the United States Courts of Appeals, 1955–1986." *Western Political Quarterly* 43(2):317–34.

Steinstra, Donna. 1985. "Unpublished Dispositions: Problems of Access and Use in the Courts of Appeals." Federal Judicial Center. https://www.ojp.gov/pdffiles1/Digitization/99990NCJRS.pdf (accessed November 19, 2023).

Sunstein, Cass R. 2006. *Are Judges Political?: An Empirical Analysis of the Federal Judiciary*. Washington, D.C.: Brookings Institute Press.

Sunstein, Cass R., David Schkade, and Lisa M. Ellman. 2004. "Ideological Voting on Federal Courts of Appeals: A Preliminary Investigation." *Virginia Law Review* 90(1):301–54.

Surrency, Erwin C. 1981. "Law Reports in the United States." *American Journal of Legal History* 25(1):48–66.

Swenson, Karen. 2004. "Federal District Court Judges and the Decision to Publish." *Justice System Journal* 25(2):121–42.

Szmer, John, Donald R. Songer, and Jennifer Bowie. 2016. "Party Capability and the U.S. Courts of Appeals: Understanding Why the 'Haves' Win." *Journal of Law and Courts* 4(1):65–102.

Szmer, John, Erin B. Kaheny, and Tammy A. Sarver. 2021. "'I Haven't Come a Long Way, and I'm Not a Baby': Task Assignment and Diversity of the Supreme Court Bar." *Social Science Quarterly* 102(6):2907–29.

Szmer, John and Martha Humphries Ginn. 2014. "Examining the Effects of Information, Attorney Capability, and Amicus Participation on U.S. Supreme Court Decision Making." *American Politics Research* 42(3):441–71.

Szmer, John, Robert K. Christensen, and Ashlyn Kuersten. 2012. "The Efficiency of Federal Appellate Decisions: An Examination of Published and Unpublished Opinions." *Justice System Journal* 33(3):318–38.

Szmer, John, Susan W. Johnson, and Tammy A. Sarver. 2007. "Does the Lawyer Matter? Influencing Outcomes on the Supreme Court of Canada." *Law & Society Review* 41(2):279–304.

Taber, Charles S. and Milton Lodge. 2006. "Motivated Skepticism in the Evaluation of Political Beliefs." *American Journal of Political Science* 50(3):755–69.

Tajfel, Henri. 1969. "Cognitive Aspects of Prejudice." *Journal of Biosocial Science* 1(S1):173–91.

Tajfel, Henri. 1970. "Experiments in Intergroup Discrimination." *Scientific American* 223(5):96–103.

Tanenhaus, Joseph, Marvin Schick, Matthew Muraskin, and Daniel Rosen. 1963. "The Supreme Court's Certiorari Jurisdiction: Cue Theory." In *Judicial Decision-making*, edited by Glendon Schubert, 111–32. New York, NY: Free Press of Glencoe.

Third Branch. 1977. "Report Released on California Unpublished Opinions." *The Third Branch: Bulletin of the Federal Courts* 9(5):6, 8.

Tiller, Emerson H. 2015. "The Law and Positive Political Theory of Panel Effects." *Journal of Legal Studies* 44(S1):S35–58.

Tillman, Elizabeth A. and Rachael K. Hinkle. 2018. "Of Whites and Men: How Gender and Race Impact Authorship of Published and Unpublished Opinions in the U.S. Courts of Appeals." *Research & Politics* 5(1):1–7.

Toutkoushian, Robert Kevin and Marcia L. Bellas. 1999. "Faculty Time Allocations and Research Productivity: Gender, Race and Family Effects." *Review of Higher Education* 22(4):367–90.

Ulmer, S. Sidney. 1984. "The Supreme Court's Certiorari Decisions: Conflict as a Predictive Variable." *American Political Science Review* 78(4):901–11.

Vladeck, David C. and Mitu Gulati. 2005. "Judicial Triage: Reflections on the Debate over Unpublished Opinions." *Washington & Lee Law Review* 62(4):1667–1708.

Vladeck, Stephen. 2023. *The Shadow Docket: How the Supreme Court Uses Stealth Rulings to Amass Power and Undermine the Republic.* New York, NY: Basic Books.
Wald, Patricia M. 1985. "The Changing Course: The Use of Precedent in the District of Columbia Circuit." *Cleveland State Law Review* 34(4):477–518.
Wald, Patricia M. 1995. "The Rhetoric of Results and the Results of Rhetoric: Judicial Writings." *University of Chicago Law Review* 62(4):1371–1419.
Wanner, C. 1975. "The Public Ordering of Private Relations—Part One: Initiating Civil Cases in Urban Trial Courts." *Law & Society Review* 8(3):421–40.
Wasby, Stephen L. 2001. "Unpublished Decisions in the Federal Courts of Appeals: Making the Decision to Publish." *Journal of Appellate Practice and Process* 3(1):325–42.
Weiss, Debra Cassens. 2015. "Are Some Opinions Unpublished to Avoid Review? Thomas Dissent Highlights the Issue." *American Bar Association Journal website*, February 4, 2015, https://www.abajournal.com/news/article/are_some_opinions_unpublished_to_avoid_review_thomas_dissent_highlights_the (accessed May 4, 2024).
Westerland, Chad, Jeffrey A. Segal, Lee Epstein, Charles M. Cameron, and Scott Comparato. 2010. "Strategic Defiance and Compliance in the U.S. Courts of Appeals." *American Journal of Political Science* 54(4):891–905.
Wheeler, Stanton, Bliss Cartwright, Robert A. Kagan, and Lawrence M. Friedman. 1987. "Do the Haves Come Out Ahead? Winning and Losing in State Supreme Courts, 1870–1970." *Law & Society Review* 21(3):403–45.
White, Bryon. 1998. "Final Report of the Commission on Structural Alternatives for the Federal Courts of Appeals." https://www.law.berkeley.edu/wp-content/uploads/2019/03/Commission-on-Structural-Alternatives-for-the-Federal-Courts-of-Appeals-1998.pdf (accessed November 19, 2023).
Whitehair, Francis P. 1947. "Opinions of Courts: Fifth Circuit Acts Against Unneeded Publication." *American Bar Association Journal* 33(8):751–844.
Zorn, Christopher. 2002. "U.S. Government Litigation Strategies in the Federal Appellate Courts." *Political Research Quarterly* 55(1):145–66.

Index

For the benefit of digital users, indexed terms that span two pages (e.g., 52–53) may, on occasion, appear on only one of those pages.

Tables and figures are indicated by an italic *t* and *f* following the page number.